THE AMERICAN HIGHWAY

A Journey Through Time Down U.S. Route 83

To Joann,
See Miles and Miles
of
Texas
on
U.S. Route 83!

TEXAS

HIGHWAY LEADING TO JUNCTION TEX

THE LAST AMERICAN HIGHWAY

A JOURNEY THROUGH TIME

DOWN U.S. ROUTE 83

In Texas

COURT BRIDGE
PUBLISHING
ARLINGTON, VIRGINIA

This book, like U.S. Highway 83 in Texas, is dedicated to the men and women who served in the Vietnam War.

Magnuson, Stew, 1963–

The Last American Highway: A Journey Through Time Down U.S. Route 83 in Texas

Includes bibliographical references, photos, maps, end notes

ISBN 978-0-9852996-3-7

Cover photo: Stonewall County, Texas, by Stew Magnuson.

Back cover photo: Prairie Dog Town Fork of the Red River, by Stew Magnuson.

Front cover Design by Brian Taylor.

Back cover and book design by Dedicated Book Services (www.netdbs.com).

Maps designed by Janis Apels.

Page 1 photo of Junction, Texas. LL Cook Company Collection. Prints and photographs collection. Texas State Library and Archives Commission.

All contemporary photos by Stew Magnuson.

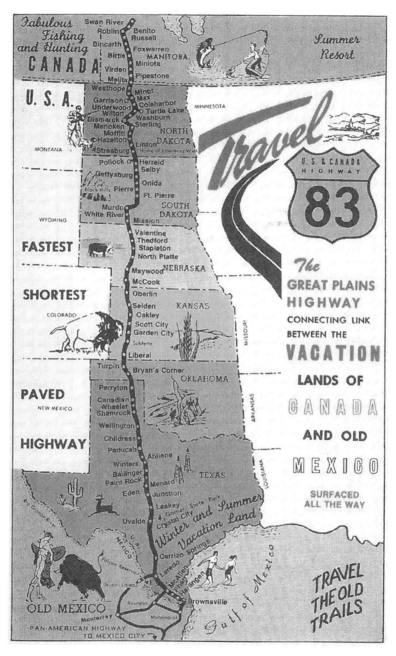

Postcard of U.S. Highway 83 printed by the U.S. & Canada Highway 83 Association, Perryton, Texas, circa 1959.

U.S. Highway 83 in Texas, Perryton to Ballinger

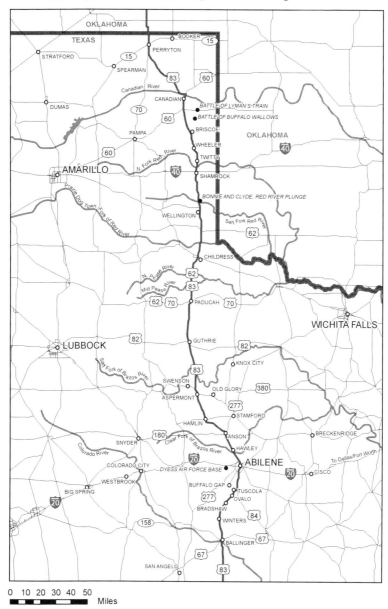

The three maps in this book are intended to guide readers, not drivers. When traveling Highway 83, please consult a road atlas for more detailed listings of roads and towns.

TABLE OF CONTENTS

A BRIEF NOTE FROM THE AUTHOR

This is a true story about a journey I took in May 2010. While I have returned to Highway 83 in Texas several times since then, I have confined the narrative to that month. It is also the final installment of a three-part series following *The Dakotas* and *Nebraska-Kansas-Oklahoma*. All three Highway 83 Chronicles works have been written as standalone books. They can be read individually, in order, or backwards, if desired.

While your narrator may come across as a "know-it-all," in fact, all of the historical vignettes found within this work come from other books or articles. Readers can find the sources I relied upon in the endnotes.

Enjoy the trip!

PRELUDE

U.S. Route 83 in Texas is a ribbon of concrete that begins in the north among the oil patches and wheat fields of the Panhandle, runs due south through miles lined with prickly pear and mesquite, slowing down only for the big speed bump known as the Texas Hill Country. It encounters the Rio Grande Valley at Laredo, then heads east until it reaches the state's southernmost tip at Brownsville.

That's 895 miles, according to the World Wide Web.

My dinged–up, dark blue 1999 Mazda Protegé is idling in a potholed liquor store parking lot on the precipice of this great highway. The folksy sing-talking voice of Woody Guthrie is on my car stereo. I just spent a few hours exploring the Oklahoma Panhandle and I could think of no better CD to play than his *Dust Bowl Ballads*. But I have planned for this moment. Woody comes out of the dashboard stereo and Bob Wills and His Texas Playboys go in. The beginning of a trip through the Lone Star State demands that I start it off "Ridin' with Bob."

If I wanted to push my car and body to their physical limits, I could make it to the road's terminus in a couple days. But I'm on a hunt for history; stories of the infamous, famous, and forgotten; vignettes found along this lonesome highway that may explain the state's unique history.

I'm an outsider, a Nebraskan born and raised, but currently residing in Arlington, Virginia. Like most Americans, I've heard plenty from the Lone Star State's proud sons and daughters about their singular place in American history and their claims that there is nothing like Texas.

It is big. No one can refute that. To wit, Highway 83 is the longest two-lane federal highway in any one state, and probably always will be until the people of Alaska decide they want to construct a longer one. And that's fine with me. I love wide open spaces and a big sky spread out in front of my car windshield. I live in a city where I can't see the sunset.

I got the travel bug early. I spent most of my young adult life living overseas, first as an English teacher, and then later as a reporter. Both of these professions were a means to see the world. I traveled to forty-eight countries before returning to America in 1999. Since then, exploring the back roads of the West has become my idea of a great vacation.

U.S. Highway 83, where Oklahoma meets Texas, is not an attractive spot to begin such a journey. It's a small collection of ramshackle bars and drive-in liquor stores where the citizens of dry Ochiltree County, Texas, can come to imbibe, or grab a case of beer to take home. The locals call this spot "The Line." One of the establishments hasn't bothered with a name. Its sign simply says, "Beer." A recent rain has served only to highlight the potholes on the loose gravel parking lots. Each is filled with shimmering water. I step out in the midday sunshine to take a few pictures of the beer joints and a concrete slab formed in the shape of Texas under a shady cottonwood tree at the state line.

"Drive Friendly—The Texas Way," a bigger green sign welcoming motorists says.

I slide back into the Protegé to begin the final leg of my trip down Highway 83. By that time, Bob Wills's *Osage Stomp*, a raucous, Dixieland-style instrumental with some mean fiddling leading the way, is pumping through the car speakers, immediately lifting my spirits. There's almost nothing I love more than driving down an American two-lane highway for the first time, just to see what I can see. I slip the car into gear, roll over the crunchy loose gravel on the shoulder and enter the Lone Star State.

TEXAS

It's May 2010 when I begin my journey under an overcast sky. The land is as flat as a checkerboard, with squares of lush green farmland interspersed with fallow fields, the rich soil that makes Ochiltree County the self-proclaimed "Wheatheart of the Nation" laid bare. A lone tan-colored pumpjack out in the middle of a field slowly dips up and down extracting oil.

Two of the nation's greatest resources are beneath the road, and I'm not referring to petroleum and natural gas, although they certainly are important.

They're dirt and water. The rich topsoil here sustained grass, and the buffalo and other grazing animals that relied on it, for millennia.

Water was another matter back then. Highway 83 is just west of the 100th meridian, a seemingly arbitrary line that marks the wet East from the dry West. Rain is a crapshoot here. When it stopped in the 1930s, this region became the "bottom of the Dust Bowl." This was not at the time the wheatheart of the nation, a breadbasket, or any such thing. It was a land of pure misery, as anything green withered away and residents choked on dust.

Salvation from the vagaries of weather lay some 400 feet below Highway 83 in the form of the Ogallala Aquifer. Its northern edge begins at about two states away at the Rosebud Reservation in South Dakota, and it will remain underneath me for another day of my journey. It touches parts of Wyoming, South Dakota, Colorado, Nebraska, Kansas, Oklahoma, New Mexico, and Texas. Some of its reserves are 3 million years old. Many call it "fossil water."

The Dust Bowl ended at about the same time as the arrival of diesel water pumps. With this new technology and a little bit of cheap fuel, a farmer no longer had to depend on spotty rains to bring in a crop. The top of Texas thrived as the mining of the aquifer began. If not for this vast reservoir and the technology required to extract it, I would be looking at a different landscape than what I'm seeing now.

I have relied on serendipity to uncover the history found along U.S. Highway 83. The road begins just north of a small town in North Dakota called Westhope. On its 1,885-mile path to Brownsville, Texas, it passes through North Dakota, South Dakota, the Rosebud Indian Reservation, Nebraska, Kansas, and thirty-four miles of Oklahoma before it reaches where I'm now driving. As I made my way south, I discovered stories through historical markers, word of mouth from locals, or in self-published books in small town libraries.

But that was not the case for Captain General Francisco Vázquez de Coronado. I knew I would be crossing the Spaniard's path several times on this trip, so I consumed as many books as I could find ahead of time. I can't be entirely sure where Highway 83 intersects with his expedition. The county museum in Liberal, Kansas, just thirty-eight miles north of here, has a piece of Spanish horse tack discovered near the town, which experts believe is a likely relic from that historic journey. Maps in reputable history books seem to indicate that in 1540 somewhere in present-day Ochiltree County, or very close to it, a dejected Coronado and his men passed through the land where I'm driving.

CONQUISTADOR

Coronado's horse walked slow enough to match the pace of the column of forty or so listless Spaniards, clergymen, African slaves, and Indians as they negotiated their way through this desolate, featureless land.

The Europeans were mounted on horses fueled by the seemingly endless grass. Grass, grass, and more grass swaying in the wind—as far as the eye could wander—with an occasional buffalo herd or arroyo to break up the monotony.

Coronado towered above the others who were on foot, but his shoulders were weighted down with discouragement. He was returning from a last, desperate journey to find wealth and glory. After three years in this vast wilderness, he had nothing. He had left New Spain a relatively wealthy man, but he would be returning considerably poorer.

Francisco Vázquez de Coronado was born in Salamanca, Spain, the second son of a well-off and well-connected family. In 1635, at the age of twenty-five, he decided to seek his fortune in the New World. Others had already done so. Hernán Cortés and his 500-man army came to Mexico in 1519 and cut a swath through the Aztec Empire, massacring and subjugating all who opposed him. His reward was land and gold.

Coronado found fortune in Mexico twenty-five years later. But it wasn't gold. He married the wealthy Beatriz de Estrada and inherited large sections of his father-in-law's properties in the New World. His first foray was to the lands northwest of Mexico City, where he became the governor of Nueva Galicia at the age of twenty-eight. But that wasn't enough for the young man, or the Spanish Empire. It was said that there were even more riches to the north. Seven great cities that rivaled the Aztecs in wealth were somewhere in those unexplored lands. This region, known as Cibola, had fueled the colonialists' imagination ever since Esteban, an African slave and the survivor of an earlier failed expedition, had returned to Mexico and told of its riches. Viceroy

Antonio de Mendoza ordered that a small reconnaissance mission be sent to gather more information, which included Esteban and a friar named Marcos de Niza. Esteban made it to the fabled city before the main party, but never returned after the Cibola natives killed him. They justifiably believed that he was the harbinger of a larger invasion. Fray Marcos ultimately did make it back to Mexico City alive. He confirmed seeing one of the fabled seven cities and insisted that it had everything the Spanish had desired.

It was no longer a matter of if there would be an armed invasion north, but when, and who would lead it. As the king's representative in Mexico, the viceroy would be responsible for selecting the conquistador. Sending away so many men in arms would be a risk and could leave New Spain vulnerable. Native peoples and African slaves were always threatening to revolt. But his countrymen were clamoring for an expedition. Many men vied for the honor of leading it, including the famous Cortés, but Mendoza tapped Coronado for the undertaking in January 1540 and named him captain general.

Among the governor's qualifications was his wealth. The crown's interest in these matters was almost always a one-way road. The king rarely provided money for such endeavors. The conquistador would have to raise the funds himself. Yet the Spanish rulers would expect their share of any riches.

Coronado spent four months preparing for the journey. He went into debt to pay his share by putting his wife's lands up as collateral. The 289 Spanish followers who believed in his dream would share in the risk and the rewards. That would either be gold, or even better, a land grant, where they could set up their own little kingdom. The wealthy colonialists were expected to not only pay their way, but contribute funds for the larger cause. In return, they were given positions as captains. The viceroy invested a considerable amount of his personal fortune as well.

The dozens of clergymen who volunteered for the trek were not out for wealth, but for souls. The Roman Catholic Church insisted that Franciscans accompany every expedition. The order produced friars in the thousands, all with a burning desire to spread the word of God in the farthest-flung corners of the known world, or die trying. To become a martyr was the ultimate reward for these earnest brothers. Military leaders such as Coronado looked upon them as a necessary burden. Fray Marcos, however, was welcomed as an experienced guide.

Coronado launched his *entrada*, or armed invasion, from Nueva Galicia in February 1540. His party's main body numbered almost two thousand. Many of them were the Spaniards' native or African slaves, who were expected to bear the heavy loads and tend to the livestock. Some women servants came as well to cook, wash, and tend to the Spanish masters' other "needs." The bulk of the force were warriors from Mexican tribes who were tasked to fight any peoples who challenged the entrada. They were a cut above the slaves and were not expected to do menial work. Cortés had made peace with tribes who had no love for the Aztecs and used them as auxiliary

Statue of Francisco Coronado at the Coronado Museum in Liberal, Kansas.

warriors to all but destroy that civilization. Coronado would do the same. Meat on the hoof in the form of cattle, sheep, and goats were part of the column, for without a handy supply of food the party would starve. A ship full of supplies for the winter was expected to sail north up the Gulf of California and resupply the invaders later.

They were on the lookout for gold; that was certain. But gold was not the endgame. The ultimate goal was the patronage system, whereby the Spanish would conquer large civilizations, putting them under their rule—converting them to Christianity to placate the church—then forcing them to become vassals. The king back in Spain would then grant the conquistadors land and peoples they could rule over—as long as he received his cut. Vassals were required to pay tribute to their overlords in labor, gold, food, or other tradable goods. It was through this system that a Spanish man could live a life of honor and ease.

But nothing went as planned.

Now, almost three years later, his listless horse plodding along through the endless grass, Coronado had given up hope.

The main party was awaiting him back in the desert lands to the west. When he returned, Coronado would have to deliver the bad news to his captains. There was nothing to the east, just some poor villagers in earthen lodges. There were no metals worth mining, no vast cities worth putting under Spanish control, or commodities of any kind that could be traded and converted to wealth. Every last Spaniard, save the priests, had gambled that they would return from their journey as lords of a new realm.

The expedition onto the vast prairie turned out to be a colossal waste of time.

And for this, Coronado blamed an Indian called the Turk.

After journeying some 1,400 miles north over five months, Coronado discovered not cities of gold, but cities of dirt.

When the party arrived at Cibola in the summer of 1540 they found only a series of pueblos, mud-brick homes scattered among the marginal lands in the desert. The Zunis were subsistence farmers. They had nothing except some blue stones called turquoise, which were of little interest. There was no life of honor or ease to be found here.

Coronado called on Fray Marcos to explain himself. He admitted that he hadn't exactly seen Cibola with his own eyes during the previous year's reconnaissance mission. All his information came from the late Esteban. Upon hearing of the slave's death, he had decided to return south. If Fray Marcos hadn't been a man of the cloth, Coronado probably would have had him executed on the spot.

Despite the setback, the Spaniards spent the next year making the land their own.

The conquering of native peoples was not without controversy in the sixteenth century. To counter those who criticized Cortés and his ruthless ways, the kingdom devised the *requerimiento*. This proclamation would be read in Spanish to the heathens and translated through any means available, most likely through sign language. It explained the chain of command. At the top was God, then there was the Pope, after him, the king of Spain. Next came the well-armed men who were standing before them riding great beasts named horses, carrying lances and loud, thunderous muskets called arquebuses. It was God's intention that Spain rule over the New World and its peoples. The end of the document told the Indians that they could either accept the dominion over them, or suffer a war.

Coronado dutifully had the document read wherever he went.

The impoverished Zunis could not provide the wealth the Spaniards were looking for, but they were forced to give up what little they had. Coronado ordered their horses and livestock turned loose on the fields. The animals ate all the stubble the natives used for their winter fuel. The captains took over dwellings and expelled the residents. Stores of corn and beans were appropriated. As winter came and the expected shipment of clothes did not arrive from the sea as planned, the conquistadors demanded that the Indians give them all their warm clothes and blankets. Though the Indians were not yet converted to Christianity, they were expected to literally give the Spanish the shirts off their backs.

Needless to say, the Spanish wore out their welcome quickly. When one of Coronado's captains raped an Indian woman and the conquistador refused to mete out punishment, one of the villages rose up in revolt. The Spanish met this resistance with brute force. The Indian allies they brought with them from the south did most of the fighting. Their payment was all they could loot and all the captives they could enslave.

All this violence and ill will proved for naught. Except for the friars who could claim to have saved some souls, the expedition was a complete bust. One party of explorers Coronado dispatched to the west discovered the Grand Canyon. But that was just a big hole in the ground. There were no riches to be found there.

Coronado's last hope was a foreign Indian he called the Turk. His real name didn't concern the members of Coronado's party. He resembled the men of that Oriental region in their minds, and so the nickname stuck.

He was not one of the Zunis; he came from the east. Whether he was a visitor, or a captive of the local natives, was not entirely clear. The Spanish communicated with him through a rudimentary sign language. The details of his life were of little importance to them, but he told them of a large civilization called Quivira. In this land there was a mighty river, with men who sailed boats larger than anything he had seen. The cities were vast, full of countless people and stone buildings. There, the men wore shiny gold metal armbands.

What was Coronado to make of this information? They had been fooled before. Their only hope was with the Turk and his tales of a wealthy land to the east.

The Spanish weren't stupid. They mistrusted Indian guides, and everything they said had to be taken with a grain of salt. Nor were the Indians stupid. They figured out quickly that a good way to rid themselves of the Spanish was to tell them that there were cities of gold somewhere off in the distance. Coronado could choose to disbelieve the Turk and return to Mexico City empty-handed, or attempt to find this elusive land and possibly return with wealth and glory for himself and the empire.

And so in the spring of 1541, the 2,000 men and numerous beasts of burden left the land of the pueblos and ventured onto the Great Plains. Feeding and watering that many mouths was no easy task. They entered what they would call the Llano Estacado, or Staked Plains. This is where they first encountered buffalo, and the nomadic Indians who followed them. If it weren't for these herds, the expedition may have starved. Hordes of the short-horned beasts were everywhere.

For the Plains tribes, it was the first time they had laid eyes on horses. They hunted buffalo on foot, and dogs pulled their travois from camp to camp. They undoubtedly looked upon the mounted Spanish captains with curiosity and envy. The Turk led them southeast over the featureless land for several days, then he began to argue bitterly with another guide named Ysopete. The two Indians did not like each other very much, and Ysopete insisted that the Turk was leading the Spanish the wrong way in hopes that they would all die of thirst. But timely rains scuttled his plans. Coronado realized too late that moving thousands of people and livestock through the harsh, dry land would be painfully slow. He decided to put together a small party to push ahead to scout Quivira. He sent the main party back to the relative comfort of the Zuni pueblos, retaining only a few dozen Spanish soldiers and friars along with a number of Indian allies, who were adequate enough to provide some protection, but not enough of a force for conquest.

Coronado traveled northwards from the lands between the Red and Canadian Rivers, up through the present-day Texas Panhandle, passing through western Oklahoma until the party reached the Arkansas River. They followed its banks until the Turk led them across more flatlands to what is now eastern Kansas. Again, they found not cities, but small settlements of round, earthen lodges where sedentary subsistence farmers and hunters dwelled, and no evidence of gold or any kind of precious metal.

When Coronado heard that the Turk was secretly urging the local Indians to attack the much smaller Spanish party to wipe them out, he'd had enough. He ordered his scout garroted.

A tourniquet of ropes was placed around the Turk's neck, and wooden handles twisted until he strangled to death.

It was a final admission of defeat. It was time to go back.

Some friars and their Indian adherents insisted on being left behind so they could convert more souls to Christianity. They were eventually killed and would wear the "crown of martyrdom."

Coronado—after passing through what would be the Texas Panhandle—returned to the pueblos, and then Nueva Galicia, with nothing to show for his two-year expedition and in considerably poorer health after falling off his horse on the way back. His wife's fortune had been squandered, and he eventually lost his position as governor. Ten years after the entrada, he died from a tropical malady.

The Spanish would show little interest in returning north for another half century. Their horses did, though. Traded from tribe to tribe over the years, the animal would find its way to a small nation of squat, stocky people called the Comanches, who first came to the Great Plains from the Rocky Mountains. Another tribe that had encountered Coronado on the Llano Estacado, the Apaches, would do the same. The marriage of the horse to these nomads would be like no other. The Spanish, when they returned, would have to contend with an agile and deadly force of their own making.

Whenever I find a small town or county historical society museum, I always stop. The Museum of the Plains on the northern edge of Perryton, Texas, is better—and larger—than most. The typical regional history museum is normally a collection of collections. A local woman with an amazing number of salt-and-pepper shakers dies, and the family donates all of them to the historical society. A bachelor farmer passes away and his perfectly preserved John Deere tractor ends up there, along with other folks' arrowheads, old bottles, wagons from the horse-and-buggy days, black-and-white photos, crockery, and such. These institutions normally have limited hours and its not uncommon to have to call a volunteer to come down and open up. But Perryton's museum has enough foot traffic to maintain regular summer hours. And inside, I can piece together the history of the top of Texas.

Hanging on the wall near the front door is a framed cover of *Popular Mechanics*, February 1920 edition, that illustrates a wave of steam-powered tractors pulling buildings across the grasslands. Out front is the grocery/post office, behind it a home, behind that a church with a steeple. The tractors blow white and black smoke.

"Everyone's got a story to tell" is a well-known cliché, but one I've found to be true on my Route 83 travels. This is also seems the case with towns. Every community has a unique story. When a branch of the Panhandle and Santa Fe Railway decided to build its new line right between the towns of Gray, Oklahoma, and Ochiltree, Texas, it marked the end of these two communities but the beginning of a new one. The magazine cover portrays a day when Ochiltree residents picked up their buildings by their foundations and moved them by steam-powered tractors a few miles north to the newly established town of Perryton.

Ochiltree was not some little dusty town that never amounted to much. It had two newspapers, a movie theater, churches, and had been there for thirty-four years despite the lack of a railroad. It had even grown famous as a

Reprinted with permission of *Popular Mechanics.*

hotbed for the nascent sport of car racing. A dried-out lake—once graded—provided a natural oval track, and promoters put up big prize money to attract motorists. Competitors in 1915 drove their Hudsons, Buicks, Pierce Arrows, and Nationals to the remote town for 250-mile-long races.

When the time came to relocate Ochiltree to the newly platted town of Perryton, the railroad magnanimously offered free lots to the aggrieved Ochiltree businessmen. There were plenty of tractors around that could be called into service. The first settlers in Ochiltree County busted the sod with horse-driven plows. Threshing machines, which separated the grain from the plant, were the first to use steam power. That saved a lot of hard work, as did the tractor. It came next, and helped break the virgin prairie into farm fields.

Rail lines grew closer, making it easier to move grain and cattle to market. Since steam-powered threshers and tractors were expensive, farmers formed co-ops, or hired crews that hauled their machines from farm to farm when the crop came in. When it was time to harvest, neighbors gathered at one homestead to help with the work.

Of course, steam-powered engines required water and some kind of fuel. Both needed to be hauled to the fields—ironically by horse—to the machine.

Popular Mechanics was intrigued by the feat of moving a town by tractor, but these were the twilight years for what has been called America's first important invention, the steam engine. About a half decade afterwards, the combustion engine had replaced it. But one tradition remains. The crews who went from farm to farm continued to offer their services even as the technology evolved. Today, custom combine crews follow the harvest north, and Highway 83 is one of their favored roads.

A barn-sized room in back of the museum features a giant steam engine tractor, perhaps one that helped move the Ochiltree buildings in 1919. Although the magazine illustration suggests that the buildings were moved in one long parade all at once, the process actually took several months.

"When every building in a town of 300 is hitched to a tractor and pulled across the prairie to a new site, astonishment is excusable," gushed the article's author, Paul H. Woodruff. Above the story is a photo of a tractor the size of a locomotive ready to relocate the Owl Drug Store. "That is exactly what happened, however, not long ago down in the Texas 'panhandle,' where they are accustomed to doing things in a big way."

As I explore the museum, I find a local petroleum company has helpfully provided a display of area's other natural resources, oil, natural gas, and helium. For decades starting in 1912, oil exploration companies came to the region and poked holes in the ground. They either came up empty, or only found natural gas. In the latter case, they just plugged up the well; there was no market for gas yet. In 1955, a driller finally hit the right stratum and the boom was on. Oil and natural gas—by then in demand—began to flow. It also turned out to be one of the few places on Earth where the natural gas contained small amounts of helium. The element is abundant in the sun but rare on Earth—where it's required to launch rockets and fill party balloons.

Highway 83 as it passes through Perryton is a wide thoroughfare, big enough to accommodate all manner of vehicles and includes ample pull-in parking, too.

I might be the only person in the world who is interested in the forgotten history of the now defunct U.S. & Canada Highway 83 Association. This organization of small-town chamber of commerce members actively promoted travel on the highway for almost six decades. But best as I can tell through my research, the association had disappeared by the late 1980s. Perryton for a time served as the national headquarters. I found one former member in Liberal, Kansas, who couldn't really point to a particular year when the organization called it quits.

From its origins as the Great Plains Highway Association to its final days as the U.S. & Canada Highway 83 Association, the LaMasters of Perryton were involved in promoting the road. Walter LaMaster Jr. was a past president of the association. Finding one of the family members is a cinch since the LaMaster Insurance/Real Estate Agency is located right on Main Street, as it has been since the day the new town of Perryton opened for business. The storefront office is warm, cozy spot, with the feel of a living room. I'm greeted by a young woman who goes in to a back office to find her boss.

Joe LaMaster comes out. He's in his sixties, with receding hair and dressed in a shirt and tie. I tell him about my project and my hopes of meeting Walter Jr., who was his uncle, but I learn that he passed on in 2005. Joe represents the third generation to run the business. It was his grandfather, Walter B. LaMaster, who, along with Judge George Perry, was responsible for distributing lots for the railroad in the new town. Perry, for his years of hard work trying to convince railroads to come to this part of the state, had the honor of having the town named after him.

Walter Sr. was a keen promoter of Perryton, and as such, traveled to McCook, Nebraska, in May 1926 to help establish the Great Plains Highway Association. He served as its Texas state director for many years. Eventually, his oldest son, Walter Jr., would join him as an ardent booster of the border-to-border highway after it became Highway 83.

Walter Jr. and Joe's father, Phil, were the second generation to take over the business. "There won't be a fourth," Joe laments. None of his kids are interested.

That appears to be why the old Highway 83 association faded away. There was a second generation of enthusiasts who took over the reins from their fathers, but there wasn't a third. While he doesn't know much about the association, Joe does have a few stories. One concerns the day his grandmother Pauline came across the plat for the new town. The main street, which would become Highway 83, was too narrow, she said.

"She told my grandfather that it had to be wide enough for a team of horses and a cart to make a U-turn. That's how we ended up with such a wide road."

The receptionist interrupts Joe and tells him that one of his clients in the southern part of the county has lost his crops to some hail last night. He gets on the phone with him.

"You know when that storm came through I was wondering if I had anyone down south," he says with the doleful voice of a mortician. His expression as he talks appears to be just as sorrowful. He assures the farmer that he will take care of his claim.

Joe has an envelope he keeps near the front reception desk stuffed with small bills. He's taking donations for a so-called "ghost sign" across the street. These painted advertisements on the side of early twentieth-century brick buildings normally advertised Coca-Cola, businesses that occupied the building, and such. They're called ghost signs today because the vast majority of them are fading away.

But not this one.

The red, white, and blue sign features the text "Keep EM FLYING

Buy Victory BONDS*STAMPS," along with an American flag flying over a bomber.

Joe and his family have dutifully kept the paint fresh on the sign for some six decades. He asks visitors and customers to chip in a buck or two. I hand over a fiver and he records my name on the back of the envelope. Keeping the small piece of the town's World War II history alive is important to Joe, who was named after his uncle Joseph D. LaMaster, a gunner in a B-24 Liberator bomber, who was killed in action flying over Austria January 20, 1945.

Joe isn't going to crow about it, but I know from a local history book I found earlier in the day that the LaMasters were one of two families in America who sent nine children off to fight in World War II. Walter Jr., LeRoy, and Henry served in the Navy. Joe's father, Giltner, Phillip and Kenneth fought in the Army. Cyrus and Joseph were in the Army Air Corps. Kathryn joined the Women's Army Corps. It was said that sister Pauline would have been happy to volunteer and make it ten children if she hadn't been married and pregnant with her first child when the war broke out. Seven of the nine LaMasters saw combat, but Joe was the only who didn't make it home. Each of the ten had earned college degrees as well.

It was a remarkable family, and I leave just a little sad that the LaMaster name when Joe retires will disappear from Highway 83 in Perryton.

I leave Perryton after lunch the following day. I stayed much longer than I expected reading local history books in the library, chatting with folks and trying unsuccessfully to track down Highway 83 Association documents. I grab a large Coke at the Dixie Dog and fill up the tank at Waterhole 83 convenience store on the south end of town, for I feel obligated to stop at any business that has Highway 83 in its name.

I'm driving on the rolling plains, a land just east of the Llano Estacado, the maddeningly uniform "Staked Plains," where Coronado and his party traversed on their way to what would be Kansas. They are a bit more topographically interesting than the flatlands to the west and today, at least, moist and lush, from the line of thunderstorms that had passed through the previous night.

Along with Bob Wills and His Texas Playboys, my Texas-only music collection includes: Stevie Ray Vaughan, The Fabulous Thunderbirds, Lightnin' Hopkins, The Tailgators, The LeRoi Brothers, ZZ Top, Anson Funderburgh and the Rockets (featuring Sam Myers), Asleep at the Wheel, Willie Nelson, Freddie King,

Johnny Copeland, Dave Alvin, Buddy Holly, Ronnie Dawson, Roy Orbison, Johnny Winter, Archie Bell and the Drells (who don't only sing but dance), Janis Joplin, The Smokin' Joe Kubek Band (featuring Bnois King), James McMurtry, The Reverend Horton Heat, Joe Tex, and one collection: Rhino Records' *Blues Masters, Volume 3, Texas Blues.* And last but not least, The Texas Tornados and Los Super Seven, which both feature Freddy Fender, who was born and raised on Highway 83 in San Benito. One town on 83, it can be argued, gave birth to a unique genre of American music. But I have along way to go before I can tell that story.

"Dave Alvin ain't from Texas," a music nerd might point out. He grew up in Downey, California, just south of Los Angeles. Alvin has no less than three songs that make reference to Highway 83 towns in Texas, so he makes it into my Texas-only collection. He is on my Highway 83 Music Hall of Fame list along with Lawrence Welk of Strasburg, North Dakota; Freddy Fender; Jeannie C. Riley; and Kris Kristofferson, who was born in Brownsville. I am remiss in not bringing some of his music with me other than Joplin's version of his "Me and Bobby McGee."

I kick off that day's journey with "On the Road Again," by Willie Nelson.

Soapweed yucca and its pointy needles growing along barbed-wire fences is a sign that I'm transitioning from farmland to ranchland. A windmill on the side of the hill is overpumping water out of the aquifer, creating streams and pools in a green pasture. Ahead is a turkey buzzard, better known as a turkey vulture, languidly circling about 100 yards ahead of the car.

The Protegé is humming along. Just a few weeks past its tenth birthday, this four-door Mazda is a workhorse. It had 123,969 miles on the odometer when I left Omaha. That's nearly five times around the globe. Five times around the equator my butt has sat in the driver's seat. I don't have a nickname for the Protegé. It's just "the Protegé." Unlike many of the Japanese carmakers that have set up factories in the United States, this one was made in Hiroshima, Japan, a city where I once taught conversational English to adults. *Consumer Reports* said of the 1999 Mazda Protegé that it "has all the verve of a BMW at half the price."

I have driven it on the streets of Toronto, Los Angeles, San Diego, Las Vegas, San Francisco, Phoenix, Seattle, Chicago, and Washington, D.C. On a lark, I drove it into the heart of Manhattan on a cold February Sunday so I could see Christo and Jeanne-Claude's *The Gates* public art installation in Central Park.

Outside, my car looks like crap, but it runs great. It creaks because I don't want to pay for new struts, so I will acutely feel every bump and pothole from Perryton to Brownsville. Sure, this would be a better story if I were flying down Highway 83 in a classic Cadillac convertible with fins, or with the wind whipping through my hair on a Harley. But the Protegé is my road warrior. It may no longer have all the "verve" of a BMW, but I can't imagine selling it. Will this be the Protegé's last trip? When I reach Brownsville, Texas, I will have a big decision to make.

I've been traveling Highway 83 my whole life. That's not an exaggeration. I was probably only a few weeks old when my parents drove me out to my dad's hometown, Stapleton, Nebraska, a village along the road nestled on the southern edge of the Sand Hills. When I was a toddler, I remember straining to see the first glimpse of Stapleton as we went up and down the hills. If we were arriving after dusk, the glow of the town lights meant we would soon be at Grandma and Grandpa's house.

Their home was on an incline on the west side of town overlooking the football field. They had a porch swing, and after dark the family would sit there and chat. I would follow the car lights out on the highway, which was just beyond the school and a vast field of corn. The white beams would emerge in the south and move silently in the darkness on moonless nights until they disappeared when reaching the edge of town. Out on the horizon, beyond the end zone, the baseball field, and my grandfather's implement shop, they reemerged as blurry red dots until the Sand Hills swallowed them up.

Where were they going so late at night?

My grandmother Bernice was a bit of a worry wart. One day when I was older, and I borrowed my cousin Devin's bike to ride out to the South Loup River, she called out to me: "Be careful. That road goes from Canada to Mexico, you know!"

"Really? I didn't know that."

While I was pedaling away and pondering this piece of trivia, she was undoubtedly imagining Canadian child molesters trolling Highway 83 for twelve-year-old boys they could kidnap and take into Old Mexico, beyond the long arm of the law.

About six months after my grandmother passed away at the age of ninety-five, I snapped awake at one a.m. with this crazy idea in my head: "I'm going to write a book about Highway 83 and the history found alongside it." This was not completely out of left field. My first nonfiction book had been published the previous year, and my wife had been bugging me about what I was going to work on next.

I knew it was a good idea because my brain refused to shut down and return me to the Land of Nod, where I would have promptly forgotten about it. I was up for hours thinking about how I could pull it off. Within months, I found myself on the Canadian border beginning the border-to-border journey.

The car drops into the Canadian River Valley. I feel like I'm in a desert oasis. There are trees lining the road, and as I pass over the bridge I see a full channel. It's the most water I've seen in a river since the South Platte in Nebraska. Looking at a map, one sees plenty of blue squiggly lines that denote rivers along Highway 83. But they are ghost rivers. They are similar to ghost towns, but instead of being abandoned by people, it's the H_2O that's missing. The Republican River in Nebraska has a trickle of water. Dams and overirrigation have turned it into a creek, and not a very impressive one. The Smoky River in Kansas: I have no recollection of it. Colorado farmers have sucked the Arkansas River dry. By the time it reaches Garden City, Kansas, it's nothing but a gravel bed. I walked right up the middle of its channel and my sneakers remained dry. The Cimarron is a dry gulch and has been since the days of the Santa Fe Trail. There were large trees growing in the center of its ancient riverbed. The same goes for the Beaver in the Oklahoma Panhandle—just a wide dry ditch.

I'm delighted to discover that the town has converted an old bridge into a walking path, so I step out of the car to stretch my legs. There are cyclists, walkers and joggers taking advantage of it. A bike path continues all the way to the town.

No one is completely certain why a river that flows so far from Canada is so named. The prevailing theory is that Canadian fur trappers were responsible. Another explanation is the Spanish word for "glen," which is *cañada*.

River valleys are some of the scenic highlights of any trip on the Great Plains, and I have been spoiled with some beautiful ones. The Souris and Missouri in the Dakotas, the White River in South Dakota, the Niobrara and Dismal Rivers and the North and South Platte in Nebraska. The Canadian rivals them. The flow is languid here. It looks like one could wade across it, but the river is notorious for quicksand, which reminds me of another story Joe LaMaster in Perryton told me.

Prior to the building of this bridge, in the early days of the automobile, a wagon master set up a business on the riverbank. When a motorist approached the river, he would offer to guide the traveler across for five dollars. That was a lot of money back then, but the first motorists were generally well-heeled, so he had no qualms about demanding such a high price for his knowledge. Many refused. Some were outright indignant. They popped the clutch and eased their cars down the bank and into the water, where more often than not they got stuck. That's when they learned the price for him to hitch up a team of horses and drag the car out was twenty-five dollars. Once the bridge was built, the wagon master took the money he'd saved and opened a gas station in Perryton.

The Texas Panhandle is a nearly perfect square comprising twenty-six counties and 25,610 square miles. The Red River War of 1874 between the U.S. Army and a Kiowa-Comanche alliance took place almost completely within its borders. It settled once and for all who would dominate this land. Two of its most famous fights occurred close to Highway 83 and south of the Canadian River where I'm standing.

HONOR AND DISHONOR

Botalye's cousin Tehan was missing. The red-haired white boy who had been captured as a child and adopted into the tribe was sent out to round up some lost horses, but hadn't returned.

Botalye, like Tehan, was at an awkward age in a young Kiowa warrior's life. Seventeen years old: no longer a child, but not quite yet a man. But there were plenty of opportunities to change that. The land between the rivers was full of bluecoats who were seeking to fight and round up the Kiowas, Comanches, and Southern Cheyennes who had broken away from their reservation in Indian Territory—along with those who never agreed to leave in the first place.

This was the tribes' home country. They had hunted the Llano Estacado and the rolling plains for generations, and it was theirs by treaty. They had agreed to come in and register at reservations to the east in Indian Territory. They would receive rations, places to live, and education for the children. But the agreement allowed the tribes to hunt the lands south of the Arkansas River until the buffalo stopped roaming there.

That time was coming sooner than anyone had predicted. White men, hide hunters, had come to slaughter as many bison as they could, stacking their skins on the back of wagons, throwing their edible tongues into barrels of brine, and leaving the rest to be picked over by vultures. The Army and the politicians were happy to let the hunters decimate the once great herds. Once they were gone, the Indians would have no choice but to give up their way of life.

Few of the tribe members took to reservation life. For those who did, the rations were inadequate. Botalye had spent time at the Kiowa reservation his nation shared with the Comanches. Nothing was as promised. The rations were meager and of low quality. The white men treated them like children.

More and more of them returned to their ancestral lands to hunt as they always did. Tensions at the reservation grew, and fighting broke out between the Army and some Kiowas one night in August 1874. Seven men were killed, and a trading post was looted. Several bands took that as a sign to leave.

Botalye departed with his uncle Maman-ti and his band's chief, Poor Buffalo. They vowed to rid the land of the hunters and return to their old way of life.

Maman-ti was one of the most powerful men among the Kiowa. He was a medicine man, a prophet, and one of the tribe's best strategists. His prophecies were communicated through an owl puppet made from one of the bird skins he carried with him at all times. While many of the chiefs wanted peace and would eventually return to the reservations, Maman-ti—and the owl—always argued for war.

But his uncle's status in the tribe didn't reflect on Botalye. In Kiowa society, young men rose to become leaders through great deeds, particularly feats on the battlefield. Botalye was also half Mexican. Even though there were members adopted into the tribe who had no Kiowa blood, such as Tehan, there were some who looked down on him.

One of the Kiowas' greatest leaders, Satanta, also held a poor opinion of Botalye. When he was much younger, he and some other boys were playing near the great chief's teepee, famous for its ochre color, when they accidentally kicked over a cooking fire. Some of the embers lit the teepee, causing most of it to burn. Even though he wasn't the only one to blame, Satanta's wrath fell on Botalye. The chief, an imposing and powerfully built man, called him a coward; years later the insult still stung. Satanta, long with another chief, Big Tree, had spent time in the white man's prison. But they were freed on the condition that they no longer make war. They had broken that promise when they left the reservation with the others.

Satanta, Kiowa chief. Taken by William S. Soule, circa 1869.

Maman-ti was Tehan's father. Fearing that his adopted son had fallen into the hands of the soldiers, he ordered his nephew and some other young men to ride out and find him.

After a day of searching the plains between the rivers, Botalye's party encountered another group who had been seeking Tehan. They reported that his horse's tracks had melded with a those of a group of cavalrymen. He had been captured, they surmised. Everyone but Botalye turned back. Undaunted, he pressed on alone, determined to rescue his cousin.

After a few hours, he encountered two older Kiowa warriors.

"Botalye, go over to that ridge there and tell us what you see," they insisted. Something wasn't right. Why wouldn't they just go over and look for themselves? Knowing in the pit of his stomach that the men were being evasive, he hobbled his horse and made his way to the ridge as the two older men stayed behind and watched. He climbed to the top of the rise and hid behind a thicket of mesquite. Peering out from their branches, he saw a short distance away an Army wagon train, lightly guarded by about twenty-five foot soldiers and ten mounted men. If it weren't for the bushes, he might have been spotted right away.

That's why the pair had goaded him. After scurrying back down the ridge, the two men told him to return to camp and bring back as many warriors as possible while they kept an eye on the supply train.

Within hours, Botalye had returned with a war party that included his uncle Satanta and Poor Buffalo. The Kiowas and several of their Comanche allies had positioned themselves on the flanks of the wagon train and were harassing its soldiers. After about twelve miles, the bluecoats would have to make a difficult crossing over a creek that emptied into the Washita River. The Kiowas saw a moment of vulnerability and attacked.

The supply train commander circled the wagons as quickly as he could, but several mounted warriors spilled through his defenses, firing their guns, filling the perimeter with smoke and dust. One of the soldiers fell dead instantly, and two others were bleeding out.

The soldiers rallied and managed to beat the horsemen back, but the siege was on. The Kiowas and Comanches knew the train was just out of range of the creek and the river, and the soldiers were cut off from their only water supply. It was hot and the sun beat down on the bluecoats as they quickly dug two trenches in a V shape. The natives sniped at them, making their job as difficult as possible. All the while, young men counted coup by charging as close as they could to the circled wagons, hurling insults, whooping, and firing their guns.

That night, Botalye and his uncle were heartened when Tehan returned to them. He had indeed been captured. He convinced the bluecoat officers that he was an unwilling Kiowa captive and offered to lead them in the dark of night to a watering hole. While doing so, he slipped away. He told his uncle that the soldiers and their horses were running dangerously low on water.

The siege continued into the following day with little changing except the amount of water inside the encirclement. The Kiowas knew the soldiers were growing desperate when they made several attempts to break out toward the waterhole. Each time they were beaten back.

That night, they saw a lithe man on a fast horse make a break. He was undoubtedly a messenger going for reinforcements, so they gave chase. His desperate dash seemed doomed. The Comanches and the Kiowas were among the most skilled riders on the Great Plains. At one point, the messenger's horse stumbled in a prairie dog hole, causing his rifle to fly out of his hand. But somehow his mount managed to stay on all four hooves.

They were closing in on him on a flat expanse when the rider came upon a buffalo herd. He rode straight into the middle of the beasts, and in the darkness and dust, disappeared.

That was the beginning of the end of the siege. It continued for another day, but the escaped rider would inevitably bring back reinforcements. There were rumors of other soldiers in the area, so the men began slipping away to return to their families. The woman and children could not be left vulnerable.

By the end of the third day, Botalye, his uncle, and a handful of other warriors and leaders such as Poor Buffalo and Satanta were all that remained. Sensing that everyone was about to abandon the siege for good, Botalye suddenly mounted his horse, took out his six-shooter, and made a mad dash for the wagon train. To their amazement, the elders saw Botalye keep riding past the wagons. His horse jumped over a rifle pit and charged through the gap between the two trenches. They heard the cracking shots inside the encirclement as Botalye emptied his gun. The soldiers had to be careful returning fire, or they might hit someone in the other trench. The chiefs watched Botalye pop back out of the dust on the other side of the encirclement and ride up to a ridge just beyond the wagons. He reloaded his gun, rode his horse in a tight circle, let out a whoop, and charged back through the bluecoats' camp, riding unscathed back to the group.

The chiefs and others were amazed. It was a coup that would go down in tribal history, they said. But don't try such a foolish thing again, they warned as they watched him grimly reloading his gun. "The soldiers will be ready for you this time."

They were shocked when he lit out again, and repeated the feat, returning once again unscathed.

Again, Botalye began reloading the gun. They implored him to stop.

"You've done enough."

"You've proved yourself a man, Botayle."

"Don't ride in there again."

His elders could only watch dumbstruck as he went back a final time. That was enough. Botalye returned this time with bullet holes in his robe and a chunk of his topknot missing. A coup didn't count if one were injured or killed.

"I could not have done it myself," Satanta said, and gave him a bear hug. Botalye had earned the respect of the revered chief as well as a new name. Poor Buffalo gave it to him on the spot. From that day forward, he would be known as He Wouldn't Listen.

Unbeknownst to the Kiowas, Comanches, and Southern Cheyennes, the circle around them was growing tighter. General Philip Sheridan had dispatched five expeditions from five different forts and decreed that any Indian caught off the reservation—man, woman, or child—was subject to attack. The Army was coming at the Texas Panhandle from almost every direction.

Colonel Nelson Miles commanded one of five columns of troops that were tracking down the renegades. His party was deep in the three tribes' territory and running low on supplies when he dispatched a wagon train to return to Camp Supply in Indian Territory so it could replenish his troops. He soon discovered that he was in the middle of a hornet's nest with hundreds of warriors reportedly in the area between the Washita and Canadian Rivers. He sent out a small search party under the cover of darkness to find out what happened to the supply train. After not hearing any word for several days, he organized a second search party, putting two scouts in charge, Amos Chapman and Billy Dixon. Chapman was half-Kiowa and a full-time scout employed at Camp Supply. Dixon was one of many of the buffalo hunters who sought temporary employment in the Army until the war died down and he could continue collecting hides. Miles, believing that the first party might have been captured and overwhelmed, told Chapman that he could take as many troops as needed. But the scout believed a small mounted party leaving at night would have a better chance of success, and he only took four privates.

The party the next day picked up the wagon train trail. They had no idea what kind of trouble it had been in. In fact, its three-day battle was over and the Comanches and Kiowas were returning to their camps.

The search party came up over a rise and found themselves less than a few dozen yards from a group of hostiles. The U.S. cavalry fought on their feet, not horseback. Sensing no escape, they dismounted with their weapons and ammunition. There was no cover at all, not so much as a mesquite bush to hide behind. They had just enough time to ready their guns when the Indians were upon them. The private in charge of holding the horses' reins was shot immediately and fell into the dust. The warriors scattered and captured their six mounts within seconds.

The five remaining men could only crouch on the ground to make themselves smaller targets. With any kind of concerted charge, the warriors could have dispatched them but to their amazement, the Indians retreated for a moment. It seemed that a cat-and-mouse game was on and they were going to be the mice. The fact that Comanches were in the party and had a predilection for torturing their victims before killing them was foremost in their minds.

Some of the Kiowas recognized the mixed-blood Chapman.

"Amos! Amos, we got you now," they yelled between charges.

Dixon may have been the one factor saving them in the first few hours. As a hide hunter, he was a formidable rifleman at long distances, and a few of the warriors had their horses shot out from under them.

Chapman took a bullet in the knee, and the remaining three soldiers were wounded as well, but not so severely. Dixon—the only unscathed member of the party—decided to risk running for the cover of a buffalo wallow. The depression in the ground—formed by bison for mud baths—was the only cover he could see. He dashed over as the Indians took potshots, kicking up dust all around him. Once he made it there, he called for the others to run over. It was a small miracle none of them were hit. But he hadn't realized that Chapman was wounded and couldn't run with them.

This predicament hadn't gone unnoticed by the Kiowas, who continued to call out to the wounded scout, who was left alone with his rifle and a shattered kneecap.

Dixon made several attempts to reach Chapman but was driven back by a barrage every time. Finally, he managed to zigzag his way over to his wounded comrade, pick him up, and carry him back to the buffalo wallow.

The sun beat down on them for the rest of the day as they contended with their thirst, their wounds, and sniping from the war party.

Relief came in the form of a late afternoon thunderstorm, which was both a blessing and a curse. The muddy water collecting at the bottom of the wallow saved the men from dying of thirst. But the storm brought in a cold front. They began to shiver, as their heavy clothes had been in their saddlebags with their horses.

The Indians let up their attacks somewhat after the storm. It was a good time to go retrieve the fallen private's gun and ammunition, Dixon decided. One of the other privates volunteered and soon came back, but reported that their comrade was still breathing. He and Dixon returned and brought the unconscious private back. He had a sucking wound in his lung.

Soon the sun set, and the men attempted to sleep in the cold mud. Sometime during the night, the wounded private passed away. They could only move his body out of the hole.

When dawn came, Dixon had no choice but to make a run for help.

The Kiowas and Comanches had by then moved off to engage a column of soldiers led by Major William Price, who was threatening an unprotected camp. Once the women and children had made good their escape, the Indian force withdrew and Price's men were able to rescue Miles's beleaguered supply train.

About two miles after leaving the wallow, Dixon ran head on into Price's advancing men. He breathlessly told the officer about the dire situation ahead. The officer dispatched the unit surgeon and two soldiers to take care of the survivors, but Dixon saw they were headed in the wrong direction and fired his rifle to grab their attention and wave them over to the location of the wallow.

As for the remaining wounded men, the gunshots in the distance could only mean one thing: Dixon didn't make it. The Indians got him. They saw three mounted men galloping in their direction. Assuming that they were the Indians, finally there to finish them off, they readied their rifles and opened fire, dropping one of the horses. Dixon saw what was happening, ran over, and shouted for the men to cease fire.

The surgeon was infuriated that he had been fired upon. He and Dixon arrived at what was certainly a pathetic scene: one corpse decaying in the sun and four wounded men caked in blood and mud. Their desperate state did nothing to damper the surgeon's anger. He gave them a perfunctory lookover but refused to tend to their wounds.

Soon, Price arrived and started hollering about the loss of a perfectly good horse. He ordered the wounded men to stay put while he sent word to Miles for him to come retrieve them. He refused to leave them weapons and ammunition, claiming that he couldn't spare any. A few of the enlisted men, taking pity on the group, gave them some of their rations, as Price left the men as he had found them.

I drive south of Canadian, where a giant green brontosaurus sculpture peers down on Highway 83/60 from atop a high hill.

The land here is pockmarked with gas and oil wells, and dirt roads leading to them. The dinosaur reminds me of all the fossil fuels lying beneath my car. Again, a turkey buzzard is making a slow, wide circle ahead of me.

Off to the west of Highway 83 is where the Battle for Lyman's Wagon Train and the Battle of Buffalo Wallow took place. It was a remarkably successful campaign for the Army, which had experienced few successes battling Native Americans on the Great Plains up to that point. The bluecoats soon drove the Comanches, Kiowas, and Southern Cheyennes back east to Indian Territory. The Red River War ended hostilities on the Southern Plains and opened the way for white settlers. Today, there are no reservations in the Texas Panhandle.

Aud the dinosaur, named after its creator Gene Cockrell's wife Audrey, watches over Highway 60/83.

As for the survivors of the buffalo wallow fight, Colonel Miles soon came to the rescue, understandably livid at the way Major Price had treated his men. The major was officially rebuked for his callowness and all six men received the Medal of Honor for their roles in the fight. Years later, a military bureaucrat revoked Dixon and Chapman's medals because they were not members of the military.

Satanta, for violating his parole, was sent to a Texas prison. He languished there for six years until the day he was informed he would never be pardoned. He killed himself by jumping out of a second-story window. Maman-ti, the Owl Prophet, was sent to a Florida prison, where he died from some unnamed tropical disease. He Wouldn't Listen, Botalye, lived long enough to tell his story to an amateur historian, an Army colonel stationed at Fort Sill, Oklahoma, in the 1930s. As for Tehan, no one ever recounted his origins—where or from whom he was captured—or knew his white identity. At the end of the war, when the leaders were being taken away in chains and the Kiowas were scattering in the chaos and confusion, he and another young warrior set out for Fort Sill. But his companion changed his mind. Not wanting to be sent to prison, he turned back, while Tehan, ever loyal to his adopted family, said he needed to go to the reservation to care for his mother. He departed alone, disappearing into the brush and from history. The Kiowas never saw or heard from him again.

U.S. Highway 60 merges with 83 for about twelve miles. As the zero in its designation indicates, it was once envisioned as a coast-to-coast highway. U.S. 83 and U.S. 60 are co-signed for a few miles before 60 branches off to the west. It will go as far as Amarillo before morphing into Interstate 40. Almost all of these East Coast–to–West Coast highways are absorbed at some point by soulless four-lane interstates. This is one reason I call 83 "the last American highway." There are only a few short stretches where it becomes one with an interstate—one twenty-five-mile span in North Dakota and another of about the same length in South Dakota.

But in both these cases, the legacy two-lane highway parallels the road, so drivers don't actually have to take the four-laners.

I am what they call a roadgeek. Railroad buffs and aviation buffs are well known. We roadgeeks maybe less so, but we are just as obsessed. We love following the federal highways and the paths of the old auto trails. We get excited finding a deserted gas station with vines crawling over it.

The story of how the United States developed its road system has largely been forgotten by the general public. I can count on one hand the number of good books written on the subject. The story of U.S. Route 83—born in 1926 but not fully completed until 1959—serves as a good example of how the nation grew its modern highways. It was an evolutionary, slow-motion process rather than a "big bang" creation. It took decades, but it transformed the nation.

Long before *homo sapiens* arrived in North America, migrating animals created the first paths. Then came the Native Americans who followed the herds, piecing together trails that would take them to sources of water or game. The Spanish created the first formal, named road in what would be Texas, known as *El Camino Real,* the King's Road, or the Royal Road, although it would be centuries before the Spanish journeyed very far north of the Rio Grande Valley. It would eventually stretch from Mexico to San Antonio. While it did not travel through modern-day Texas, the first major trail in the region connected the Spanish Empire in Santa Fe to the United States' trading center in St. Louis. By 1821 some intrepid traders had made the journey on the Santa Fe Trail, although the Spanish authorities frowned on it. Mexican independence opened up the trail, and it thrived for almost twenty-five years. More roads were created as oxen pulled supply trains from fort to fort. Their wheels cut grooves that could be followed by anyone including pioneers, Native Americans, and bandits.

The easiest and most efficient way to move people and goods on the Great Plains would be by rail. One of the first railroads to come to the region did its best to follow the Santa Fe Trail. The railways actually created more roads as teamsters hauled goods and passengers to far-flung settlements and ranches, creating paths that radiated from the whistle stops. These rudimentary roads were nothing but mud-filled ditches after it rained.

The State of Texas, meanwhile, saw road improvement as a matter for the counties. Localities would have to pay to grade and improve highways as they passed through. Commissioners passed special taxes to cover the costs; residents could either pay up or contribute by doing some backbreaking work to improve the local byways.

It wasn't the automobile age that ushered in the Good Roads Move-

From *Hamlin Herald*, April 25, 1930

ment, but rather the first bicyclists, who wanted better streets to practice their hobby. They made little headway until the motorists took up the mantle. A host of emerging industries, as well as local business leaders, backed them up: car manufacturers, petroleum pumpers, cement mixers, rubber factories. They made an alliance with the small-town chamber of commerce types who knew that better roads would bring economic development to their communities just as the railroads had. Of course, if there was someone in Washington lobbying for it, there was someone probably lobbying against it. The railroads, for example, weren't excited about taxpayer money going to a conveyance that would compete with their passenger trains.

The federal government had about the same attitude as the State of Texas: roads were a local matter, and the states and counties should take care of them. Frustrated, movement adherents began to develop their own roads without federal help. The Lincoln Highway in 1913 was the first coast-to-coast named highway, running from New York to San Francisco. Soon there were hundreds of these auto trails, some of them more aspirational than real. Boosters only had to draw up a map, then have volunteers mark the road to make it a reality. The Lincoln had blue and white signs with a capital "L." They were nailed on trees, stuck on posts, or painted on rocks. If a motorist drove more than a few miles without seeing one of these markers, they were more than likely lost.

As most of the nation's traffic was oriented east to west, many of these road boosters wanted a highway running north to south. They created a Great Plains Highway that ran more or less on what would be U.S. 83, except that it veered northwest to Regina, Saskatchewan, and took a more easterly route on its way to terminating in Laredo. Almost 200 businessmen gathered in McCook, Nebraska, on May 10, 1926 to create the Great Plains Highway Association.

In these parts, it was the Dallas-Canadian-Denver Auto Route, denoted with D.C.D. in white letters on a black background. The D.C.D. came from Dallas and hooked north at Childress, Texas, following what would be Texas Highway 4, and later Highway 83, up through Perryton. It was hoped that drivers wouldn't think they were taking the long way to the Mile High City via the *nation* of Canada.

The federal government finally saw the light in 1916 and passed the Federal Aid Road Act and began distributing some funds to states to help improve their highways. But as is the case with free money from the feds, there were strings attached. For example, the money couldn't be put toward a road that didn't connect to one in another state. And the state had to have a Department of Roads staffed with qualified civil engineers to administer the funds. That would seem like a no-brainer. But in fact, several states, including Texas, had no such agency.

Good Roads boosters from throughout the state pressured Governor Jim Ferguson to create a new Texas Highway Department. Ferguson was one of the most corrupt politicians to ever live in the governor's mansion. He never had any interest in building roads, until Washington passed the act, which would apportion funding based on the amount of highway miles in each state. As the largest state in the union at the time, Texas was therefore in line to grab a big pot of money. Suddenly, Ferguson was very interested in developing good roads. Texas created its highway department in January 1917. It was the fourth from last state to do so. It probably wasn't surprising that one of Ferguson's first acts was to have the state's motorists mail in their wheel taxes to a bank he just happened to own.

The newly formed department created some roads of its own, at least on paper. The Del Rio-Canadian Highway extended from Ochiltree to Del Rio on the Rio Grande by way of San Angelo. This route would eventually be Texas Highway 4, extending all the way down through the Lower Rio Grande Valley and on to the Gulf of Mexico. It more or less set the direction the present-day Highway 83 would follow.

I come to an intersection where Highway 60 verges to the west. If I were to follow it for another forty miles, I would be in

Woody Guthrie's second hometown of Pampa. I've never been there, and I'm a major fan of his music, but I will have to leave it for another time.

I have no real itinerary. Other than I'm expected back at my real job on a certain day. And my time off to explore Highway 83 will have to include somehow getting back to Arlington, Virginia, from Brownsville, Texas. I've actually thought about selling my car for whatever I could get for it and flying back one-way. At this point of the trip I'm inclined just to drive back. That will take a few days. Putting those considerations aside, I have only two hard, fast rules. One, I want to see all of the road in the daytime. So wherever I am when the sun goes down is where I check into a motel. The second is that I stop in every town long enough to at least take a few pictures.

How far should I go on this first full day of driving?

My experience in North Dakota, South Dakota, Nebraska, Kansas and Oklahoma, has proven that it always takes longer than I expect. I stop every few miles to take some photos. I meet an interesting person and the conversation lasts an hour. I tell myself I'm going to take a quick look inside a local museum, but I end up staying a lot longer than anticipated. And if I come across an antiques store, I must stop. I'm not in a rush, yet hard choices must be made. What constitutes a Highway 83 town? There are often signs pointing me right or left to towns seven or eight miles to the east or west. My rule of thumb is that if I can see the town from the highway, then I must stop and explore at least a little bit.

With this in mind, I blow through Wheeler, Texas, a one-time oil boom town where the fourth man to walk on the moon, Alan Bean, was born. Highway 83 as it passes through town is named after its most famous son. I have been a space nut since I was five, when I sat in front of the TV for days watching the first moon landing in 1969. Do I stop and see if I can track down his childhood home? Nope. I stop long enough to take some pictures of the town square, and I keep going.

My rule to take a few photos of every town is challenged again when I pass a wide spot in the road with a sign that says "Twitty." I pull the car over looking for something, anything of interest. There is no central business area that I can discern. I suspect this is one of those teeny-tiny towns hanging on with only a handful of residents. A middle-aged man with a sandy colored mustache pops out of his door to see who has parked in front of his house.

"So is this a town?" I say.

"This is Twitty, Texas!" he declares, a hint of defiance in his thick drawl, then fades back into his home. Apparently, I wasn't deemed a threat, or I wasn't whom he was expecting. Or maybe I hurt his feelings.

Up ahead is Shamrock, Texas, where Routes 83 and Route 66 connect. I should be there within a few minutes, but I catch sight of an abandoned stretch of the road as I enter the North Fork of the Red River Valley. Serendipity strikes again! I park the car on the south side of the river and, ignoring a "Private Property" sign, squeeze gingerly through a barbed wire fence and walk along a crumbling stretch of concrete that was once Highway 83 for a few hundred yards. Yet another turkey buzzard circles above me in a blue sky broken up only by the cotton candy–like cumulus clouds marching across the horizon. I glance down into the thickets for an old Highway 83 shield sign, but no luck.

This is actually an important unmarked natural boundary, and I'm glad I stopped here. Spring water keeps this watercourse and the Canadian River full year-round. The Ogallala Aquifer has been beneath my car since the Nebraska-South Dakota border, but this is where it ends on Highway 83. While it stretches down to Odessa on the west side of the Panhandle, those south of here along 83 are not so fortunate. Groundwater is patchy over the next few hundred miles and ranchers and farmers must rely on rain.

I remember my grandfather telling me about this vast underground ocean that lay directly beneath Stapleton and stretched from the Rocky Mountains to Nebraska. He relished the tap water and said it was the best tasting on Earth. Being a kid, I imagined a huge underground cavern with a large body of water sloshing around. The aquifer is actually stored in porous wet dirt and gravel.

As the environmental writer William Ashworth noted in his 2006 landmark book on the aquifer, *Ogallala Blue*, "The fourteen million acres of crops spread across its flat surface account for at least one-fifth of the total annual U.S. agriculture harvest. Five trillion gallons are drawn from the Ogallala annually .... If the aquifer went dry, more than $20 billion worth of food and fiber would disappear immediately from the world's markets."

Or perhaps we should say, *when* the aquifer goes dry. The water being pumped out cannot be replaced. We're like a thirsty kid sucking up a Slurpee through a straw. And just as at 7-Eleven, there are no free refills.

The old bridge is in remarkable shape and I take several pictures of traffic traveling over its replacement to the east. I head back to the car, thankful that I didn't get an ass full of buckshot. This is Texas after all, and "Private Property" signs are serious business. The whole expedition took another forty-five minutes out of my day.

After a few minutes, I cross over Interstate 40 and enter Shamrock, Texas. I have reached the Mother Road.

Route 83 and Route 66 have the same background and birthday, but their "brand-name recognition" isn't quite the same. Think John Wayne and Robert E. Morrison. The Duke had a brother who produced and directed a number of movies, but who remembers him?

Few remember Thomas H. MacDonald, either. Yet his impact on the lives of Americans is profound. More than any other person, he was credited with taking Americans out of the mud and onto decent roads. He was an Iowan who, from an early age, hated traveling on the state's crummy roads. By the time he was a civil engineering student at the University of Iowa, he had already decided that improving highways would be his life's work. He became the state's highway commissioner when it had a paltry $5,000 annual budget, and then went on to chair the American Association of State Highway Officials.

The Federal Aid Highway Act of 1916 was only one step in the creation of the federal system. When Congress named MacDonald the director of the Department of Agriculture's Bureau of Public Roads in 1919, he was ready to take charge. He was single-minded in his cause, believing that road building was the second most important task the government could perform, after educating children. He was allowed to keep his AASHO chairmanship—a real conflict of interest. That paled in comparison to the power Congress eventually bestowed upon him. He was allowed to directly negotiate contracts with states, bypassing congressional appropriators. In other words, the Treasury had to pay up on any contract he signed—an amazing abrogation of power on the lawmakers' part.

He set about creating standards for road work. There were many unanswered questions about roads, and the states were going their own ways. How wide should a road be? What paving material was best? He began validating standards at a test bed. All along, he was the public face of the Good Roads Movement, traveling from city to city to advocate for better highways and a national system, despite the deep opposition from the railroads.

The final law needed to put his master plan in place was the Federal Aid Highway Act of 1921, sponsored by a Colorado senator but basically written behind the scenes by MacDonald. At long last, he had the power to coordinate highways in America. A board of twenty-five AASHO members was charged with putting together the draft map of the federal highway system. The organization was under plenty of pressure to please everyone. With 28,000 or so small towns in America, every one of them wanting to be on one of the new federal highways, they weren't all going to get their wish.

When the draft came out in 1925, there was plenty of howling. First of all, the colorful, descriptive names the associations had put so much time into marketing were going to be replaced by numbers. The Lincoln Highway was now Route 30. The Dallas-Canadian-Denver road would become Highway 287. Such three-numbered highways would be considered "secondary," less important roads.

Even worse was when there was no road at all. The North Dakota lawmakers complained that there was a Route 85 in the western part of the state and Route 81 in the east, but nothing down the middle. They requested three more roads in the state's center. When the final map came out in 1926, it got one: Highway 83. There were only twenty-five men on the commission, but one happened to be from North Dakota. Maybe that helped.

ASSHO was also lobbied hard to create a Chicago–to–Los Angeles road following several old auto trails. There were plans to call it Route 60 or perhaps 62, but road enthusiasts in other states wanted those numbers. Its proponents settled on 66 just because it sounded good.

As for Route 83, the final draft had it stopping just short of Pierre, South Dakota. Through the rest of the 1920s and 1930s it extended southwards. The Great Plains Highway Association held on for a few years, but soon adopted Highway 83 as its own. The auto trail pole markers came down and the icon shield signs with numbers went up in their places. By 1931, Route 83 was appearing co-signed with Highway 4 in Texas. By 1939, it had completely supplanted the state highway except for the final few miles to the Gulf of Mexico.

Meanwhile, MacDonald's power only grew. When he visited a state capital, local leaders rolled out the red carpet and catered to his every wish. He was reportedly a dry, ponderous public speaker. But they would erupt with fawning applause in hopes of grabbing a bit more of that big pot of money he controlled. In Washington, he was a true autocrat. The only one who was permitted to ride the elevator with him was his personal secretary. His employees spoke only when spoken to in his presence. He would go on to serve in five presidential administrations. Like J. Edgar Hoover at the FBI, no one dared fire him.

After crossing the interstate, I drive over a giant white federal 66 shield sign painted on the concrete at the intersection of these two great highways. Of course, no giant U.S. Route 83 sign is painted there. No matter how much I hope, U.S. 83 will never reach the fame of U.S. 66. The Mother Road attracts tourists from all over the world who want to connect with the America of a bygone era. They remember the song. They might know the TV show, or perhaps they read John Steinbeck's *The Grapes of Wrath*, in which the protagonist Tom Joad eased his family's jalopy onto 66 for the first time and declared, "We stay on this road right straight through."

The beginning of Chapter 12 about the refugees fleeing the Dust Bowl is more like poetry than prose: "66 is the path of a people in flight, refugees from dust and shrinking land, from the thunder of tractors and shrinking ownership, from the desert's slow northward invasion, from the twisting winds that howl up out of Texas, from the floods that bring no richness to the land and steal what little richness is there. From all of these the people are in flight, and they come into 66 from the tributary side roads, from the wagon tracks and the rutted country roads. 66 is the mother road, the road of flight."

Route 66 is featured in the first third of the novel. Like the Mississippi River of Mark Twain's *Huckleberry Finn*, it becomes a character in the story—a living, breathing entity, but instead of water flowing, it is a stream of Dust Bowl refugees heading to California.

Then the dust settled, the war was won, and Bobby Troup wrote the song "(Get Your Kicks on) Route 66" for this new age of optimism and prosperity. Americans were soon loading up their cars with their children again—not to move to California to work in squalor as farm laborers, but to see Disneyland. Traveling on America's highways was fun!

For four years on CBS, viewers watched Tod Stiles and Buz Murdock travel the country in a Corvette convertible on the *Route 66* TV show. Each week presented a new story in a new setting.

Tod and Buz were hoboes with a great set of wheels—"rubber tramps," as they are called today. Route 66 itself was almost never portrayed or mentioned beyond the first few episodes, but no matter, the title represented freedom, adventure, and escape.

As Americans watched Tod and Buz on TV from 1960 to 1964, the road itself was beginning its decline. Interstates and turnpikes began to bypass the old highway. In 1985, the renamed American Association of State Highway and Transportation Officials decided that enough of the route was gone to kill it off. The mother road was dead, "decertified" as the bureaucrats termed it.

Long live U.S. Route 83, the Last American Highway! It's not decertified, and probably never will be. It's still (mostly) two lanes through the heart of America.

What U.S. 83 needs is a catchy song. I've been singing a rockabilly tune in my head for days. I just need the Brian Setzer Orchestra, Lucinda Williams, or JD McPherson to record it.

Highway 83,
That's the place for me
Travelin' down the Plains,
I've never felt so free!

Oh, who am I kidding? Route 66 has brand-name recognition. Highway 83, not so much.

At the corner of these two great highways stands the old Tower Conoco Station and U-Drop Inn, an art-deco style building constructed in 1936 that the town had the foresight to preserve. I come too late in the day, and the Chamber of Commerce visitors' center within is closed. I wish it were open so I could go in and say, "Hey! How about a little love for the border-to-border highway!"

Decertified? The thousands and thousands who seek out the old road and travel it by car, bus, or motorcycle each year couldn't care less. They come from the East. They come from Europe. The come from Japan. Along with the gas station, Business 66 going east to west through town has a string of old 1950s–era motels to offer those looking for Steinbeck's "great western road."

In 1956, there were spots on Highway 83 that were still gravel. In fact, it wouldn't be until September 1959 that every last inch of the road was paved. A thirty-mile stretch in the Nebraska Sand Hills from Stapleton to Thedford was the last portion to be sealed.

Not long after, the U.S. & Canada Highway 83 Association began producing postcards, brochures, decals, and restaurant placemats promoting tourism along the road. "PAVED ALL THE WAY!" they declared. "Travel the Old Trails," they said, suggesting that 83 followed the cattle drives of the 1800s, which isn't the case. But it certainly added an air of romanticism to driving the route.

In the mid-1960s, a retired school principal and a passionate member of the U.S. & Canada Highway 83 Association, Ira Laidig, drove solo from his home in Oberlin, Kansas, south to Texas. He had three goals: drum up support for the association, encourage the Texans to form a state Highway 83 Association, and have the chambers of commerce or city councils along the road sign a petition asking Washington lawmakers to replace Highway 83 with an interstate. Congress had already authorized the creation of an Interstate 27, but the appropriations committees had failed to fund it.

He kept a running single-spaced, typed report on his interactions with the community leaders as he traveled down to Brownsville, Texas, and back.

"Stayed in Perryton and called on the LaMasters, who are not only boosters, but Walt is on the highway association as a representative from Texas. They will do what they can but their relationship with the Chamber of Commerce is such that this can be very limited."

"Spent some time in Shamrock at the chamber's office and with Sam Pakan the strength in Shamrock. Mrs. Neeley is secretary in the office, but is merely a figure head with little or no authority. Pakan was very much interested in all things presented, such as petitions, state association, finances and things of that nature."

Laidig happened to be in Childress when a regional industrial development meeting was taking place. He attended and did his best to drum up support. He talked to many people there and may have done some good, he writes, "But they couldn't see the forest for the trees." He found that most were more interested in their east-to-west road, U.S. 287—the old D.C.D. auto trail, the shortest route from Dallas to Denver. He stopped at the corner of U.S. 83 and U.S. 287 at the famous Gay's Café, where he spoke to the husband and wife owners, Mr. and Mrs. Gay, who were supportive: "They are very much aware of the potential of 83 and Childress's slowness in seeing this."

Laidig seemed to be dropping in on these city and town leaders without any appointments. Sometimes no one was around. "On to Hamlin where I found the office closed...."

"... Returned to Aspermont, where through pure accident I got in contact with a lively energetic group of young fellows. They want to do things and are ready to move in any possible [way] to promote 83."

In Abilene he met with a group of twenty-five men and women. "They are and should be the leaders in this area. Abilene would like the national meeting in the near future. Was much pleased with the meeting there. Best by far of any meeting in Texas..."

"... Spent some time in Garner State Park[.] This is an excellent park with all kinds of facilities, accommodations and could be more promoted and advertised. In fact little is known of this park on 83."

Uvalde, he reported, "was the one of the least active towns along 83 so far as 83 is concerned. They as most towns are much more interested in roads running east to west.... The new president gave me every consideration and promised action on the petitions."

In South Texas, Laidig reported strong support in Crystal City and its neighbor Carrizo Springs. He attended several meetings in Laredo, which had hosted the national Highway 83 convention in 1963. The leaders of this border city were even more enthusiastic to promote tourism in the area, which was a major gateway to Mexico.

But as for the remainder of the Rio Grande Valley, he found little or no interest in the association. "Spent the evening and night in Mission. Called on the manager. He is a new man, his name is Charles Hakes. We can never expect so much from the valley as they sit in the receiving end and will get most of the traveling public of the area without effort. They do seem interested at least to the extent of being courteous."

At San Benito he complained that "all the towns in the valley are quite anxious to have advertising, activity and improvements along 83 so long as it does not cost effort, money or involvement, which might cause questions to be raised."

At Harlingen, he found outright opposition to any petition that would designate Highway 83 an interstate because they wanted the same for Highway 281, which ran north to San Antonio.

Finally at Brownsville, he found the city manager and assistant manager out of town. The "girl in the office Rachel Torres was a very efficient and informed young lady," but alas there wasn't much he could do except drop off information.

Laidig traveled over the bridge to Matamoros, Mexico, where he reported that plans to build an International Peace Garden— similar to one found near 83 on the North Dakota border with Canada—had stalled for lack of funds.

Laidig's petitions went nowhere, fortunately. The towns in Kansas for the remainder of the decade lobbied their lawmakers and governor hard to fund the building of Interstate 27, but it never happened. The 27 designation was eventually appropriated for a stretch of interstate from Lubbock to Amarillo, Texas.

North of the border, the association's Canadian members were lobbying their national government to extend Manitoba 83 all the way to Hudson Bay. They, too, were unsuccessful.

Of course, I'm glad the association's efforts to destroy and decertify Highway 83 and replace it with a homogenous four-lane superhighway came to nothing. On the other hand, it's too bad the Canadians failed. Driving from the Gulf of Mexico to Hudson Bay would be a fantastic road trip.

Shamrock's main commercial strip is actually on Highway 83, not old Route 66. The tallest water tower of its class in Texas looms over its downtown as I hightail it south. I'm burning daylight, and I have one sight to see before the sun sinks.

Ten miles south of Shamrock, I find what I am looking for—a steel bridge that has been replaced by a modern bridge to the east. The truss bridge's steel beams that create an archway over the Salt Fork of the Red River are intact. I park at a picnic area on the west side of the new bridge, where hundreds of swallows have already pasted their mud nests. They dart in and out as I make my way to the old bridge on the other side of the road. Construction crews have blocked the bridge off with a pile of dirt to keep motorists off it, but it's still walkable.

I'm here just in time, not only to take pictures in the soft light of the evening, but to see this bridge at all. In a few more months, it may be completely gone. The Texas Department of Transportation has it slated for destruction. Collingsworth County residents have been fighting to preserve the bridge for some five years, but despite their outcries, the end is near. Proposals to turn it into a pedestrian-only bridge—similar to what Canadian did with its wagon bridge—never came to fruition, mostly because of a lack of funds. That is too bad. These old steel bridges have their own kind of beauty and they are disappearing from the American landscape.

This I knew before arriving because I had done my research ahead of time. For one of the most notorious incidents to happen on Highway 83 in Texas occurred here on the night of June 10, 1933, when the gravel road was in the process of being paved. Clyde Barrow, in the fading evening light, failed to see the detour sign and sent his car skidding off the pavement and onto the old dirt road. The Ford V-8 crashed through a barrier and flew into the ravine.

THE RED RIVER PLUNGE

Clyde Barrow only knew one speed: breakneck. He had a hellhound on his trail; there was little choice but to drive fast.

Daylight was fading as he came barreling north up a recently paved section of Highway 83. His girlfriend, Bonnie Parker, sat next to him, and his loyal teenage lackey William Daniel Jones, better known as W.D., was in back of the Ford V-8, one of the fastest cars one could buy—or in Clyde's case—steal.

Clyde was a small-time crook who had graduated to cop killer and had become so infamous that there was no place to hide anymore. All he and Bonnie could do was run.

And so they drove from town to town, camping out in the brush at night, staying at the farmhouses of the rural poor who were either sympathetic to their plight, or simply didn't know the identity of Texas's most notorious criminals. Sometimes they stayed in motor courts, the relatively new single-cabin hotel rooms that were popping up on the outskirts of towns to cater to travelers driving the new highways. The motor courts were preferable to the traditional brick hotels found in town squares; it was easier to make an escape from these roadside "motels." But roomy cabins and comfortable beds were becoming more and more risky since the duo's pictures had been printed on the front page of nearly every daily and weekly from Lubbock to Texarkana and states beyond.

Clyde had no choice but to drive, and drive fast. Keep moving or die. The Barrow Gang robbed gas stations and small town grocery stores, not to strike it rich, but just to survive. They had been on the lam for almost fifteen months. How many times had they crossed or driven down Highway 83? Too many to keep track.

Two months earlier, Clyde, his older brother Buck and his wife, Blanche, Bonnie, and W.D. had escaped a shootout in Joplin, Missouri, that left two lawmen dead. They ended their flight in a motor court at the intersection of 83 and 66 in Shamrock. Since then, they had traveled dusty roads in Texas, Kansas, Oklahoma, Arkansas, Louisiana, and Indiana, and had even taken a "vacation" in Florida.

It all started in the slum known as West Dallas. Clyde was twenty years old and had already experienced a few run-ins with the law. He had made several attempts to "go straight," but he was on the Dallas police's "list," meaning every time a major crime was committed in the city, they showed up at his place of employment and hauled him in for questioning. That didn't sit well with employers, who had their pick of men needing jobs during the worst years of the Depression.

When Bonnie spotted Clyde at a party of a mutual friend in 1930, he was nattily dressed, with a little money to flash and a nice car (both ill-gotten). He wasn't tall, but she was quite petite. It was love at first sight for the pair, and Bonnie soon became enamored with this dangerous boy with the wavy brown hair and mischievous brown eyes.

It wasn't her first relationship. Bonnie had been married at fifteen to a blond muscular boy slightly older than her, who also dressed well and had a mysterious source of money. He disappeared on her after a few months and never returned.

Like many West Dallas working-class girls, she dreamed of a better life, something akin to the glamorous movie stars she saw at the local theaters. But she had no hope of any education beyond high school. And when the stock market crashed in 1929, it hit the working poor particularly hard. Even finding a job as a waitress or store clerk was tough.

The pair's time together was brief. The police arrested Clyde in front of Bonnie's family one morning. Her mother, Emma, never stopped pleading with her daughter to give up on Clyde. But Bonnie worshipped him to the end.

The arrest resulted in Clyde being sentenced for robbery to the brutal Eastham prison farm, a living hell for anyone unlucky enough to be sent there. The farm had one purpose: to grow as much cotton and corn from slave prison labor as it could under the most inhumane conditions imaginable. Clyde and the other prisoners were forced to run the two miles to the fields in the morning, work ten-hour days with little rest and a meager lunch, then run two miles back as guards riding horses with rifles watched their every move, and beat those who they believed were slacking off.

Back in the overcrowded dormitory, the slight Clyde was raped repeatedly by a fellow prisoner and one of the guards' favorites, Ed Crowder. After a year of being tormented, Clyde took a rival prison goon up on a promise to take the rap if Clyde could knock off Crowder. Clyde lured the hulking bully into the bathroom one night and brought a pipe down on his head. It all went as planned. Clyde's ally took the blame, claimed it was self-defense, and received no punishment. Clyde had killed his first man.

But even after getting rid of Crowder, Clyde was still facing another thirteen years in Eastham, if he could survive that long. He was wasting away on the starvation diet, toiling under the brutal Texas sun. Even worse, the letters from his sweetheart Bonnie started to become less frequent. She had apparently found someone new. Clyde's family was petitioning the governor for a pardon or a parole, but he had reached the end of what he could take. Like a beaver forced to chew off a leg to escape the jaws of a fur trap, Clyde took an ax and chopped off two of his left toes to get out of work. It was the only way to escape the relentless pain that would lead to an inevitable death. Little did he know that the governor intended to parole him within days.

Out of prison, and back with Bonnie, Clyde made a few attempts to find a legitimate job. But nothing worked out for the ex-con, who now had a pronounced limp.

Clyde Barrow and Bonnie Parker in Joplin, Missouri, circa 1934. Library of Congress photo.

One thing Bonnie loved about Clyde was that he was a take-charge kind of guy. He wanted to lead his own criminal gang. Clyde was no criminal genius, though—far from it. During one of their first capers together, he was forced to leave Bonnie behind to be captured by police. She was eventually let loose after a grand jury believed her "unwilling accomplice" story.

Most of Clyde's bank robberies were botched. And when one was successful, it netted a paltry sum. Wannabe criminals joined his gang, but the smart ones left once they figured out that they weren't going to strike it rich running with the Barrow Gang.

William Daniel Jones wasn't one of the smart ones. He was sixteen years old and knew the Barrow family from West Dallas. He didn't have a lick of sense, but he worshipped Clyde, and that was a good enough reason for Clyde to keep the kid around.

As would be expected when there are guns being brandished, eventually folks started getting killed. Only days after W.D. joined the gang, he and Clyde were attempting to steal a Ford when its owner ran out and grabbed Clyde by the collar as he was trying to drive off. Clyde killed his pursuer with a bullet in the neck—all just to see if W.D. had the guts to steal a car. No one was supposed to get hurt. But things tended to go horribly wrong when Clyde was calling the shots. Soon Bonnie and Clyde, along with W.D., were fulltime fleers, perpetually on the run.

They tried to keep a low profile in the town of Joplin when his older brother Buck and his wife, Blanche, came to meet them. But the local cops came calling, and they had to shoot their way out of the predicament. The result was two more law enforcement officers dead. Clyde swore he wouldn't go back to Eastham. But after the killings, the prison farm wouldn't be his end. He knew he would die in the electric chair or in a swarm of bullets. Bonnie knew it as well. She was determined to share his fate.

While the Barrows were inept bank robbers, they were good at one thing: escaping. It was more than just dumb luck, though. They knew that the best weapons could be stolen from National Guard armories. They took machine guns and other military-grade arms. Small-town law enforcement officers were normally armed with revolvers. Clyde, Buck, and W.D. stole only the most powerful cars. V-8s were the best. The cops didn't have anything nearly as fast. The gang could drive and blast their way out of almost any situation.

Clyde always took the wheel, for he had to be in charge and in control. Given the way he drove—the powerful cars, the poorly maintained country roads—it was far more likely that Bonnie and Clyde would die in a jumble of twisted steel, wrapped around a tree, than at the hands of the law. They both knew that their luck would one day run out. It was near the bridge on Highway 83 that would mark the beginning of the end for the notorious duo.

The battery acid poured out from the smashed engine compartment and trickled down Bonnie's right leg. It began to eat her flesh, and she passed out from the excruciating pain.

They had not landed in the water, for there was little of that in these dry summer months in the middle of the Dust Bowl. Clyde, stunned but still conscious, reached out of the smashed car window to try to pull himself out. He felt a pair of hands take his. Sam Pritchard lived less than 100 yards from the highway, and along with his wife and extended family who were over for a visit, had witnessed the accident. His son, Sam, and son-in-law, Alonzo, pulled the two men from the wreckage. Trickier was getting the unconscious and barely breathing woman from the car. They rushed her up to their home, where Sam's daughter Sallie poured baking soda on the long burn, stopping the acid from stripping away more of her skin.

The driver of the wrecked car insisted that the family not go to town to fetch a doctor, and then returned to the damaged vehicle in full sight of everyone to retrieve his guns. That was suspicious enough to prompt Alonzo to slip out and drive to Wellington to alert the local police. But no one had any idea that those they'd saved were the notorious Barrow Gang.

When chief of police Paul Hardy and county sheriff George Corry stepped inside the house, Clyde and W.D. had the drop on them and took them hostage. But not before a jumpy W.D. emptied his shotgun at Sam's daughter Gladys, believing that she was reaching for a gun, when she was only stopping her daughter from running outside. The blast winged her hand. She was fortunate to escape serious injury.

Clyde and W.D. took the two lawmen hostage, hijacking their car to drive to Oklahoma to meet Buck and Blanche. Bonnie was in agony, but taking her to a hospital was out of the question. She lay across the officers' laps as W.D. kept his pistol trained on them from the front seat. Since Hardy and Corry had treated her so kindly, Clyde decided not to kill them. After meeting up with his brother, Clyde instead left his hostages tied to a tree at the side of the road.

Bonnie and Clyde had escaped once again.

Wellington, Texas, is where I spend the worst night of my life.

There is nothing particularly bad about the town, or what I can see of it as the afternoon light begins to fade. It just happens to be where I end up when the sun goes down. There isn't a large selection of motels in the town of some 2,200 residents. I pick out one that looks like it dates back to at least the 1950s, secure a room, and eat at a diner just south on the highway. They pull up the sidewalks early in some of these small towns, so it's not a bad idea to find a hot meal before the best places close up, or it's gas station microwave burritos for dinner.

"Home of the Skyrockets," a giant billboard on 83 declares, with a firework exploding. I'm a fan of unique high school mascots. I make a mental note to look around for some T-shirts.

I return to the small motel room, which like the exterior looks like it could use an update, with bland walls, old carpeting, a boxy TV and shower. I'm on a budget, and I've stayed in much worse on this trip. I thought I would relax a bit before heading out to drive around town, maybe find a local watering hole.

But first I have to call my wife. We had a huge argument the night before I left on the trip and I haven't spoken to her for several days.

She went to an adult education class on doing voiceover work because she thought it might be interesting. She came home excited because the instructor said she had a wonderful speaking voice. He also gave the class the soft-sell on some voice acting lessons. As she described him, I recognized the teacher for what he was: a salesman peddling his voice coaching side business, not an adult education teacher. But I don't say anything.

She was doing it. She was all in. She told me about all the extra money she could make doing voiceover work as she repeated back the sales pitch. And then she said the words no husband wants to hear: "Now don't get mad when I tell you how much it costs…$3,500."

The argument was on.

It was seemingly about money—a common topic of contention among couples. Hardly worth mentioning, really, but it actually wasn't about money. It was about the fact that we couldn't have children.

We found each other late in life. I had made it well into my forties without ever being hitched. But this was my wife's second marriage. Her first was tumultuous, and she knew having a child with her husband would be a mistake. She was in her late thirties when we married, the time when magazine articles warn women that their biological clock is ticking. We began trying right away, and reading and practicing everything we could for tips to make it happen. As the months went on, the disappointment and tears came regularly. After a year, it was time to see what medicine had to say. We went to the best fertility doctor in the greater Washington, D.C., metro region.

We were both tested, prodded, and poked, our bodily fluids collected in little jars over the course of several weeks. The doctor gathered all the data and sat us down in his office and sketched out on a blank piece of paper what he thought the problem was. He concluded that my wife had a hormone problem, one that was somewhat common for women her age. She had the eggs; they just weren't dropping. As he began to explain some of the options my wife began to sob. Amazingly, the best fertility doctor in town didn't haven't any tissues on his desk, and had to run off to look for some.

I held her hand and I sat and listened to all the options that would cost a pile of money that we didn't have. Each had a low percentage of success.

The months leading up to my departure for Texas were rough. We were both in mourning for the children that we would never have, although she would have had to waterboard me before I would admit that I was suffering, too.

Fifteen thousand dollars for a twenty percent chance of having a child. We could have scraped up the money somehow, but then what if it didn't work out? I didn't think she could survive the heartache. The guilt was already eating her alive. She said she couldn't go through with it. I said, okay.

It was my job to be the man: keep things happy. Continue to be positive. I had asked the doctor if something could change as far as the hormones were concerned, and if she could still become pregnant. "Absolutely," he said. I heard that, but she didn't.

When we encountered a cute baby in a stroller on the sidewalk, I pretended it wasn't there. Cute babies on TV. Not there. But tears came at random times. She asked me several times if I wanted to leave her for a younger woman. I said "no, of course not." She looked for an infertility support group, but couldn't find one that really matched what she was going through. The other members were still actively trying to become pregnant. She shared with me their stories of all the money they had paid the fertility specialists to become mothers, but to no avail. Where did they find this endless well of cash, we wondered? We told ourselves that we would never want to put ourselves through that emotional roller coaster.

Meanwhile, her job was not going well. Her boss was incompetent. Her career in international development, which she had began late in life and accrued massive student loan debt to pursue, seemed to be going nowhere.

"Two treatments for the price of one!" A woman on a radio ad chirped enthusiastically as I sat in my dentist's waiting room. "Come on. Let's have a baby!" she said. There were apparently enough of us for there to be a radio spot for fertility treatments. They were advertising it as if it were Lasik eye surgery. I told her about the ad. She still refused.

I called my friend Bob Atherton, a marriage counselor in Omaha, about all this. He told me that both of us were in mourning, not just her. I realized the moment that he said it that it was true. It was okay to drop my façade and let her know that I was suffering, too. It was part of the grieving process, he said.

By the time I packed my bags for Highway 83, I had yet to confess this. Here I was leaving by myself on a big adventure, spending the profits from my last book on some vague plans to write another, while she stayed home in our tiny one-bedroom apartment in Arlington and went to her crummy job.

Given all this, the right thing to do when she said the words "three thousand five hundred dollars" would have been to jump up and down enthusiastically, run and grab the credit card from my wallet, and say, "Anything for you, baby! Whatever you want!"

But I am a horse's ass. Not only did I not do that, I convinced myself that the argument was her way of sabotaging my trip by making me miserable. So for revenge, I have maintained radio silence for the first few days of the trip. While my best friend is a marriage counselor, I'm sure that he wouldn't approve of any of this behavior.

When I reach her on the phone the conversation picks up where it left off. After some discussion, I tell her that if she really wants to take voice lessons, she can. She informs me that she had already made up her mind to do so and she doesn't need my permission.

But that doesn't solve anything.

She pauses. "I want to know how you really feel," she says to me, with an inflection that makes it a question.

I feign ignorance. "About what?" I say, as if I that would help postpone the conversation.

"I want to know how you really feel about me not being able to have a baby?"

And then I tell her. I repeat what Bob has told me: that we are both mourning, and that it is a normal stage of grief. And I finally confess that I am hurting just as much as she is. And my voice cracks just a little, enough for her to hear.

There is silence. And then I hear the sobs coming from the other end of the line. Deep, sorrowful sobs. And I feel utterly helpless. I'm 1,800 miles away, unable to reach out and hold her in my arms, tell her everything is going to be okay. The motel room feels like a jail cell.

I don't know if I had ever felt so low in my life, lying in a queen-sized bed in tiny motel room in faraway Wellington, Texas, dim light, listening to my wife tell me that our marriage is over. She wants me to leave her for a younger woman.

"No, no, no!" I say. Telling her that I don't want that. Thinking to myself that Bob is wrong. Very wrong. Why have I listened to his advice?

Nothing seems to stop the tears.

We talk for another hour. I tell her about all the great kids we know who were adopted, which isn't the first time this has been discussed. She is against it. I drop it. I'm still hoping she will come around to the idea someday.

When we finally let each other go for the night, I feel that nothing has been resolved. Those deep sobs haunt me, and will for the remainder of the trip.

Wellington's brush with the notorious Bonnie and Clyde is one of the town's claims to fame. And I understand the local history museum has some relics from that violent, mad night. I arrived too late in the evening and will leave too early in the morning to see them, though. I drive around the town square in the dawn light, hours before anything will open. The town seems empty and forlorn, but maybe that's just me. This calls for some blues, and the spare guitar picking of Lightnin' Hopkins begins the day.

I have entered the heart of cattle country now. I have miles and miles of barbed wire, mesquite, and turkey buzzards ahead of me. Plenty of time to go over the previous night's conversation in my head. What comes after grief? Isn't it acceptance? Was that the purpose of the Heartbreak Motel? Will something positive come out of this as Bob predicted? He never told me *not* to confess my true feelings of grief when we were 1,800 miles away from each other. Although I'm sure he would have advised against it.

And there is that same turkey buzzard ahead of me, flying in languid loops above the highway, waiting for someone like me to come along and squash a prairie dog, lizard, bird, or some kind of critter. Barbed wire, mesquite, and buzzards. Aside from the road and the sky, they are the three most common objects I will see for the rest of the day.

The vultures are such a frequent sight that I have some crazy idea in my head that this is the same one, somehow maintaining a holding pattern just a few hundreds yards ahead of my car.

He's not actually looking for roadkill. He's sniffing it out. *Cathartes aura* uses its sense of smell to find carrion. Since he's so large, a seventy-inch wingspan on average, he's easy to spot. A highway such as this is one long smorgasbord for buzzards. They prefer the recently deceased rather than carcasses that have reached the point of putrefaction, so he's no doubt looking down on my dark blue Protegé hoping that I will provide him a quick and easy breakfast. I do my best to avoid running over critters, though.

The other constant on my trip on Highway 83 from the Dakotas down to Texas is barbed wire. Except when I pass through towns, it's often on either side of me—three strings of it or more, so prevalent that it is easy to overlook. One can't ignore the importance of this invention to the development of the Texas Panhandle and the Great Plains. Gun enthusiasts will claim that the Colt six-shooter tamed the West, but it was really barbed wire.

The steel fences protected claims, kept cattle from drifting away, and prevented them from eating crops. Patented in 1867, the invention caught on quickly but at first was a cause of conflict. The Fence Cutting Wars pitted large landowners against homesteaders and landless ranchers who were accustomed to grazing their herds on public lands. The big outfits strung the wire across roads, cutting off access to areas they didn't control, leading to organized gangs of fence cutters. Sometimes those gangs squared off against vigilantes hired by the big ranches, and the bullets started flying.

By 1884, Texas had passed a law mandating prison sentences for fence cutters, but the law also required landowners to place well-maintained gates every three miles and to remove fences that weren't on their property. That seemed to please most everyone, and the so-called war died down.

I have a healthy respect for the fences. I have only two scars on my body, both from barbs, both wounds suffered while visiting my grandparents in Stapleton, Nebraska. I was about five years old when I was playing with some kids at the school grounds there. They were on the other side of the fence in a pasture near the playground equipment. I tried to slip under it but I got punctured in the left lower abdomen. I went bawling back to my grandparents' house.

When I was a teenager, I tried to slip through the wires on a friend's ranch west of town, and a barb sliced a three-inch gash on the side of my left thigh. It amazingly didn't draw much blood, and I didn't do much about it other than put a bandage on. It left a bulbous scar. This is what happens when a city boy comes to the country.

Of the turkey buzzards, the barbed wire, and the mesquite, however, by far the most annoying is the latter. I'm really beginning to notice the roughly ten-to twelve-foot tall trees lined up along the fences. They are just big enough to block my view. Honey mesquite is not an invasive species. It is native to the land. Its edible seeds saved many a starving animal and explorer. The oily wood burns a long time. Its role in barbecue is the only thing I knew about it before reaching this part of Texas.

Ranchers hate it. The trees' deep roots suck the water tables dry, leaving little for native grasses. But as many have pointed out, ranchers have a great deal to do with its proliferation. Prairie fires that were once part of the natural cycle on the Great Plains and kept the number of trees in check are not welcomed today. Prairie dogs, once the trees' natural enemies since they consumed so many of the seeds, have now been nearly wiped out by cattlemen who consider them pests. Poorly managed ranges where there is overgrazing have also let the trees prevail over the grasses.

But the ranchers fight on. The Mesquite War has been ongoing for decades. This fight is man versus nature. But try eliminating a tree that has roots reaching as far down as seventy feet. At least from the road, the trees seem to be winning.

The Prairie Dog Town Fork of the Red River is an unexpected pleasure. I'm amazed and a little sad that the state, the county, or whoever is responsible, has not built a turnoff so drivers can pull over and take in the beauty of this valley, where the cloudless blue sky touches the dark green mesquite-lined banks. The channels are the color of uncooked pinto beans—the result of oxidized sandstone found in the rock outcrops to the west.

I park the car on the south side and walk over the bridge, which features a wide shoulder. Traffic is light, only a car or truck coming every couple minutes, leaving me in peace to take in the rippled patterns that the water has carved into the red sand. The river is only a few inches deep here—so shallow a lone beer can lying in the mud still sticks out from the water. This, the main channel, meets up with the Salt Fork to the east and flows on to the Mississippi.

The Red River, the Brazos, the Rio Grande. Just about every one of these rivers I'm going to encounter in Texas is included in the name of a western movie, book or song. But not the Pease. "Across the Pease River." Nope. Just doesn't have a romantic ring to it.

Paducah, Texas, is the most disheartening spot on Highway 83.

It's not that I'm unfamiliar with sad, dying small towns. Empty storefronts are common on the Great Plains. I've seen plenty of them during my travels on Highway 83. But nothing prepared me for Paducah.

I thought that a town in Kansas called Gem, a true misnomer, was the worst case of rural blight that I had ever seen. Its dirt road main street was one long string of empty building and churches. Its schoolhouse—surrounded by barbed wire fence—sat forlorn on the edge of town with every window broken out.

But the thing about Gem, Kansas, was that it never really amounted to much. It peaked at a few hundred residents before the Depression. Paducah, on the other hand, was once a grand town with a grand town square.

On the western side where Highway 83 passes sits the M. B. Moses Co. 5-10-25¢ & $1.00 Store, a beautiful two-story building that once housed the First State Bank. Closed. Its second-floor windows boarded up. Next to it, the florist. Closed. On the northeast corner, the Cottle Hotel, a full block long, three stories tall. Closed. The first floor boarded up, the upper floors open to the elements.

J. E. Norris Appliance and Furniture Co. on the other side of the street. Empty. Antonio's Mexican Café features an elegant couple dancing in full regalia hand-painted on the window. Closed. Love Bridal & Gifts. Closed.

Down the street a half block from the square is the most disturbing of these ghost businesses: a nameless implement store that looks like it was abandoned at 6 p.m. on a Saturday evening and simply never reopened. The window is broken out, and I peer inside, where shelves are stocked with plastic motor oil bottles and cans of solvents. The counter and chairs feature an inch of West Texas dust. There are tires, a wooden barrel. A four-foot tall safe. A sad-looking, faded American flag droops from the wall. The ceiling is brown with water damage. Not only has no one cleaned out the business, no one has bothered to nail up a sheet of plywood to cover the gaping hole.

The east side of the square appears to have a local newspaper still operating, but it's not currently open. The entire north side of the square is a long string of closed businesses.

I don't see a single soul.

"No Skateboard Bicycles Rollerblades on Sidewalk. Fines Up To $200." A city sign reads. Are you kidding me? They should be paying kids to ride their bikes and skateboards on the sidewalks. It would give this depressing place a little life.

In the middle of the square is a big, Art Deco county courthouse. A historical marker informs me that it was built in 1929 for $150,000. "A four-story brick and terra cotta building that looms over the square. Stepped blocks project from a central mass, with carved eagles, stylized figures of justice and liberty, and inscriptions above each of four entries. The unusual design, which has drawn comparison to an Egyptian temple, makes it one of the most distinctive buildings in the region," the marker reads.

It actually looks like a fort. I can almost see cannons sticking out of it to protect a harbor. It has a well-kept lawn with green grass, and there are a few pickup trucks parked along its edge, meaning that if I went inside I would find some human beings and I could ask them what the hell happened to Paducah.

But the fact is, I already know.

I can imagine Saturday morning here on the Paducah town square a century ago with hundreds of farmers and ranchers in town for their once-a-week trip to take care of business. Depending on how far away they lived, it would take them an hour or two to make it in their horse-drawn buggies. A few automobiles may have been parked alongside them, but not too many yet.

The children would find their townie friends or cousins and run off to play, while their dads went for a haircut and their mothers shopped at the general store to stock up on some essentials. If they were lucky, the kids might have a nickel to spend on candy. The bank was open and had long lines. The men gathered on the sidewalk, smoking, jawing about the weather, crops, politics.

A second historical marker informs me that the early settlers here were mostly Civil War veterans who arrived about twenty years after the end of the conflict. The majority of them had fought for the South in Texas units. But there were Unionists as well, some of whom became wealthy ranchers. "On occasional trips to town [they] verbally refought the war on the courthouse square but lived peacefully together to build a great country," it said.

Then Texas Highway 4 was built running north and south. It wasn't a great road—it was dust and gravel—but it made driving to town in cars and trucks that were rapidly replacing the buggies all the more convenient and much faster.

Texas Highway 4 was supplanted by Highway 83. The feds also placed U.S. Highway 70 here, one of the coast-to-coast highways, and the town would call itself the "Crossroads of America," one of about a dozen other communities to make that claim.

Before arriving here, I had passed by the Walmart Supercenter in Childress, about thirty-two miles to the north. It would be easy to blame Paducah's decline on the big-box store, but like many prairie towns, the seat of Cottle County was in a rapid state of decline before it arrived.

The town's population almost hit 3,000 residents in the 1950 Census. It has been sliding ever since, losing almost 300 people every decade. Every abandoned house, every closed business has continued to degrade the tax base. The roads got better, the cars safer. The speed limits went up. The hospital closed in 1985. Good thing the ambulance can make it to Childress within a half hour. That is, if the patient has thirty minutes to spare.

One can see the businesses on the town square falling like dominoes until there was no reason to come here barring some pressing business with the county. There might be enough money to save one or two of these beautiful old buildings, but not all of them. Weather, gravity, lack of upkeep will destroy each of them one by one. The courthouse will be surrounded by rubble.

Gem, Kansas, I decide, is not the most depressing place on Highway 83. That near ghost town never amounted to much. Paducah's town square once thrived. And that makes it all the more sad.

Most agree that the southern border of Cottle County marks the end of the Texas Panhandle. Geographically, there is no change in the landscape when I cross into King County. Yet there is something different. The mesquite trees have been chopped down and their gnarly branches placed in stacks along the fences. There is a serious, ongoing effort here to fight the pernicious trees. I'm now driving through the 6666, the legendary Four Sixes, a vast ranch that takes up most of the county.

I don't want to overreach and say this is "the heart of cattle country." That would not only be a cliché, but too many other spots can make that claim. I can say, however, that this land gave birth to no fewer than two Marlboro men.

The man who sparked the idea for the advertising icon never got paid a penny by the Phillip Morris Company. Clarence Hailey Long appeared on the August 22, 1949, cover of *Life* magazine. He wore a white cowboy hat and frayed kerchief and had a cigarette pointing straight out of his mouth. The only word that accompanied the photo was "cowboy." Inside was a photo spread about ranching in the West.

The black-and-white portrait of the leathery-skinned ranch foreman from Paducah squinting into the sun caught the attention of a Chicago ad man, Leo Burnett, who had been trying to figure out how to sell Marlboro's filtered cigarettes to men. That was a challenge. On the masculine products scale, they were on par with nylons and lipstick. As a test, he found a cowboy hat, a bandana, and a male model and replicated the Long photo in a Chicago studio. He knew immediately that he was onto something. What could be more emblematic of manhood than the tough, independent cowboy?

Long's picture inspired an ad campaign that would not only make men want to smoke filtered cigarettes, but endured for decades, even as evidence grew that smoking was linked to lung cancer. The Marlboro man became an American archetype. The company changed its mind every few years about whether it should use male models or real working cowboys to serve as its symbol of masculinity. One magazine ad infamously showed a dude wearing his spurs upside down.

Then an advertising executive with Burnett's agency spotted a handsome young cowboy at the 6666 ranch. His discovery settled the matter.

COWBOY TO THE BONE

Glenda Jo Rees, undergrad at Texas Tech University in Lubbock, had a thing for cowboys. Her interest in ranch hands was a sort of inside joke among her girlfriends. She would soon be graduating with a teaching degree and never truly pictured herself living that kind of country lifestyle. One of her cohorts showed up at her dorm room with a picture of the Marlboro man clipped from *Life*. The hat, the blue eyes, the handsome, rugged look and the cigarette: here was the ideal cowboy for her.

"Oooh. I'm going to marry him someday," she joked as she taped it up on her wall.

The man in the photo took on a life of his own as the weeks passed. One friend located an article in a magazine profiling him. He had a name—Carl "Big-un" Bradley Jr.—and he was no phony male model. In fact, he lived at the famous 6666 ranch 100 miles east of Lubbock. He was a third-generation cowboy born and raised near the tiny town of Knox City. His uncle gave him the nickname "Big-un" and his little bother the name "Little-un," the article said. He was now a foreman.

Glenda graduated, the picture came down from the dorm room wall, and then she was out, more or less on her own. Using her parents' home in Westbrook as a base, she spent the summer interviewing for teaching jobs in small West Texas towns.

One of her college friends invited her to Stamford over the July 4th weekend, when the town hosted one of the region's most famous rodeos of the year. The Stamford Cowboy Reunion, a three-day rodeo, quarter horse show, dance, and Independence Day celebration, had been held every year since 1930 and

Carl "Big-un" Bradley at the 6666 Ranch, 1968. Taken by Tom Ryan. ©
Dickenson Research Center, National Cowboy & Western Heritage Center,
Oklahoma City, Oklahoma

attracted thousands from all over the area. This was a real working cowboy's rodeo and not for the so-called "arena trained" types who had never worked on a ranch.

During the first night's dance, Glenda and her friend found themselves standing right in front of the Marlboro man himself. He really wasn't a "big one," standing at 5′11″, and he smoked menthols, not Marlboros. He was thirty years old, eight years her senior, and plainly unattached by the way he was playing the field. Being a local celebrity—and handsome to boot—he had his pick of dancing partners. Meeting him there wasn't outlandish. His hometown was only thirty-five miles to the north and he had been attending the celebrations since he was a boy. He did the Texas two-step with a bunch of gals as the country-western band kept the dancers moving. Glenda's friend caught his eye, and he escorted her home the first night.

The third and final night of the festivities, he danced with several other young women, and despite Glenda's best efforts, didn't pay much attention to her. Finally, something clicked, and in the waning hours of the dance, he asked her out on a date.

The courtship lasted six months. Big-un was everything the image on the magazine implied. He was cowboy to the bone. He drove a pickup when he wasn't on the back of a horse. He woke up long before the sun rose to go to work and didn't knock off until late at night. The health and well-being of cattle was his life. He said he had no use for any man who was unkind to a horse. The only time he would take a break from his duties as a 6666 foreman was for the occasional photo shoot or TV advertisement.

While he wasn't a giant as his nickname suggested, he was strong and sturdy. His friends and fellow cowboys still called him Big-un. The only one she ever heard use his given name, Carl, was his mother, and that was her God-given right. His folks lived a few miles from Knox City on a dusty dirt road out by the Brazos River among the pastures and oil rigs. His father, "Banty," was a leathery old cowboy himself, and his mother May had spent her life working under the sun as well. It was a simple but clean home—no phone and few modern conveniences. Glenda couldn't say that Big-un was on his best behavior when he went home because he was always the same. He was exceedingly polite, had impeccable table manners, and treated women with respect. His mama had taught him well.

May told Glenda how Carl began riding horses at age three and proclaimed from then on that he would be a cowboy just like his daddy. The only thing Glenda found surprising about the family was that Carl's brother had no interest in tending cows and was working in the construction business. As for Big-un, he never wavered in his goal of becoming a ranch hand. His mother kept a scrapbook full of clippings she had started even before his notoriety. Glenda was amazed when she flipped through it. He was co-captain of the football team, served as president of the school's Future Farmers of America chapter, and had been voted by the senior class as the most popular student. Glenda had met many boys of this type at Texas Tech: the homecoming kings, football stars, those who were destined to be lawyers, politicians, or important businessmen in their communities. But this was not a family that dreamed of higher education, and Big-un wouldn't have had any interest in it anyway.

How did this soft-spoken man with such humble beginnings—living out here in the middle of nowhere Texas—end up on the pages of *Life* magazine and on the television screens of millions of viewers from sea to shining sea?

It all began at the 6666—a place where time seemingly stood still and cowboys practiced their trade much as they had a century ago. There were bigger ranches in Texas, and some even more famous. Many of them had similar origins.

The Four Sixes' founder, Samuel "Burk" Burnett, started in the cattle business when the land was still wild and dangerous. An invasive species in the form of longhorn cattle had come from the south, escapees, so to speak, from Spanish rule. They were there for the taking, unbranded, belonging to no one, fattening up on unclaimed land. All a cowboy had to do was round them up, put his brand on them, and deliver the "beeves" to a spot where they could be transported to markets in the East. That would be in Kansas, where the Kansas Pacific Railway was making its way west.

It was in this brief "open range" time in 1866 when a seventeen-year-old Burk Burnett went on his first trail drive north as a hired hand. The following year he made the trip again, but this time as a trail boss, taking a herd north for his father. The destination was Abilene, Kansas, where the Chisholm Trail ended and cattle were loaded onto boxcars for the trip to the Chicago slaughterhouses. The Comanches, Southern Cheyennes, and Kiowas still posed a danger. An Osage raiding party had made off in the middle of the night with dozens of cattle and a few of their spare horses. They would never be able to retrieve them. For the rest of the trip, Burnett had to worry about his remaining horses. If they were stolen, that was the end of the operation. But he made it.

With his savings, Burnett invested in a herd of 100 longhorns that came along with the right to use a brand comprising four sixes. He made several more trips in the early 1870s.

The Comanches ran the greatest empire the land had ever seen, but once they were finally defeated in the Red River War and permanently relocated to Indian Territory, the hide hunters were free to move in and finish off the great bison herds. From 30 million to almost zero. The buffalo were hunted nearly to extinction within a generation.

The Comanches were allowed back into Texas for a seasonal, supervised hunt in the fall of 1878. The government assigned a trail boss and some soldiers to oversee the party. The hunters would hopefully come back with plenty of bison meat to supplement the meager diet that they had to live on at the agency. The journey lasted weeks, but they didn't find one single buffalo. They survived on what few antelope they could find. By the time they were forced to return, they were slaughtering their horses to avoid starvation. If there was any hope for the Southern Plains Indians that they could return to their old way of life, it was extinguished on that trip. If there were no buffalo, there was no reason to return.

About this time, Burnett realized that the days of trail drives and open ranges were coming to an end and he began buying property, at first near Wichita Falls, Texas. Corporations were swooping in to buy property as well. Big money from Europe and the East was being invested to take advantage of the cattle business. The longhorns, with their stringy meat, had been replaced by more docile, more palatable breeds such as the Hereford.

Burnett married Ruth Lloyd, the daughter of a wealthy Fort Worth banker who had cattle ranches of his own. They had three children; only one, Tom survived until adulthood. After working his way around his father's ranches, from line rider to foreman, Tom struck out on his own.

While animal husbandry seemed like a sure bet on a land that had supported grazing herds of bison for several millennia, that wasn't always the case. Along with market vagaries, the weather caused many operations to go belly-up. At the onset of a severe drought, Burk Burnett and a few other enterprising cattlemen struck a deal with Comanche Chief Quanah Parker to allow them to lease land at the Fort Sill Reservation, where rain was more steady. They arrived with satchels full of cash and made sure everyone in the tribe received a piece of the action. Leasing lands from Indians was a legal gray area. But as long as the cattlemen paid on time—and with cash the Indian agents couldn't control—most of the Comanches were happy.

Burnett ran cattle on Indian territory until the federal government announced at the turn of the century its plans to turn over the so-called "excess land" to settlers. He traveled to Washington to lobby President Theodore Roosevelt to give the cattlemen a reprieve. Teddy was a former rancher, and saw Burnett's predicament. He gave the Texas ranchers two years to vacate the lands.

By then, the drought had ended and Burnett was already casting his eyes toward King County. The cattle industry was by then taking shape with barbed wire and windmills used to control herds. The new fencing prevented overgrazing. Cattle could be moved from one pasture to another as needed and when winter storms struck, it prevented them from drifting away. The windmills tapped into groundwater, so livestock no longer required constant access to streams or rivers. Trains began to make their way to these previously remote lands, and it was easier to move livestock to market.

Burnett was soon the head of a cattle and business empire. He bought out his neighbors and acquired most of King County. The county seat, Guthrie, became a company town, with most of its residents under his employ. The supply store was owned by the ranch as well, and much of the cowboys' pay was spent there.

Burnett built a ten-room mansion on the property, which also served as company headquarters. He stayed there on visits but resided in Fort Worth, some 230 miles away. He had financial interests in banks and the railroad that would soon come to Paducah. He arrived there by train in his personal car, and would travel the final thirty miles to his ranch by buggy and later a car. And as a bit of icing on the cake, oil and gas were discovered underneath the Wichita Falls portion of the 6666 ranch, giving Burnett and his descendants even more income.

Burnett made some enemies in his dealings. He encountered a rival cattleman in the men's room at the Paducah Hotel. Who drew first was a matter of controversy, but Burnett shot him dead. A jury found it self-defense.

Burk Burnett passed away in 1922, having acquired some 333,000 acres of land spread throughout the Panhandle. The beneficiary of the two Burnett cattle empires, which included his son Tom's holdings, was Burnett's only grandchild, Anne, who also lived in Fort Worth. She was the rarely seen owner by the time Big-un had signed on as a ranch hand. The real brains of the operation was the ranch manager George Humphreys, who had run the outfit for decades. While Humphreys did a lot to bring modern ranching practices to the Four Sixes, much of the basic work was carried out as it had been since the turn of the century. Cowboys would go out for days and weeks to tend to the cattle while riding purebred quarter horses raised on the ranch. Big-un was eventually made wagon foreman. The chuck wagon was where the cowboys gathered for meals and to get their orders from the boss.

There were many legendary ranches in Texas. Some of them more famous than the 6666, but for some reason it seemed to attract more attention than most. The Western artist Tom Ryan arrived in 1963 and made his career out of portraying the cowboys working on the land.

An ad man who worked for Leo Burnett—no relation to Burk Burnett—arrived that year to film footage for a soap commercial. He spotted Big-un and knew immediately that he was exactly what the guys who had the Marlboro account were seeking—a real cowboy who was good-looking enough to give the Hollywood male professional models a run for their money.

The agency offered Big-un a full-time contract and a part in a Hollywood movie. Acting would mean quitting his job, so he turned the role down. He worked on a freelance basis, receiving from $150 to $1,500 depending on whether it was a print ad or TV commercial. When the ad men wanted a locale other than the Four Sixes, they would pay his way to other western spots, such as the South Dakota Badlands, to shoot the film. That was as much of the outside world as he would ever see. Big-un always returned to the Four Sixes to do what he loved best. He wasn't *the* Marlboro man. The ad agency found other working cowboys to replace the models.

Glenda and Big-un's courtship lasted six months. By the time they married, she had found a job teaching home economics in Guthrie. She rarely saw her husband, who was up before dawn and back after sunset. After dinner, he would go straight to bed. He would work weeks on end without taking a day off. He rarely went to church on Sundays. Simply knocking off for a day was a foreign concept to him—the cattle didn't take a day off. The only real vacation he would allow himself was the three-day annual festivities in Stamford.

They made enough money to get by, with the Marlboro ad money going into a savings account. Big-un did have ambition, although it would not mean a change to his daily routine. He dreamed of having his own little ranch someday.

Soon, Glenda was pregnant, which meant an end to her teaching. Now that there was a child, he confessed that he should have taken that movie job. By the time their son Carl Kent was born, the savings had dried up along with the ad work. The government had abolished cigarette ads from TV, and as for the print ads, the agency had found a new face.

After Humphreys retired in 1969, Big-un quit the Four Sixes. He and Banty ran a herd on some leased land near Knox City for a while. He then ended up as a hand on his best friend Bill Flower's spread west of Aspermont, a town about thirty miles south of Guthrie on Highway 83. Big-un's dream of working for himself on his own property was as distant as ever.

They had been married for five years and Carl Kent was twenty months old when Big-un left the house alone about three in the afternoon to do one more chore. There was always some work left undone in Big-un's mind, and as long as the sun was still up, he couldn't sit still. There was a wild bronco that needed to be tamed, and probably a few other little jobs.

When Big-un didn't come back after sunset, Glenda started to get a bad feeling. She called Flowers and told him she was worried. There was no need to be, he said. Everyone knew you couldn't pry Big-un off a horse with a crowbar. But he said he would pop down to the pasture and have a look anyway.

He and a hired hand found the horse's legs and saddle blanket sticking out of a recently dug stock tank, but no Big-un. The bronco had lost its footing and drowned, and presumably Big-un along with him. Swimming was one of the few skills he didn't possess. It may not have mattered. When they found his body the next day, it looked as though his head had struck a rock.

Guthrie has a population of about 160, but when I pull into town, it looks like about 155 of them are away. This is a company town, and reportedly the majority of homes are owned by the ranches and rented out to their employees. There is a courthouse, a school (presumably the kids are bottled up inside), a couple of abandoned gas stations, and the 6666 Supply House. Quarried from local stone, it's a solid little building, where Big-un Bradley certainly spent a lot of money—perhaps on his menthols.

Big-un's funeral in Knox City was said to be about the biggest anyone had ever seen in those parts. Cowboys and admirers came from hundreds of miles around to pay their respects to the Marlboro man, who had died in the saddle at age thirty-six. He never lived to see the day when the icon was embroiled in controversy, when smoking was all but banned except outdoors and in private homes. Today no fewer than five models who portrayed the Marlboro man have died of smoking-related diseases, giving rise to the cigarette's nickname—cowboy killers. It was a wildly successful ad campaign, but for a product that causes premature death. These days, the Marlboro man as an advertising icon has disappeared in the United States.

I thought out here miles and miles from the nearest supermarket, the supply house would be stocked up a little better. Its offerings are sparse. I'm about to make a major detour to visit Lubbock, and I buy a cold Coke for the journey west. Forgoing a half day on Highway 83 will hopefully be worthwhile. I intend to meet the people who published my first nonfiction book at Texas Tech University Press—folks with whom I have corresponded or spoken to on the phone numerous times, but never met face to face. And then I will take on all the sights having to do with Lubbock's most famous son, Buddy Holly. But most of all I want to meet the man who organizes a yearly motorcycle ride down the length of Highway 83.

I've driven 100 miles due west of Highway 83 to meet Brent and Brenda Jackson at an International House of Pancakes in Lubbock.

Every year, for four days in early March, the couple organizes and leads a motorcycle rally down the entire length of Highway 83 in Texas.

Brent is a big bear of a man with a thick Texas drawl. Brenda, a blonde, is half her husband's size. They sit across from me, sipping coffee, and tell me how they came to organize the annual tribute to the nation's Vietnam vets.

He was a motorcycle cop in the nearby town of Levelland twenty years ago, a role that first nourished his love of two-wheelers. After marrying Brenda, Brent forgot about riding for a while. Then health reasons forced him to move into the less strenuous role of police dispatcher.

When his father died in 2002 and left him a small inheritance, he bought a 1999 Yahama Royal Star and decided to take it on an inaugural trip south on Highway 83 to the Hill Country, a region considered a biker's mecca in Texas. On his way there, he stopped at a small park near the town of Eden in Concho County to stretch his legs and get a drink of water. He noticed a small plaque with the image of Vietnam imposed over a Texas flag, and an inscription in English and Spanish.

Texas Vietnam Veterans Memorial Highway
US Highway 83
In gratitude to the thousands of men and women who
served our country during the Vietnam War, the people
of Texas dedicate this highway which runs across the
state from the southernmost tip to the northernmost

*point. It is our hope that all those who travel U.S. 83 will
pause to remember those who gave up their lives or their
youth or their hopes in that long and bitter conflict. We
vow not to forget those who did not return to us and
we pledge to remember the sacrifices of those who have
come home.*

"I didn't know Texas had such a thing. I was really happy that
Texas had done something for the Vietnam vets," he says. "Those
poor guys. Those that got welcomed, it wasn't a good welcome.
Most of them didn't get anything."

The story behind the plaque that inspired Jackson goes
back to early 1982 when an Army Vietnam vet, Pablo Aguillon,
was driving north on U.S. Highway 281 from the Rio Grande
Valley to San Antonio. Every seventy miles or so, there was a
sign reminding him that it was designated the American Legion
Memorial Highway.

Aguillon was one of the lucky ones. As an engineer, he
never saw combat, but many young men from his hometown of
Crystal City, a community of about 8,000 along Highway 83, did.
The town had sacrificed more than its fair share, with nine of
its young men losing their lives in the conflict. The town was
about ninety percent Mexican-American and ten percent Anglo.
Eight of those who died from the town were Chicano and one
was white, so the toll matched the makeup of the community.
Aguillon worked for a nonprofit as the local veterans' service
officer helping vets navigate the Department of Veterans Affairs.
Every day, he saw the emotional toll the war was continuing to
take on the men he served. He was also commander of Crystal
City's American Legion Post No. 396, so he had nothing against
the organization. It was just that designating U.S. 281 as such
made it sound as if it was honoring the organization, not the
vets, who might or might not be members. And he later found
out that it was so named in 1960, when the Vietnam War was just
beginning. So did the highway really honor *all* veterans?

Highway 83, which ran along the side of his hometown, was the obvious choice for his plan. It traversed the entire length of Texas, and unlike the east-to-west Interstate 10, it cut right through the communities it served, including twenty county seats, instead of bypassing them.

Seven short years after the fall of Saigon, the nation was still reeling from the effects of a war it did not win. Honoring Vietnam veterans for their service was not on many people's agendas. As Aguillon would say in written testimony to the Texas House Transportation Committee: "We join a myriad of Americans, especially Vietnam veterans in a quest for recognition. We feel, like our forefathers before us, we answered the bugle call indifferent to whether or not the cause was just. Unlike our forefathers, however, we were not welcomed back with ticker-tape parades and prancing majorettes. We were avoided like the plague and to date some of us are still waist deep in rice paddies fighting an invisible enemy—our inability to forget."

Aguillon started a letter-writing campaign, beginning first with the state's senators, John Tower and Lloyd Bentsen, and his local congressman, who were all supportive, but they pointed out that it was up to each state to name federal highways within their borders. It was not a federal matter.

During an American Legion 15th district meeting, which encompassed much of the Rio Grande Valley, the other posts unanimously approved a resolution designating U.S. 83 in Texas as the Vietnam Veterans Memorial Highway. This region covered Highway 83 from Crystal City down to Brownsville. He didn't necessarily need this endorsement, but it showed he had widespread support.

Aguillon found a ready ally when he met in April 1982 with Ernestine Glossbrenner, legislative district 44's representative to the Texas House. A Democrat and a pioneering feminist in the once male-dominated legislature, she discovered that to give Highway 83 the designation in Crystal City did not require a law to be passed, but a simple application with the state's

Pablo Aguillon at the Vietnam Veterans Memorial Highway dedication ceremony, July 4, 1984. Courtesy of Pablo Aguillon (top). Brent and Brenda Jackson, Lubbock, Texas, May, 2010 (bottom).

Department of Transportation. But that action would at best designate Highway 83 a memorial highway in Zavala County, where Crystal City was located. Legislation could take care of the remainder of the highway, so she readied a bill that would call for it to be dedicated to Vietnam vets from end to end.

As the Texas House convened in 1983, Aguillon received a stinging letter from W. H. McGregor, the Texas American Legion department adjutant in Austin, demanding that Aguillon ask Glossbrenner to withdraw the legislation. The proposal should be put to a vote in the Legion's executive committee during that summer's upcoming state convention, he said. "This is necessary because the highway goes through more than just your one city or District," he added.

"We feel that if you introduce a bill in the Legislature as indicated it would open up a can of worms and we might lose the designation we already have on our present highway. We would very much appreciate it if you would consider asking your State Representative to withdraw this bill until it has gone through the proper channels within The American Legion," he wrote.

Reading between the lines, it was obvious the Legionnaires' leadership didn't want a road competing with Highway 281. Plus, McGregor was arrogantly assuming that the American Legion spoke for all veterans. It was shortsighted and appeared to disrespect the Vietnam vets. The fact of the matter was that organizations like the Veterans of Foreign Wars and American Legion were struggling. The World War I and World War II vets who were the backbone of the clubs were dying off, and few Vietnam veterans were interested in taking their places. Aguillon knew that waiting for the state convention would kill the momentum, and they wouldn't let it pass anyway. The legislature convened only in odd-numbered years, so he would have to wait until 1985 until trying again.

Aguillon's response was equally terse.

"In April of 1982 I met with Rep. Glossbrenner and related to her our intentions. She immediately expressed a desire to help us to the greatest extent possible. Eventually and after looking into the necessary steps she decided to introduce legislation in the form of House Bill No. 287, we did not ask her to do so, so in view of this we cannot ask her to withdraw this bill."

Despite intense pressure from the American Legion higher-ups, Aguillon soldiered on without their endorsement, and the bill received a hearing in the Transportation Committee on April 19, 1983. It sailed through the House and then the Senate, passing there 30-1. Governor Mark White signed it into law in June 1983.

Glossbrenner reminded a reporter that the highway ran through one of the state's largest Hispanic populations, in the Rio Grande Valley. "In the Vietnam war, we had more Mexican-American casualties than their representative proportion in the population. Of course, in every war, all Texans have done their best to aid their country....We do not have a proud record of welcoming home our Vietnam veterans compared to other wars," she added.

One by one, the plaques went up along Highway 83.

It was almost twenty years after Aguillon's victory when Brent Jackson discovered the one in Eden. Somewhere along that trip, he struck upon the idea to ride the whole length of 83 as a sort of personal thank-you to the veterans. He initially thought it would just be himself, with Brenda driving a pickup truck behind him as a backup in case there were any breakdowns, but word of his plan got out, and he had four other bikers join him at the state line north of Perryton in early March 2003.

They gathered on one of the broken cement parking lots near the beer joints in early March, and with no fanfare took off south on a nearly 900-mile journey.

There wasn't much planning on the initial trip. Two of the riders had to split off at Guthrie and head back west to take care of some unexpected business, leaving just three riders and Brenda. The whole trip took three days. They pulled up to the border crossing in Brownsville at midnight.

"It was dark. It was lonely. It was creepy, but we had made it," Brent says.

Not knowing the area very well, he had mistakenly made hotel reservations in Harlingen, some thirty miles back up the road to the north, so the weary riders had to double back.

Over the next year, he created a website for the event and had twenty-seven riders sign up. It was better organized then, with a schedule stretched out to four days. Numerous residents and chambers of commerce in towns such as Perryton, Childress, Hamlin, Abilene, Junction, Eden, Leakey, Uvalde, and Laredo hosted water breaks or barbecues along the way. Supporters gathered to wave flags and cheer them on as they arrived in town. Local law enforcement would customarily meet them and provide escorts through the larger cities. Brenda hauled one of two support trailers that carried broken-down bikes. She provided first aid and other assistance as needed.

Every year the numbers grew until there are now more than 100 bikers. Riders come from all over Texas, and the world. One San Antonian working in for an oil company in Africa flies back every year to participate. There is another American couple living in Germany who make the trip. In Crystal City, Pablo Aguillon has joined them and drives along in a pickup truck.

Brent recalled riding through the Hill Country and looking in his rearview mirror. The headlights stretched out as far as he could see. Many riders are Vietnam veterans, although they have had World War II, Korean War, and Iraqi War vets come along. Some riders have to drop off; others join the rally where they can. "The only requirement to go on this trip is to be respectful of our veterans," he says.

The last day takes the riders from Laredo to Brownsville, where they end the ride at about noon at the Veterans Park in the shadow of the statue of Sergeant José Lopez, a Mexican-American Medal of Honor winner. One year, the ride ended with 148 participants.

Brent vows that he will continue organizing the ride as long as he can. "It's the least I can do for the vets who have done so much for us," he says.

I wake up the next day back on Highway 83 in Aspermont at the Hickman Motel. It looks like another beautiful day on the last American highway. A hiccupping Buddy Holly is coming through the car stereo. Naturally. I found time to stop by the Buddy Holly Center in Lubbock the day before, and I have been listening to him almost nonstop. It's too bad that the city leveled his old neighborhood in order to build a Walmart. Walmart: The destroyer of downtown Paducah, Texas, and the childhood home of Buddy Holly. That is now two marks against it.

Cattle have given way to cotton as I drive south. Although it's too early in the year to see the crops, the level plowed fields are everywhere. Cotton is Texas's number one cash crop.

The story of Jones County, where I'm entering, is not unlike those of its neighbors. After the bison and Native Americans left a void, cattlemen came to fill it. But in Jones County's case, farmers came as well. It didn't take them long to figure out that cotton was an excellent crop for this dry land. And very soon, the cotton fields outnumbered pastures.

I drive into the Radium Gin Mill, which looks abandoned, but only because it's spring. There are empty racks where giant cotton bales are hauled. I drive past on old shotgun shack, a long house that I have only seen during my travels in Mississippi and New Orleans. I wonder if sharecroppers once inhabited it. The old system, practically indentured servitude, was the norm in Texas up until the 1940s, when modern machinery eliminated the need for field hands. Some of the cotton grown here will be shipped north on Highway 83 to Liberal, Kansas, which has a seven-acre warehouse to store it.

Jones is the county and the county seat is Anson. Anson Jones was the first president of the Republic of Texas. Anson—the town—is both famous and infamous for dancing. It is famous for hosting a big yearly ball where cowboys and cowgirls come from miles around to swirl and twirl the night away in 1800s garb. It also gained national notoriety for an ordinance that banned dancing. Anson is also the hometown of Jeannie C. Riley, a woman who left for Nashville to pursue her dream of becoming a singer. She had a smash hit record, "Harper Valley P.T.A.," about small town intolerance and sexual liberation, but would later become a born-again Christian. When I think of Anson, I think of irony.

Highway 83 sweeps around the impressive courthouse dominating the town's square. Its beautiful, red-brick opera house—still in use—is one of the first buildings I notice. It's a grand structure and an architectural jewel. Along the west side it appears that most of the storefronts are occupied. Anson seems to be doing much better than Paducah, I think, but then I drive past a big pile of rubble on the southeast corner—a prime spot on the square. That is rather unsightly, I think, and park the car to do some exploring. I wonder if the building is being demolished. I don't see any heavy equipment, though, just a large pile of bricks. A man walks up and stands there. And stands there. And stands there. He's not just looking it over, he seems to be in deep contemplation. He finally walks away.

I stroll a block or two south and discover Wilson Ranch Furniture, a store unlike anything I've ever seen. There are deer-antler chandeliers, deer-antler table lamps, deer-antler side tables. Sturdy wood bed frames varnished without any paint. Cowhide sofas and longhorn cattle horns suitable for hanging on a wall or placing on the grille of a 1975 Cadillac. Floor lamps made from old horseshoes. This is hunting lodge décor. Or perhaps for a man's den. I have a hard time imagining many women who would want a deer-antler light fixture hanging over her dining room table.

There are also rows and rows of beads, and the clerk behind the counter, Margie Gray, a big mane of brown hair, zebra patterned eyeglass frames she looks over, chats with me in a broad Texas drawl as she makes a pair of earrings. She tells me that the rubble on the corner was an old pharmacy that had been empty for several years. After a night of gusty wind, the townspeople woke up to find it collapsed.

I'm not an engineer but I think I can guess at what happened. I live in a 1940s-era garden-style condominium made of brick. My condo board had recently embarked on a repointing project. After sixty years the mortar between the bricks was starting to deteriorate, and tuck-pointing, which involves removing the old material and replacing it, has to be done about once every half century, or the building loses its integrity. It is a painstaking and expensive process. I didn't know about any of this before it was explained to me at a condo board meeting. I thought brick buildings were solid. The big bad wolf couldn't blow the third little pig's house down, after all.

Who in these small towns can pay the bill to have tuck-pointing done for all the old brick pharmacies, general stores,

Masonic halls, and churches? If most of these were built in the first half of the twentieth century, aren't they all due to collapse in the next few years?

I tell Margie about my trip, and she insists on calling the local newspaper editor to come down and interview me. I have a picture in my mind of the *Western Observer*'s owner and editor in chief: middle-aged to elderly, a matronly, gabby woman who knows everyone in town. Or a rotund, male equivalent. And I base this stereotype on the many small town, weekly newspaper publishers I have known.

And then Tiffany Waddell walks in the store. Tight shirt, blue jeans, clutching a notebook in her hand, a camera dangling off her shoulder. If I didn't know she was the owner of a newspaper, I would guess she was about eighteen years old. She is pretty, with the look of a 1970s runway model. If I hadn't been told differently, I would have guessed that she was an intern or perhaps a recent college journalism school grad getting her foot in the door as a reporter at a small-town paper. No, she is the editor, publisher and co-owner, along with her husband, who I gathered from Margie was away in the service.

She is actually twenty-five. She started working at the paper with no journalism training at twenty-one. Six months later, the previous publisher offered to sell the business to her and her husband, K.T.

I think back to when I was twenty-one. I was working at my college newspaper producing poorly written Joan Jett record reviews, still taking wild guesses when it came to correct usage of "their," "there," and "they're."

I sit down on a cowhide sofa and she interviews me about my trip down Highway 83 and what I'm trying to accomplish. The conversation takes a turn as Margie mentions some pushback Waddell is receiving from local leaders.

I know from experience that there is a fine line to walk publishing a small-town newspaper, where there is no separation between "church" and "state" because the owner and the editor-in-chief are one and the same —the "church" being the higher calling of journalism and the "state" being the advertising side of the business. Tick off the local powerbrokers and chamber-of-commerce types with an exposé about small-town corruption and suddenly the advertising base disappears. Tiffany recently began annoying the county government by re-running some of their public notices that it had only been posting on a seldom-read website. She felt the county was deliberately trying to keep the public in the dark about matters like the re-selling of supposedly abandoned private property, construction contract bids, and voting redistricting.

I have fantasized about running my own small-town newspaper, thoroughly embedding myself into a community, being my own boss, writing a weekly column containing nothing but my musings, with no one to tell me that it wasn't worthy of publication. I envy Tiffany Waddell. Anson must be one interesting town to get to know.

DANCIN' IN ANSON?

Mercy Torres stood up to speak at the standing-room-only city council meeting.

She couldn't have been any more of an outsider. She was a Catholic Mexican-American woman from East Los Angeles who now called Anson her home, and it was her job to convince six middle-aged Protestant white men to drop what she considered an antiquated city ordinance.

No one at the packed Anson city council meeting that night was old enough to remember why dancing was against the law in Anson 353 days of the year. The original law was passed in 1933, and most assumed it was because the devout Christians in town simply believed back then that dancing was sinful.

Because that was still the case.

Members of the fundamentalist Church of Christ had an alliance with the Southern Baptists for decades. Together they ran the town. The mayor, all but one council members, the school board, and the chief of police all attended one church or the other. Along with dancing, alcohol sales were also forbidden, a situation still relatively common in West Texas counties. But the times were changing back in March 15, 1987, when the meeting was called to order.

Torres was president of the Footloose Club, a recently organized alliance of local residents who wanted to overturn the ordinance. Its name was inspired by the movie *Footloose*, a big hit a few years before in which a Chicago teen, Ren McCormack, played by Kevin Bacon, finds himself in a similar town. He challenges the status quo and, through the sheer force of his dance moves, defeats the town's uptight citizens.

The Footloose Club was hoping for a similar victory. It had organized after one concerned mother discovered that her fourteen-year-old daughter was pregnant. The teens in town had nothing to do but get into trouble. Why couldn't they have a chaperoned homecoming dance or prom like all the other kids in Texas? She thought. She called around and found enough parents interested to call for a meeting. In a local diner, they formally organized the club and elected officers. Torres, college-educated, a one-time dance instructor, experienced in organizing for social change, and the wife of a local physician, became their leader, along with Paul Davidson, a deputy editor at the *Western Observer* newspaper. He was a guitarist and member of a local band who had come to Anson after marrying a local gal. Almost every member was an outsider—not born and raised in Anson, and definitely not a member of one of the two churches.

The club's first act was to actually hold a dance. They wanted to prove that the local teens could handle a well-supervised party. They found one reluctant husband of a member to agree to open up his spacious but dirty tractor shed. The club spent hours cleaning the place up for a Valentine's Day dance they called the Renegades' Ball. Davidson's band, Bittercreek, would provide the country-western music. The club had gone through considerable effort to obtain a copy of the original city ordinance. The town clerk was a Church of Christ member and staunch supporter of the status quo. She did everything she could to keep the books shut, but eventually had to let them see it. It simply stated that "dance halls" and "public dancing" were prohibited. The law was vaguely worded and didn't seem to outlaw dances held on private property. The fine was fifteen dollars, which may have been considered stiff back in the Depression years, but was a joke by 1987. While fifteen bucks may have been laughable, the town cops were known to show up at nonofficial proms and demand that they be shut down. No one knew of any cases in which a dance organizer had spent the night in jail.

For the local teens, living in Anson meant crushing boredom. There had once been a movie theater. Closed. There had once been a roller skating rink. Closed. There was the opera house, worthy of being on the National Register of Historic Places, but it seemed to serve no purpose other than making the town square look pretty.

The official school prom was a "banquet." The students sat and ate a dinner as if they were at a Rotary Club luncheon. Ironically, the late night spot to secretly rendezvous, smoke cigarettes, drink beer, and fool around in the backseats of cars was the Church of Christ parking lot.

This wasn't the case in other Jones County towns such as Hamlin, or nearby Stamford, which hosted the three-day Stamford Cowboy Reunion wingding every July Fourth. Back in the 1950s, an up-and-coming Elvis Presley played the Stamford High School gymnasium—twice. The town leaders in Anson would have had a fit if they had seen the future King of Rock 'n' Roll swivel his hips. Jeannie C. Riley, Anson's most famous hometown girl, had to have her uncle drive her twenty miles to the town of Truby to make her public singing debut. "Harper Valley P.T.A." was a song about uptight small-town folks who felt the same way about miniskirts as Anson's leaders felt about dancing.

The Renegades' Ball went off without a hitch despite a stiff, cold wind out of the north and a drafty venue. The local kids showed up in the hundreds. It was rumored that the Church of Christ and Baptist parents had forbidden their teens from attending, but the huge turnout seemed to indicate that many came anyway. The club members stopped the kids from congregating outside the shed and they were closely watched. It was vitally important that nothing untoward happen. No drinking, no smoking, no steamy windshields in the cars outside. The chaperones patrolled the parking lot to make sure the rules were upheld.

The cops drove around in their cruisers several times, but made no effort to stop the dance. The Footloose Club won this battle, but the ultimate victory would have to be at city hall. The law wasn't enforced that night, but what about the next time?

The city council meeting pretty much went as expected. The attendees were surprised to see crews from Abilene television stations in attendance, harbingers of the media frenzy to come.

Torres stood before the council and laid out the group's request. She assured the six men that the group was not out to open a "dance hall." They wanted the high school students to be able to hold a school-sanctioned prom in the city limits. They were concerned—just as the council members surely were—that idle teens were trouble-bound and that well-chaperoned dances were something positive. And while she respected their religious beliefs, she reminded them that imposing them on others who did not feel the same was a violation of their civil rights.

The councilmen and mayor listened politely, then threw back responses that seemed to indicate that they hadn't heard a word she had said. What if we dropped this ordinance and someone came to town to set up a dance hall? One councilman said if a town could outlaw prostitution, it should be able to outlaw dancing. Dancing was almost as bad as prostitution, he claimed.

The low point came when a local fundamentalist preacher stood up to speak. "In thirty-one years of counseling, I've talked to young people who were unwed mothers and unwed fathers, and I've asked them, 'Where was the point of your downfall?' Nine out of ten told me, 'It was on the dance floor.'" For the Abilene television crews, the preacher's quote was gold.

The council attempted to "table the matter until further review," which the savvy club members knew was just a tactic to permanently blow them off. They demanded that the council deliberate and give them an answer. That was met with a promise to do so, but with no timetable. The club members demanded a deadline. The council reluctantly agreed to give them a "yes" or "no" answer by the next meeting.

Until the television cameras showed up that night in 1987, most folks in West Texas were probably unaware that the small town of Anson had banned dancing. In fact, most of them would have been shocked. If it were famous for anything, it was for a ball that had taken place the weekend before Christmas for the past fifty-three years.

Lawrence Chittenden was a wallflower at the big dance. It was 1885, and the easterner stood watching as the cowboys, dressed in their finest clothing, twirled the eligible young ladies in their satiny dresses on the wood floor at the Star Hotel's dining room. All the tables and chairs had been cleared out for the soiree.

There wasn't much to Anson back then even though it was the county seat. There was the two-story Star Hotel, its rival the Tipton Inn, a rudimentary court house, a post office, some typical businesses of the day—dry goods store, blacksmith–livery stable—and a few dozen homes lined along its dirt streets. A railroad had yet to reach the town.

When it became known that a well-liked cowboy intended to marry a local gal the weekend before Christmas, the hotel's proprietor, M. G. Rhoads, organized a dance to go along with the celebration, and invited everyone to come. What better way to liven up a dreary month?

A dance was a big deal for the residents of Jones County. For lonely cowboys and ranchers it was an opportunity to escape the isolated life on the plains, and a chance to meet some eligible young ladies. They would not be attending in their scruffy work clothes. Boots were polished, and if too worn, were put aside for something nicer. This called for their Sunday best. The same went for the ladies, who spent the day getting their attire just right.

One of the many locals to accept the invitation was Chittenden. Twenty-three years old, tall and lean, with a black mustache and gray eyes, he managed a ranch for his uncle a few miles from town.

The dance floor was tiny. There was only about enough room for six couples, a fiddle player, a percussionist playing a tambourine, and local cowboy, William "Windy Bill" Wilkinson, to call the quadrilles. There was a line outside in the salon for those waiting their turn to kick up some sawdust. Chittenden chatted with some of his neighbors there, sometimes stepping into the dining room to take in the festivities, but he never asked any of the ladies to dance. He preferred to watch.

Chittenden had come to Texas on a lark in 1883. He had left his job at a New York newspaper and was spending idle days in the city when members of the Swenson family invited him out to Jones County. Swante Magnus Swenson was a railroad and cattle baron who had turned over day-to-day management of his largest ranch to his boys, Eric and Swen. The wealthy Swensons split their time between Texas and New York. Chittenden, age twenty-one, had recently made the ranchers' acquaintance after his wealthy uncle Simeon bought 10,000 acres adjoining the Swenson Land and Cattle Company.

Investing in the cattle business was where all the smart money was going in those days. Eastern and European investors, many of whom never laid eyes on their land holdings, were buying up vast tracts of western Texas, Kansas, Nebraska, and Wyoming, where cattle bought for a few dollars were selling for forty-five dollars per head back east.

Chittenden accepted the Swensons' invitation, borrowed some pocket money from his uncle, and made an agreement to write some travel articles for a New York newspaper.

While a guest on the Swensons' ranch, he became smitten with the cowboy way of life and the wide-open spaces. He returned to New York with a new calling in life. His uncle, recently ousted from Congress after serving four terms, was looking for something to do as well and agreed to his nephew's

Larry Chittenden

plan. The pair set about buying cattle, horses, fencing, and all the necessary equipment to set up a cattle operation on the property, which was about eight miles north of Anson. They hired cowboys and a foreman, who all knew a lot more about animal husbandry than they did, and soon enough, the newly named Chittenden Ranch was up and running.

Every boom has a bust, and the cattle industry was no different. Many of the big-time investors lost their money during droughts, or when supply outpaced demand. With every fall in beef prices, a little bit more of Jones County's ranchland was plowed under to plant cotton. But unlike the absentee ranch owners, Chittenden stayed on to manage the operation himself and he weathered the vagaries of the cattle business. He planted wheat to diversify the operation and to serve as feedstock, experimented with new breeds of cattle, and raised horses and mules to keep the money flowing when cattle prices tanked. When his uncle passed away in 1889, he was wealthy enough to buy the ranch from the estate for $37,000.

Meanwhile, Chittenden had not given up the love of writing that he had nurtured during his time as a reporter in New York.

At nights, he spent hours under the light of a lantern reading or composing poetry.

Most of the ranch house he reserved for the manager's family. He remained unmarried and took only one room for himself, where he slept, wrote, and gazed through the window at his vast holdings. He kept a collection of hundreds of books to keep him company.

All along, he continued to contribute articles about life in the West to New York newspapers. He also began to dabble in what would be called cowboy poetry—verse written about life on the range using the slang of the day. Perhaps believing that there wouldn't be any interest in such poems in the East, he sent these to Texas newspapers.

The 1885 dance at the Star Hotel was such a success, it became a tradition. Chittenden attended it for three straight years—always watching, never dancing. As he observed the locals spinning to Windy Bill's calls, he began to form some couplets in his head.

At his desk back at the ranch, he dipped his pen in an inkwell and began to write a poem that would be known as "The Cowboys' Christmas Ball."

The big-city papers out East all took their turns parachuting in a national correspondent to cover the "No Dancin' in Anson" controversy. National Public Radio's *All Things Considered* show sent a reporter, as did newspapers in England and Australia. Comparisons to the hit movie *Footloose* were inevitable, given the opposition's choice to name their movement after the film. Most of the anti-dancing crowd began to shun the media, save one. The actor John Lithgow played the uptight Reverend Shaw Moore in the movie. The out-of-town reporters found a worthy equivalent in a Church of Christ minister named Leon Sharp. He was happy to share his views.

He told one reporter: "I believe that dancing is an activity that promotes what the Bible calls the sensual nature of man," he said.

"I feel like some dancing per se is vulgar. The music and some of the rhythms, appear to me to be the result of native dances that were intended to lead to sexual activity."

The congregations were far from monolithic in their opposition to dancing. The police chief was a Church of Christ member, but he and his wife were enthusiastic participants in the Christmas Ball.

As a human interest story, the episode often made the front pages. Not lost on many of these reporters was the irony that Anson had a dance hall. The original ball lasted until 1891, when the Star Hotel burned down. A few years later, Chittenden went to a New York publisher and offered him his collection of poetry. The book, *Ranch Verses*, was a huge hit, eventually running through twelve printings. "The Cowboy's Christmas Ball," which described the "lively gaited sworray" and the colorful characters who attended the dance, was by far the most popular poem in the collection, and soon enough, was being set to music. Chittenden was called the "poet-rancher" and became the toast of New York salons. As the years went by, he bought homes in Connecticut, New England and the Bahamas, spending less and less time on the ranch.

In the dreary days of the Depression in 1934, an Anson high school teacher and folklorist, Leonora Barrett, decided to recreate in dress, song, and steps the pioneer dances of the 1880s that had made Anson famous. The ball was originally conceived as a fall festival, but word arrived that Chittenden had passed away at age seventy-one. In memory of the man who put Anson on the map, she moved it to the weekend before Christmas, the traditional date of the Cowboys' Christmas Ball.

Forty years had passed since the last soiree—long enough for the event to be classified as nostalgia, but not so long that some of those who were at the original dances couldn't attend and provide their expertise. The ladies and cowboys did their best to come in period dress, and the songs and dances of the day were played. The revival was such a success that it continued, with attendees coming from farther distances as the dance's reputation grew.

Barrett had plowed ahead with her plans despite the law on the books prohibiting dancing. The good Baptists and fundamentalists in town wanted nothing to do with the celebration, but they turned a blind eye to it.

As the ball grew, the organizers trademarked the name, created an association, and set out to build a dance hall dedicated to the event with the help of the Works Progress Administration. It was quite a commitment considering the no-dancing law, so the organizers went to the city council to have the ordinance changed. The best they could do was obtain an exception for their event for three days of the year. So Pioneer Hall, the purpose-built dance hall, was closed to the Footloose Club.

As the media attention grew, tensions in town rose accordingly. Preachers went as far as to say that the club was doing the devil's work. Ansonites who traveled out of town found themselves laughingstocks. No one could believe that a town would prohibit dancing at a school prom. Not only that, the Texas attorney general declared publicly that the law was unconstitutional. In light of that, the city council and mayor decided to change the ordinance—for the worse.

The Footloose Club was incredulous when the new law was released without any public debate. The council claimed that it had notified the public about a public hearing (by posting it on a bulletin board at 5 p.m. the evening before the snap meeting) but no one had caught wind of it.

Where the old law was vaguely worded, the new one had twenty-two clauses—each one seemingly designed to discourage a dance from actually taking place. A permit would have to be issued by the city, and the county clerk would have to determine if the organizer was "of good moral character." Plus, no dance could be held within 300 feet of a church. With more than a dozen houses of worship in town, that precluded just about every spot, including the high school gymnasium, which was across the street from the First Baptist Church. And the fine for breaking one of these new rules had been increased for inflation—from fifteen dollars in the 1933 law—to $250.

Torres and Footloose organized an unofficial spring prom dance twenty-three miles to the south, near Abilene. Davidson with his band debuted their new song 'No Dancin' in Anson,' but the fight was not over. Footloose had a backup plan, which for the town elders would be the equivalent of "going nuclear." They called in the ACLU. The town leaders, diehard conservatives to the bone, were apoplectic. As far as they were concerned, if the devil did have an advocate, he would manifest himself on Earth as an attorney for the American Civil Liberties Union. The preachers' condemnations from the pulpit were swift: the Footloose leaders were under the sway of Satan.

The town became more polarized than ever. More than two-thirds of the voters in the last election had chosen anti-dancing candidates, so the pro-dancers were clearly in the minority.

Meanwhile, Davidson's job at the *Western Observer* was precarious. The owner of the paper was a Church of Christ member. He would eventually be fired. Dogs were poisoned. The proprietor of the restaurant where the group met was pressured to kick them out. Anyone who had a business and supported Footloose kept his mouth shut.

But all it really took was one letter mailed to the town's attorney from an ACLU lawyer in Austin. After a couple paragraphs spelling out various court decisions that protected dancing—even topless dancing—as a form of free speech, it ended with a thinly veiled warning that a lawsuit was coming.

The town simply didn't have the funds to wage an expensive legal battle in the courts. By the time the next city council meeting came around, the mayor and four of the council members let the lone Methodist on the council save face for the town. He came out in favor of loosening up the new town ordinance and "convinced" the others that removing some of the restrictions wouldn't do any harm. Pretending to "see the light," they changed the law and the fight was over.

For the first time in more than forty years, the padlocks to the Pioneer Hall were opened on a weekend that didn't fall before Christmas. Davidson's band was the opening act at the victory dance, where they played "No Dancin' in Anson." A nationally known country band, Mason Dixon, waived its fee to be the main act. Hundreds of attendees came from miles around to celebrate. In the middle of the band's set, the musicians brought Davidson, Torres, and the other leaders on stage to take a bow. For the now jobless Davidson, it was one of the happiest moments of his life.

One wonders if the spirit of Lawrence Chittenden was standing by a wall in back, taking it all in.

U.S. 83 at Abilene veers either east or west as it continues south, forming a beltway, the top of which is Interstate 20. I forgo that route and take Business Highway 83, which doesn't cut through a particularly scenic part of town. The first buildings I encounter are scrap yards with signs announcing that the establishments buy copper, brass, and catalytic converters. Metal recycling lots are not pretty, but these seem to be fairly well hidden, perhaps by design.

At about 117,000 people, Abilene is by far the largest city I've encountered since leaving the border in Canada.

As I drive farther south, there are businesses devoted to the automobile, but no sparkling car dealerships. More like collision repair and auto glass replacement shops, auto part chain stores— "Get in the Zone: AutoZone"— construction machinery rental, and all sorts of businesses catering to folks from the country: a horse trailer sales lot, feed stores, farm machinery, and boot repair, along with a self-storage lot, monument carvers strategically located next to the boneyards, 7-Elevens, liquor stores, the Mrs.

Baird's Pies industrial bakery, about a half dozen cafes that have gone belly-up, an instrument maintenance company called The Instrument Maintenance Company, and a muffler shop called The Muffler Shoppe. There's not a Bed Bath & Beyond mall-type store to be found, but there is a lot of nuts and bolts business going on here.

The Western Way Saddle & Tack store, with its red fiberglass horse perched majestically facing the highway, is a windowless, cinder-block building with what appears to be a historical plaque next to the door. Determined to read every marker I can find along the route, I pull up and take the bait.

"On March 2, 1836, Texas declared her independence from Mexico, wild Comanches roamed the plains, rangers protected frontier settlements, and this building was not here yet," it reads.

I see now that its is signed by the "Texas Histerical Committee."

Larry's Better Burger Drive-In would probably qualify for historical status in the minds of its thousands of loyal customers who have made their way to the hamburger stand for the past fifty-eight years. It sits between a gift shop that has gone out of business and a monument shop that sells headstones for the graveyard behind it.

There is no indoor seating, or outdoor seating for that matter. The seating is in your car, if you choose to eat there, but none of the customers do this. They bend over and give their orders through a small sliding glass window to middle-aged women, pick up their orders in white paper bags at a second window facing the highway, then drive off. The old neon sign is faded. Corrugated steel awning painted blue and white keeps the sun and the rain off customers; rusted columns hold it up.

"Are you writing about this?" a petite black woman asks, spotting my notebook. "You better. This is the finest food in town," she says, laughing.

I find the owner, Larry Olney, who invites me to the back and sits at a small wooden desk with a couple pictures of cowboys hanging behind it.

He's seventy-one years old, wears jeans and a yellow-and-blue-checkered short-sleeved shirt. He's tall, and has to stoop over to hand customers their orders. Two tufts of gray sideburns descend from his purple baseball cap. He looks at me through thick bifocals. He has owned the stand for forty-three years.

"Bought it in 1967. It was already old when I got it. Think it was built in 1952—that's what they tell me. I worked in restaurant wholesale. The guy who had it wanted to get rid of it. I ran it; kept my job for a few years, then I wound up just doing this."

"You ever get bored?

"Oh yeah. I'm tired of it right now. I got to do something. I still like to do it. I don't have to do it. It's old and its wore out. But that's okay. We still sell a lot of hamburgers. We got a good business. Some customers have been eating here their whole life. It's just an old, cheap, crackerbox hamburger stand that was built years and years ago. It's still plugging along. Its day is almost here. It's wore out. Me, too.

"I got a boy, Danny, who may take it over. He helps me a good bit. I'll probably turn it over to him some day. If he can keep it open. It's old. It's hard to keep up with the regulations. I'm kind of under the grandfather clause a little bit. The city, and nobody else, wants to put me out. I got too good a reputation. They would rather just let me run my course. 'Cause it won't be long. There won't be no more like this. It will run its course one day, and that will be the end of it."

A chicken wholesaler comes in and gives him a sales slip.

"Most of the salesmen are like him. I don't even give them my order. I just let them come in and do it themselves. We're

Larry Olney, May 2010

plugging along. Come by again some day. We might be here. You never can tell."

When I tell him that I'm writing a book about Highway 83, he asks, "Where's that?"

"You're on it, now."

It turns out that no one calls it "Business 83" here. It's Treadaway Boulevard, and for about a mile it runs parallel to the traditionally black neighborhood in town, the Carver community. Of all the towns along Highway 83, Abilene has the largest African-American population, at about 9,500. I stop at the Mount Zion Baptist Church to take a picture of the historical marker. Established in 1885, this is the oldest African-American church in the city—although the building is not in its original location. It has been here since 1940. About a block north was the Abilene Negro High School, which was open until desegregation in 1968. I will later find in the city library a collection of remembrances from some of the town's black residents. These recollections are predictably depressing and disturbing to read, especially for someone like myself who was born in 1963 and never experienced segregation firsthand: bigotry was rife. The testimonies don't paint a complimentary portrait of pre–Civil Rights–era Abilene, but to be fair, the stories echo those of that time found in many southern and northern cities.

"The buckle of the Bible Belt" is Abilene's nickname. Three religiously affiliated universities call it home: Abilene Christian University (Church of Christ); Hardin-Simmons University (Baptist) and McMurry University (Methodist).

Founded in 1881 by cattlemen wanting to ship livestock on the Texas and Pacific Railway, Abilene, Texas, was named after Abilene, Kansas, the northern terminus of the of the old Chisholm Trail.

Abilene, Abilene, prettiest town I've ever seen, the old song goes. It probably wasn't referring to the Business 83 section of town. I've got Dave Alvin's song "Abilene" from his live album, *Out in California* playing almost nonstop as I explore the city. It's not about the town, but rather a down-on-her-luck dancer named Abilene.

Just to the west a few blocks is the city's more charming downtown with the Grace Museum and restored Paramount Theater. These streets—when they were nothing but dust and mud, and Abilene little more than a playground for drunken cowboys—were the scene of many shootouts. It was a wild, wild West town, and getting ranch hands liquored up was a lucrative business.

The most famous gunfight involved two former Texas Rangers, brothers Frank and Walter Collins, and a local hothead saloonkeeper, Zeno Hemphill. Frank was a city alderman and his bother Walter, a deputy sheriff. They arrived the evening of January 8, 1884, at Hemphill's establishment on Pine Street—possibly to have a drink or two. Frank was immediately intercepted by Hemphill, who was out on bond awaiting a trial for murder. The saloonkeeper didn't care much for a new city ordinance prohibiting gambling and told Frank in no uncertain terms. Someone threw a punch, then guns were drawn. Walter tried to step between the two and took a bullet from Hemphill that killed him on the spot. Frank reeled from a gunshot wound but managed to fire and kill Hemphill.

Frank Collins lingered for two months before succumbing to his wounds. The so-called Pine Street Shootout marred Abilene's reputation at a time when the town was struggling to attract newcomers.

Not as well known, and much more unusual, was the day two of the town's three newspaper publishers squared off on San Jacinto Day, 1885. Just about every town in the west of any size had at least one newspaper, and many had two—one Republican and one Democrat. Sniping at each other in print was common, and in fact, constitutes one of the more entertaining parts of reading frontier broadsheets today. C. E. Gilbert of the *Abilene Reporter* and W. E. Gibbs of the *Magnetic Quill* decided that the "sword was mightier than the pen"—as the town's third newspaper editor put it—and faced off in a duel.

One of Gibbs's bullets grazed Gilbert across the forehead. Gilbert responded with a bullwhip loaded on the ends with buckshot to give it extra weight. It landed a blow on Gibbs's right arm that was hard enough to render the appendage useless. That was enough, the onlookers decided, and both men agreed to end the face-off. Each would later claim that the other was forced to retreat.

The Wild West town began to calm down when the respectable, church-going citizens began to outnumber the saloonkeepers, ruffians, cowboys, and prostitutes. A tough Irish-American Confederate army veteran named John Clinton arrived to keep the peace as the town marshal. He cut his teeth as a lawman in notorious Dodge City, Kansas, so he came with considerable experience. His job was made a bit easier when Abilene voted to go dry in 1902. Not that ridding the town of legal alcohol solved everything. There were bootleggers and underground saloons to deal with. He killed only one man in the line of duty, and reportedly stopped carrying a gun from that day forward. The citizens' initial misgivings about appointing a Roman Catholic to the post were soon forgotten. He served thirty-seven years and was on duty the day William Jennings Bryan arrived in town.

THE HORSELESS CARRIAGE

Young Eddie Rickenbacker entered the hotel lobby in Abilene with his hat in his hand, hoping to meet one of the most famous politicians of his day.

He had a tough task as the regional salesman for the Columbus Buggy Company of Columbus, Ohio. It was 1909, and the carriage maker was now offering a vehicle that no longer required a horse to pull it. The four-passenger Firestone-Columbus Model 76-A was a departure for the company, which had previously toyed with simply mounting gas or electric engines on traditional buggies and operating them with a stick. This new model resembled rival automobiles—although no one would call them that it this West Texas backwater. They were simply "horseless carriages" and a novelty only affordable to rich folks.

Eddie had a plan, though. He always had a plan.

William Jennings Bryan, the three time presidential candidate for the Democrats, was arriving for a big speech and Eddie would offer to transport him around town free of charge. Eddie wasn't all that interested in politics. But he had already worked out surefire methods for selling automobiles. One was simple: Race on Sundays, sell cars on Monday. Just about as soon as men had invented cars, they organized competitions to see who could go the fastest and farthest in the new contraptions. But there were few if any other automobiles to compete with in Abilene, let alone a developed race track. The other strategy was to offer test drives. Bryan was not a prospective car buyer, but if he agreed to be chauffered around town, the throngs there to greet him would have to take notice of the horseless carriage, Eddie reasoned.

Nineteen-year-old Eddie, the lanky son of impoverished immigrants, knew just about everything there was to know about this upcoming technology. In fact, he'd had a hand in designing the 76-A.

His father, William, was a Swiss German-speaking migrant who wound up in Columbus, Ohio, working in a brewery. It was a good, steady job, or so his mother, Lizzie, thought when she met her countryman in Ohio and married him. It turned out William was ill-tempered and ended up going from job to job until he was reduced to being a day laborer. Lizzie was more industrious and managed to keep a roof over the heads of her children as they came one by one.

Eddie was the second son and the third child of eight. He grew up a ruffian on the industrial side of Columbus, the leader of his own little gang that specialized in theft and pointless vandalism. He also showed signs of being a daredevil at an early age. Dangerous mischief was his gang's specialty. He once—and only once—tried to fly off his home's rooftop employing a bicycle and an umbrella. His posse stole a small cart from a gravel mine and repeatedly rode it down into the pit until an accident left a deep gash in his shin.

Poverty fueled his rebellion as the Rickenbacker siblings were forced to go to school in rags and mismatched shoes. The other wounds came from his father. William thrashed Eddie when he misbehaved, which didn't do any good. William and Lizzie were convinced that their second son was heading to reform school.

It all changed overnight when William got into a fight while working at a construction job and was beaten so badly he went into a coma, then later died. Eddie instinctively knew, at age thirteen, that it was time to forsake his childish ways and become the man in the family. He promised his heartbroken mother that he would straighten out. She worked out a deal with the truant officer, and the boy was allowed to quit school and go to work in the city's factories. He turned out to be a more serious and steady worker than his father. He could charm his way into any job, and had a series of them, eventually landing in the machine shop for the Pennsylvania Railroad, where he learned to work with a lathe to make parts.

It wasn't long after when he joined a crowd gathered around a horseless carriage salesman. The man parked a new Ford Model C on the street and began to extol the virtues of this new way of going from point A to point B.

It was a tough sell. Automobiles at that time were temperamental machines that took a tremendous amount of skill to operate. Some were powered by steam, some by electricity, and a few by gasoline. They were hard and dangerous to start. A driver could break a hand if he cranked it wrong. They overheated. They offered little in terms of safety—engineers were too preoccupied with making sure they worked than thinking up items like seat belts. Tires constantly went flat or wore down on the streets. And the roads were a mess. Hitting a pothole too fast could eject a driver or passenger.

So when the Ford salesman asked if anyone would like to go along for a ride, not a single prospect raised his or her hand. Only a skinny kid with a penchant for danger, wearing threadbare clothes, volunteered. The salesman took Eddie along anyway. As the wind blew through his hair and the Ford gathered speed, it became another life-changing moment for the boy. He began hanging around the numerous car makers in Columbus. There were some forty of them at one time or another, all vying for a piece of this upcoming market. The city was known as the "Buggy Capitol of the World" because of all the manufacturers there, and the entrepreneurs in town wanted a piece of the future.

He found work sweeping the floors at Evans Garage, which had recently branched out from making bicycles. It was a quarter of the pay that the railroad offered, but he was soon doing a lot more than handling a broom. He took a correspondence course in automotive engineering and learned to read technical drawings. Within a year, he was working down the street at the Oscar Lear Motor Company, which was manufacturing cars one hand-crafted part at a time. One of the owners and the chief engineer,

Lee Frayer, took Eddie under his wing. He let him build parts at first, then graduated him to the design team.

In 1906, the company entered its automobile in the Vanderbilt Cup auto race on Long Island, and Frayer brought Eddie along as his mechanic and co-driver. It was the first time Eddie had left the Columbus city limits.

The cup and other races were far more than competitions where men vied for bragging rights and prize money. They turned out to be essential for the development of the automobile. Engineering teams pushed themselves hard ahead of the races to make the most durable and fastest machines possible. Every crash or breakdown was a chance to learn what went wrong, and to come up with fixes that would improve their cars. Winning a high-profile race like the Vanderbilt Cup, which attracted teams from the United States and Europe, would not only bring in $10,000 in prize money, it would bring in sales and publicity.

Mechanics at that time were co-drivers, sitting in the passenger seat, with no seatbelts or windshields, hanging on for dear life. For a danger junkie like Eddie, it was exhilarating. The very first automobiles that raced at the turn of the century went seven and a half miles per hour. Six years later, the top speed at the Vanderbilt Cup was sixty-one miles per hour. By the time "Fast Eddie" retired from racecar driving, they were in the nineties.

Frayer's team didn't win the cup, but the news of what they accomplished at the race attracted the attention of the larger and well-financed Columbus Buggy Company, which hired them away. At the age of seventeen Eddie Rickenbacker was named the firm's chief of design. Soon he was being dispatched all over the United States to assist salesmen in the field. He was renowned for being able to put his ear up to an engine and immediately diagnose what was wrong. The machines "spoke to him," he would say. Soon, he was selling and racing the cars full-time in Texas.

Eddie approached Bryan in the hotel lobby.

He was a stout, jowly man with a rich baritone voice that had made him the most famous orator of his time. He had campaigned in a Benz back in 1896 when he was running against McKinley, so he readily accepted the younger man's offer. Bryan sat directly behind Eddie while two others in his entourage grabbed the remaining seats.

Bryan waved to the onlookers as Eddie took him from event to event, culminating in a big speech at the hotel. Local papers took photographs of "the Great Commoner" in the car—the best possible publicity they could ask for.

The gambit resulted in a nibble. A local rancher approached Eddie and said if he could take him and his family back to their home the following day "just outside of town" without the machine breaking down, he would buy a car. Eddie accepted the challenge, not realizing that "just outside of town" in Texas terms was about eighty miles. The road, if it could be called that, was nothing but wagon-wheel ruts. Eddie suffered two flat tires on the way there, but the rancher didn't hold that against him.

Eddie Rickenbacker drives William Jennings Bryan (back, driver's side) in Abilene, Texas, 1909. Other passengers unknown. Courtesy of Auburn University Library.

He did, however, lose the bet. Just as they were approaching the gate to the ranch, an axle hit a tree root and snapped. A horse team had to haul the automobile to the house.

The cowboys at the ranch headquarters had never laid eyes on an automobile before. They gave the disappointed young salesman a hard time about his horseless carriage that had required horses to finish the trip. But like most folks, the ranch hands took an instant liking to Eddie. Soon enough, they were goading him to ride a horse for the first time. Always the risk taker, Eddie didn't hesitate. He immediately kicked the horse in the ribs, and his mount bucked him off heels over head. Such a calamity could have snapped his neck and killed him, but that would turn out to be the story of Eddie Rickenbacker's life. He would use up the lives of a dozen cats before he passed from this mortal coil.

The cowboys the next morning helped him build a fire. Eddie heated up the axle until it was red hot and pounded it back to shape. The repair was good enough for him to drive the rancher back to Abilene without incident. That may have convinced the Texan that automobiles were the future. Despite Eddie losing the bet, the rancher ordered three 76-As.

Eddie Rickenbacker would continue to be a pioneer in auto racing, and would participate in the earliest Indianapolis 500s, but go on to even greater fame as an aviator in World War I, making twenty-seven kills in the skies above Europe and earning the Medal of Honor. He accomplished what few of the early military pilots managed to do: survive the war alive. Even as a company executive—co-founder of Eastern Airlines—he cheated death by surviving two plane crashes. He was once shipwrecked and survived in a life raft for twenty-four days. He lived long enough to watch the establishment of the national road system and the interstates, fly in a jet, see men land on the moon, and watch race cars top 200 miles per hour. Perhaps the most surprising thing about his life was his death. In 1973, he passed away of natural causes.

I take a spin around Abilene's beltway so I can claim that I have truly touched on every part of Highway 83. There are a surprising number of strip bars visible from the bypass for a town known for being so devout. The southwest side of the bypass is where the big malls and chain stores sit, along with Dyess Air Force Base. The buildings thin out on the northern section where most of the Interstate 20 traffic passes by. These four-lane expressways radically altered U.S. cities. I'm just old enough to remember going shopping at a downtown department store in Omaha. I also remember when the eighth biggest shopping mall in America opened up out west along the interstate when I was about five. Within a few short years, retail downtown was dead, and everyone was heading to the suburbs to shop. This trend played out all over America and in Abilene.

Highway 83 encounters four interstates in Texas, and this is the second of them.

President Dwight D. Eisenhower on June 29, 1956, signed the legislation that would be the death knell for many federal highways. The Federal-Aid Highway Act of 1956 created the so-called "superhighways" that would speed Americans between cities on four lanes instead of two. It would create a 41,000-mile-long network of "limited access" roads that would touch almost all of the nation's cities with populations over 50,000. The feds would pick up ninety percent of the costs.

Remarkably, the president signed this transformative piece of legislation while lying in a hospital bed at Walter Reed Medical Center, where he had just undergone surgery for ileitis—not at some big ceremony in the Rose Garden. Like its predecessor, the Federal Aid Highway Act of 1921, it was a law that would have an enormous impact on Americans' lives.

Eisenhower, as a young Army lieutenant shortly after World War I, volunteered to travel in a convoy traveling the length of the New York–to–San Francisco Lincoln Highway, which had been laid out in 1912. The arduous journey took sixty-two days, much of it spent pulling trucks out of the mud. Decades later, Ike said that experience, and seeing the German autobahns, prompted him to sign the 1956 legislation.

Today, drivers occasionally see a blue sign bearing five stars reminding them that this is the "Eisenhower Interstate System"—but it should rightly be called the "MacDonald Interstate System." It was Thomas MacDonald's Bureau of Public Roads that had formulated the idea. In 1938, at the behest of Congress, the bureau produced a report, "Toll Roads and Free Roads." It laid out a vision for superhighways not unlike the German autobahns. The chief had traveled to pre-war Germany to witness these new roads for himself. He was impressed, but could see that they were intended to rapidly transport troops and military vehicles. That was a colossal waste of money, he believed. As for the United States, they would be practical in large cities, but not for remote areas. The volume of rural traffic would never justify them, he said. Nevertheless, the report mapped out what would be a nationwide system, one that would be paid for by tolls and included six nationwide long-distance limited-access roads.

Meanwhile, Pennsylvania set about creating the nation's first four-lane, limited access turnpike. With a big check from the Works Progress Administration intended to give men jobs during the Depression, additional funding from the state, and technical advice from MacDonald's cadre of engineers, it was completed in a little more than two years and opened to motorists in 1940.

When the war was over, lawmakers wanted more four-lane highways. The Federal Highway Act of 1944 authorized the creation of an interstate system to supplant many of the federal highways. But authorizing in Washington is not the same as funding. Congress over the next few budget cycles

Thomas H. MacDonald, father of the modern U.S. highway system

appropriated a paltry $25 million, about enough to build fifty miles of superhighway. The proposed map languished as the roads in and around cities began to crumble. No one predicted the massive population and economic boom that would follow the war, nor the increases in automobile and truck traffic that would ensue when rationing was lifted.

President Harry S. Truman wanted MacDonald to stay on the job. He had reached retirement age and had served under five presidents, but change was coming. The roads bureau was taken from Agriculture and put under the Department of Commerce. MacDonald now answered to two superiors. All along, he never wavered in his belief that superhighways in underpopulated regions would be a waste of money.

MacDonald had lorded over the Bureau of Public Roads (now renamed the Public Roads Administration) for thirty-four years. The chief amassed the power to take the nation out of the mud and onto good roads. As the 1944 plan languished, the federal highway system become overtaxed and the newly elected Eisenhower laid the blame on MacDonald, who was already three years past retirement age. The president asked him to retire from public service in 1953. MacDonald continued working at Texas A&M University, where he led a highway research center, and died in 1957 at age seventy-seven, just as road crews began to grade the first of the new highways. Eisenhower didn't create the Interstate System, but he pushed for it during his presidency. The 1956 law he signed kicked in the necessary billions to build it. A gas tax, rather than tolls, created a permanent fund to keep it maintained.

Today, MacDonald's impact on Americans' lives has been largely forgotten. Google the words "Thomas H. MacDonald Memorial Highway" and nothing pops up—not a single road dedicated to the father of the federal highway system.

I leave the beltway where Highway 83 merges with Highway 84 then heads south of Abilene. The Protegé labors as it begins to climb a hill, the steepest I've seen for days. It's part of the Callahan Divide, a small chain of hills that extends a mere twenty-six miles.

About ten miles south of town is the appropriately named Hilltop Station. I have seen dozens of abandoned old gas stations along the road. They have been mostly replaced by big, shiny new convenience stores that sell hundreds of items. The stone building boasts a couple of 1980s era pumps, so my first impression is that it's closed. But a sign is advertising fuel at the current prices. It's still open. I could use some gas, so I turn around and head back.

I'm surprised when a man pops out of the door and asks if I need to fill it up. Wisps of gray hair protrude from his scalp, and a blue button-down shirt exposes some gray chest hair and a potbelly hanging over his jeans. This is a full-service gas station. I'm also just barely old enough to remember full-service gas stations, where friendly men asked if my folks wanted to "fill'er up" and cleaned the windshield and windows as the gas pumped. By the time I was old enough to drive, full service was almost a thing of the past. I'm in shock and almost at a loss for what to do as he carries out a task I feel that I should be doing myself.

So we chat as I take some pictures.

His name is Lloyd Smith. He's a sixty-eight-year-old lifelong bachelor who took over the gas station from his father. He farms and ranches in the evening and pumps gas here in the daytime.

The station has been here since 1940 and has never closed. He rattles off all the brands that were once sold here: Sinclair, Gulf, Premier, El Paso, Conoco, Philips, Kerr-McGee. There is no brand now. Just unleaded gas for $2.69.

"I'm the last of the Mohicans," he chuckles to himself.

I'm sure I have passed dozens of stations that have sold gas along the highway for decades, but I doubt any have been in the same building for seventy years. This is a real "filling station."

Lloyd doesn't take credit cards. He doesn't offer to wash the bugs off my windows, either. It's just gas. And some air for the tires if needed. He complains that "its hard to compete." But he has no competition up at the top of the hill. It is a lonely spot; no other businesses are nearby. He doesn't have any kids who will inherit the station. Like the Larry's hamburger stand, it may be the last of its kind.

U.S. Route 84 was one of the original roads designated by the highway commission in 1926, but originally it only extended from Georgia to Alabama. Like 83, it evolved through the years. It begins in the east near a small town not quite on the Atlantic Ocean, swoops through the deep South, and begins a northwest climb beginning at Abilene until it ends on the southern edge of Colorado. Tracing its path, it appears as a wide grin on the U.S. map. Highway 84's time together as the same road as 83 is brief, as it splits off on its way to the capital in Austin and on to Louisiana, while I head south to the tip of Texas.

I am forced to pull over again as I spot an abandoned business, the Highway 83 Car Wash. The place is overgrown with weeds and mesquite. Of course, every small business that goes under represents a dream that died hard for someone. I have to wonder who thought it was a good idea to open up a car wash out here miles away from any town. They had to have a good source of water, I reckon, and maybe they thought they could capitalize on it. The outfit appeared to have one bay where drivers could pull in, drop some quarters in a machine, and blast the dust off their vehicles. It's not the type of business where you have to be around all the time. Even so, it didn't make it.

Soon I'm rolling into Winters, a town I was looking forward to seeing. "Welcome to Winters. Home of the Blizzards," a bank sign announces. It ironically declares that the temperature is 91 degrees. The town was also the home and birthplace of Baseball Hall of Famer Rogers Hornsby, perhaps the second greatest hitter of all time behind Ty Cobb. As I enter the outskirts I look for a sign to the effect of "Hometown of Rogers Hornsby," but find none. Something pointing the way to his house? Nothing. Perhaps the town hasn't embraced its most famous son because his family were outsiders and their time in Winters was brief.

Hornsby's ancestors were among the first Anglos to settle Travis County, Texas, the eventual location of the state capital,

U.S. Highway 83 in Texas, Ballinger to Laredo

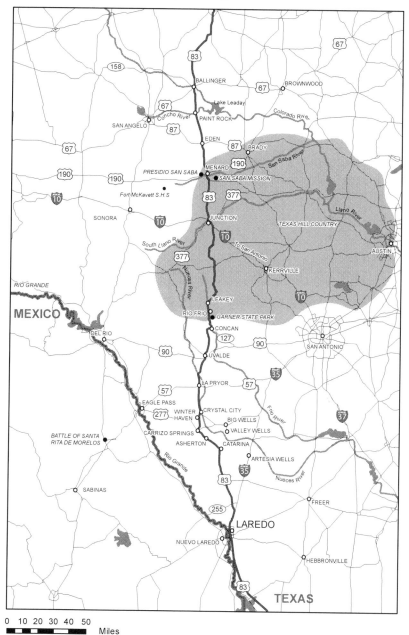

0 10 20 30 40 50
Miles

Austin. The first settlement in the area, the town of Hornsby Bend, was named after them. Rogers' father, Ed Hornsby, and his uncle Daniel ventured out from the family enclave after all the prime land was taken there. Ed and his wife, Mary, bought a section of land in Runnels County two miles south of Winters from Daniel and moved there with their first four children. They eked out a living farming and raising a few cattle. About four years after they arrived, Rogers was born in 1896. When he was two and a half, Ed unexpectedly died at forty-one. Shortly thereafter, Mary and the five children moved back to Travis County to live with her parents.

So Rogers had no memories of Winters. He didn't spend his formative years there, or learn to play baseball in the town. Few in town probably knew the family well. Maybe that's why there is no sign for the man who retired with the second-highest batting average of all time.

It's a few short miles to Ballinger, the county seat of Runnels County, and what looks to be a great spot to stretch my legs and take some pictures. It's a town of some 3,800 residents with a large downtown and plenty of grand old buildings built in the first half of the twentieth century. An antiques store beckons to me. In fact, they all do. I have loved antiques stores, antique malls, flea markets, and thrift stores my whole life. Even if I don't buy anything, I consider each a walk through an uncurated museum. But this one truly is calling out to me, and anyone who happens to be passing by. The stucco building is painted in gaudy colors, mostly orange. "Stop Here Now!" one of the signs hand-painted on the side of the building commands me. "This Means You!"

"ONEOFAKINDUNIQUEANTIQUES.COM," reads another. "Whoa!"

You had me at "antiques," I think. No need for carnival barker tactics—in my case anyway.

I step in and find behind a cluttered counter a middle-aged man who apparently has a penchant for old signs. I know immediately that this is my kind of antiques store. It's crammed with old porcelain gas station, soda pop, and beer signs, and it has a booth devoted to Elvis Presley.

I don't have room for giant Sinclair Gas Station signs in my small condo in Arlington, Virginia, nor would my wife be excited about me bringing one home if I did, but I am on the lookout for old federal highway signs for Route 83. I ask the owner if he has any, and he's quite sure he doesn't. I also collect a category known as "true space," toys or memorabilia connected to the U.S. space program. I strike out on both accounts, but a tattered, relatively plain concert poster catches my eye. It reads:

DANCE
Stagecoach Inn
Stamford
Sat. May 31
9:00 P.M. TIL 1:00 A.M.
IN PERSON
TOMMY ROSS
"When I Drank Texas Dry"

There isn't a picture of this Tommy Ross, whom I have never heard of, yet this is a unique find. The store has lived up to its name.

Stamford is the closest town to "No Dancin'" Anson, and while it isn't on Highway 83, this poster is too cool to pass up. The proprietor wants five bucks. Sold! I resolve to find out more about Tommy Ross and his "hit" record later.

South of Ballinger are two notable photo ops. One is a giant, 100-foot-high white crucifix on top of a hill. The other is the Colorado River, which I am absolutely dumbfounded to come across. Wow. I had no idea, I think as I get out of the car to take some pictures of the legendary river.

(I'll feel pretty stupid that night when I look at my atlas and realize that it's not THE Colorado River, just *a* Colorado River. No rule against using a name more than once, I guess. It turns out that this Colorado is the longest self-contained river in Texas at 862 miles. Water flowing south of the Callahan Divide ends up in its channel. Water flowing north goes to the Brazos.)

The towns of Paint Rock and Eden get the short shrift as I head south, not really knowing where I am going to hang my hat this evening. I had plans to spend at least a night in Abilene, but I ended up pushing through town. Paint Rock is famous for Native American pictographs painted on cliffs near the Concho River, but they are on private property and an attempt to phone the owners and see them is unsuccessful. I stop long enough to take a picture of the Paint Rock Wool Warehouse, a red brick building along the road. It is the first sign that I'm entering sheep country. It was this industry that brought the first roads to this sparely populated region. The herders needed a means to transport their livestock to railheads in Abilene or San Angelo.

I press on through a mesquite forest—that same damn turkey buzzard circling about 100 yards in front of my car—until I enter a steep valley approaching the town of Menard.

On the outskirts is a classic Texas dance hall, Club Victoria, likenesses of two black guitars displayed on either side of the sign. The parking lot is empty since it's daytime. There are two quintessential Texas experiences: the Texas dance hall and a Friday night high school football game. It being May, there is no chance I will attend the latter, but I'm still hoping to see some foot-stompin' Texas music somewhere along 83.

When I reach the bottom of the valley I spot the Motel 83. "Color-TV-Cable," the sign reads and advertises a room for thirty-four dollars. The sun won't be setting for several hours, but this is the first motel I've come across named after the highway. I feel compelled to stop and spend a night here.

Just beyond the motel parking lot is a brown sign. When traveling on highways, brown signs are the best. They can designate only a few things: a historic site, a park, or a wildlife refuge. I live for brown signs. This one reads: "Presidio De San Saba."

It's the dying light of the day, the best time to take pictures, so after checking into the motel, I head out as soon as I can. The Presidio San Sabá sounds intriguing. I drive west on U.S. Route 190 for a few short miles and follow the signs to—a golf course? As I pull in, a pair of white golf carts are gliding along the fairway carrying a foursome. I follow the road until I see what appears to be the ruins of an old fort made of mortar and stone with prickly pear and tall grass growing along its cracks.

Aside from how this historical landmark ended up in the middle of a golf course, I wonder what the rest of the story is with this place.

THE CROWN OF MARTYRDOM

Corporal José Vasquez and the other soldiers in his detail took in the horrific scene from the top of the valley overlooking the mission. Hostile Indians occupied every clearing. More were coming over the ridge to the north on foot or horseback. The stockade built to protect the mission was ablaze, and a plume of smoke spread out in a black cloud over the San Saba River. The Indians dashed in and out of the mission's buildings, emerging with looted goods. The air crackled with the sound of muskets popping off rounds. The Catholic priests and the three dozen others living there couldn't be seen. God have mercy on their souls, for the attackers were mostly Comanches.

Vasquez was standing alongside Sergeant Flores and seven other Spanish soldiers, horse reins in their hands, assessing the bleak situation. They had left the relative safety of the presidio a few hours earlier on a scouting mission when a messenger arrived from the fort with orders from the commander, Colonel Diego Ortiz Parrilla. The Mission San Sabá was under attack. He and his men were to proceed there immediately to "determine the intentions of the Indians" and reinforce the handful of soldiers guarding the compound if necessary. As for the first part of the order, the natives' intentions were very clear. As for the second, they were too late. There were hundreds of Indians between themselves and the mission. The road leading there was overrun with them. The men all agreed that there must be 1,500 warriors within their sight, and that many of them were armed with modern French muskets. That was a shock. None of them had ever seen so many guns in the hands of the natives. They had to wonder whether French agents were behind this attack.

Vasquez was a twenty-six-year-old foot soldier who had served in San Antonio and other missions in the northern reaches of New Spain, but he had never experienced anything like this. He carried a musket and a bayonet and was protected by a thick white leather breastplate. The Spanish had long ago abandoned the shiny steel armor of the conquistador age and replaced it with cowhide thick enough to stop an arrow, thus earning dragoons such as Vasquez the nickname *soldados de cuera*, leather soldiers.

The nine men rode down the hill to see if they could somehow help the beleaguered mission. But coming from the opposite direction on the road was a column of Indians on foot, walking three abreast like a European regiment.

The Indians opened fire. Vasquez and two of his comrades fell on the road. Vasquez hadn't been hit—perhaps it was his horse. He looked over and saw the two others bleeding from their wounds. The other soldiers dismounted and fired a volley, but that was all they could manage as the attackers advanced. Stuck between the river and the bluffs, they retreated into a gulley.

Before Vasquez could get back on his feet, a warrior with his face painted black and white thrust a lance into the right side of his chest, piercing his leather. The Indian left him bleeding on the road, then joined the others in pursuit of the six remaining Spaniards.

Vazquez crawled into a thicket next to the river, where he immediately passed out.

Despite the abject failure of Francisco Vazquez de Coronado's expedition to find cities of gold in 1541, the Spanish Empire had pushed onwards to occupy the region north of the Rio Grande. But it wasn't just there for the taking. The Apaches and a dozen or more other tribes considered this their traditional lands. They raided the colonies, stole livestock, killed and kidnapped. The French, from their territory in the east, encroached on Spain's claims and vied for influence with Native American nations in the north such as the Wichitas.

The kings in Madrid handed out land grants to those who dared to carve out a life in the inhospitable and untamed lands. While no one had found cities of gold there, the Spanish needed to occupy the territory to serve as a bulwark against French and British territorial claims. The settlers had to scratch out a living as subsistence farmers and ranchers, sometimes with little or no army to protect them.

But there was one almighty power on the Spanish side: God. The Catholic Church and its various orders, mostly the Franciscans, were charged with saving the souls of the Indians and ministering to the spiritual needs of the colonists. Seminaries in Spain produced thousands of priests whose sole mission was to go out into the wilds of Spain's many colonies and convert the heathens. It was dangerous work for these brothers. Many became martyrs.

During the 217 years between the Coronado expedition and the attack on the San Sabá mission, the Spanish had inadvertently handed over the horse to the Indians. It transformed their way of life.

Prior to the Comanches' taking over the southern Great Plains, the Lipan Apaches were the most powerful tribe in these lands. They were one of six loosely affiliated Apache tribes spread throughout the Southwest. They had migrated over the centuries from the Northwest and through the years developed separate dialects and customs, and were sometimes known to fight one another. When the Spanish first pushed north of the Rio Grande, the Lipan Apaches resisted the encroachment.

For the Spanish, there were two possible solutions to the Apache problem: make peace, or make war. As for the second option, it was hardly feasible. The king's army in the north was poorly equipped and thin in numbers. The Apaches—if they gathered all their bands together—could amass a horde of thousands of warriors. A Spanish garrison protecting a mission might quarter a hundred soldiers on a good day. The Apaches would raid, and the Spanish would send out punitive expeditions to track down the culprits, often with little success.

The brothers of the Catholic Church believed peace was the better way: build missions in the wilderness and convert the "savages" into Christians.

The Spanish established San Antonio in 1717 as the northern-most outpost in Texas. The settlement at first comprised of a contingent of Canary Islanders and black slaves, and its existence, when surrounded by so many hostile tribes, was precarious. The local Payaya tribe, which soon converted and became known as the "mission Indians," helped boost its numbers. The mission

Indians were taught how to farm, weave, build homes, and tend to livestock.

For every mission there was a presidio, or fort, somewhere nearby. As far as the civilian government was concerned, the military was not only necessary to protect the citizens from Indian transgressions, it served to send a message to rivals in Britain and France that this was Spain's land.

The Lipan Apaches, meanwhile, had no friends. They were hounded by the Comanches and their allies to the north and harassed by Spanish soldiers in the south. By 1749, they made a strategic decision to cease raiding the Europeans and ally themselves with the Spanish. Amazingly, the peace held for five years. But for the friars, this was not enough. The idea to expand the mission system north came from powerful church leaders. The Apaches weren't fighting, but neither were they becoming good Christian mission Indians. As for the civilian leaders, they wanted to explore and settle the region northwest of San Antonio. Building a fort there would make a statement to the French and their Wichita and Comanche allies.

Prior to making peace with the Lipan Apaches, the Spanish had fought two battles with the tribe in the San Sabá Valley. They knew the territory well and believed it to be the heart of Apache country. There was reportedly silver in the nearby hills as well. So when the time came to choose a location for the new mission, the fertile valley was the only location seriously considered.

The Apaches who came to San Antonio to trade promised that they would meet the Spanish there, convert to Christianity, and learn to farm. The missionaries took them at their word. Whether the friars ever consulted their intended neophytes about the location isn't known. But they probably would have told them that the valley was now too close to the Comanches' territory.

Spanish civilian and military leaders were skeptical. A series of missions had been built along the San Antonio River under similar circumstances, but they had failed to attract any adherents.

After years of bloodshed and hard feelings between themselves and the tribe, officials doubted the friars would succeed.

Establishing a mission and fort required the permission of the viceroy of New Spain, located in far-off Mexico City. Correspondence between the two cities took months. The mission would have to find a rich benefactor. Spanish kings expected wealth to flow from the colonies to Spain, not the other way around. The civilian government would have to authorize the building and manning of the presidio. It took three more years of negotiations between the Franciscans and the government before the plan came together.

The governor of Texas was among the skeptics. He sent one last letter to the viceroy opposing the idea. He didn't believe the Lipan Apaches would lay down their arms to become peaceful farmers. Nevertheless, the friars got their way.

Colonel Parrilla had risen through the ranks of the Spanish army, fought the British in Cuba, helped put down a Pueblo revolt in New Mexico, and was by then the commander of the presidio protecting the San Xavier Mission, some 100 miles northeast of San Antonio. He was ordered to close down everything there and lead his group of soldiers, their wives and children, missionaries, mission Indians, servants—plus cattle, horses, and sheep numbering in the thousands—to the previously chosen spot along the San Sabá River some 150 miles due west.

The caravan included six Franciscan friars, including the mission president, Father Alonso Giraldo de Terreros, the cousin of the mission's wealthy benefactor, Don Pedro Romero de Terreros.

They arrived in the picturesque valley on April 17, 1757. Having made a five-day inspection of the area and finding no Apaches, Parrilla favored abandoning the project altogether. That option was completely unacceptable to the brothers. The colonel then began to squabble with the Franciscans about the fort's location and purpose. The colonel wanted to co-locate it and the mission for safety reasons, but the friars insisted that the structures be set about three miles apart to show the natives that they came in peace. The two parties couldn't even agree on which side of the river their respective compounds would occupy. The fort was built on the north side and the mission on the south, meaning the river would have to be forded every time one journeyed between them.

Colonel Diego Ortiz Parrilla

The valley was a good choice for farming and ranching. The bottomlands were fertile, and there was water and grass nearby for the animals, and timber for building. Fed by aquifers to the north, the river never went dry. *Nuez de la arruga*, the wrinkled nut, also known as the pecan, grew on majestic trees along its banks. The first structures were built with mud and logs. Militarily speaking, the Presidio San Luis de las Amarillas, its formal name, was not an ideal location, nestled in a valley with hills to the north and south that gave attackers an advantage.

After weeks of hard work, the Mission Santa Cruz de San Sabá and the presidio were standing. They were rudimentary structures, but they would be improved upon as time went on with stones quarried from the nearby hills. The most important item was to erect the stockades as protection.

Now, all they needed were some godless Apaches to baptize.

The Indians eventually came in small bands. They camped outside the mission, accepted the friars' gifts, and made promises to return someday and take up the plow instead of the war club. Then they disappeared.

The visits resulted in optimistic letters being dispatched to Mexico City and beyond. This foray—farther north than any other established mission—was being monitored in Madrid and the news being relayed to King Ferdinand VI himself.

As the months wore on, the friars grew more pessimistic. There were a grand total of two Apaches living at the mission. Feeling that they could of more use elsewhere, three of the brothers departed, leaving only Father Terreros and the two other friars, Father Santiesteban and Father Molina.

Finally, in mid-June, the day they had all hoped for arrived in the form of some 3,000 Apaches—a massive gathering of dozens of sub-tribes, including the women and children. They camped out along the valley. The missionaries were overjoyed. But they soon found out that the Indians were only there to rest a few days before pushing north to hunt buffalo and make war against their rivals. A band of Comanche and Tejas Indians had recently killed one of the Lipan Apaches' most influential chiefs in a skirmish along the Colorado River.

The chiefs let the priests baptize an elder and minister to some of the sick. They said they would come back just as soon as they had finished the hunt and exacted revenge on the northern tribes. The friars chose to believe them. Just as suddenly as they appeared, they vanished.

Some of them came back after a week, their larders full of buffalo meat—what happened up north, they wouldn't say, but they seemed to be in a hurry to go south.

The months wore on with no natives stopping by the valley. Father Terreros, in letters written to the viceroy in Mexico City, began to acknowledge that the situation was hopeless. Life at the mission and fort became tedious. The viceroy seemed to think that there was still hope, so he ordered the campaign to continue. By the beginning of the next year, as northern winds brought bone-chilling temperatures, Colonel Parrilla began to hear rumors of war parties gathering. Small bands of Apaches would arrive, accept the missionaries' hospitality for a few days, then quickly head south ahead of a gathering storm that the Spaniards were only beginning to understand.

Colonel Parrilla had received intelligence late in the summer of 1757 that the Comanches were planning to attack the Apaches in the San Sabá Valley, but autumn and most of winter had passed, and nothing came of it.

The Comanches at the start of the sixteenth century were a relatively small, hapless tribe that had been pushed out of the Great Basin by rivals and were occupying a tiny corner of the New Mexico mountains. Then they discovered the horse. In a very few short years, they mastered the animal and became some the greatest mounted warriors the world had ever seen.

One of their key skills was the ability to shoot arrows with amazing accuracy from atop a galloping horse. Woe be to any nation that did not become their ally. As the tribe ventured out onto the Southern Plains, they laid claim to the great buffalo commons and jealously guarded this vital food source against any encroachers. The Comanches became a highly organized society whose leaders set themselves up as middlemen in the lucrative trade for European goods, including firearms. They captured men and women from rival tribes and sent them south to New Spain to serve as slaves. They ruled through a sophisticated blend of diplomacy and terror. In a Comanche raid, adults not taken as slaves were often tortured and mutilated. Infants, being of no use to them, were slaughtered. The tribe's reputation weighed heavily on the minds of the fort's occupants, as there were some 260 civilians living inside, most of them the wives and children of soldiers such as Corporal Vasquez.

On the night of February 25, a band of unknown Indians swooped into a nearby pasture where the horses, sheep, and cattle were kept, and scattered them into the brush. Sergeant Flores, Corporal Vasquez, and the rest of the detail were charged with recovering the livestock. As they went after the animals, they saw signs of Indians everywhere. The tracks indicated a large group on horseback and on foot driving the animals away. Another patrol went after the marauders but never caught up with them. They returned after twelve days having recovered only one horse.

The news spread through the Presidio like a cold gust of wind. Parrilla's men were already spread thin. One detail had left for San Antonio to escort a supply train of pack mules. Another dozen men were protecting the livestock in a pasture twelve miles to the east. The colonel immediately dispatched a handful of men to protect the mission. Six more were sent to warn the supply train. They were attacked on their way there, and two were severely wounded. Parrilla sent more men to reinforce the train. The presidio had 100 soldiers stationed there, but in fact Parrilla had fewer than half that many on hand.

The colonel and his entourage rode hard and fast downriver, where he pleaded with Father Terreros to abandon the mission and return with him to the relative safety of the fort. Only a few dozen souls remained there, including the two other friars, servants, stewards, some mission Indians, and the two Apaches who had converted to Christianity. Terreros insisted on staying. The stockade was strong, he said. For Parrilla, the friar's stubbornness was hard to understand. The two had made plans to travel to Mexico City together to discuss the relocation of the mission and fort. They had already sent a letter requesting permission to go there. It was clear by that time that the whole campaign was a failure. To wear the "crown of martyrdom" was the highest honor for the Franciscans. But why put his life in danger for a lost cause?

Parrilla left eight soldiers behind to bolster the mission's meager defenses. He returned to the presidio and prepared for an assault with only three dozen soldiers and a handful of armed servants there to protect the women and children.

The next morning, hundreds of Comanches and their allies swarmed over the San Sabá Mission.

Corporal Vazquez awoke to the sound of muskets firing in the distance. He reached to feel his chest wound and came up with blood covering his fingers. He was certain that he would not live much longer. He lay halfway between the fort and the mission. Both were certain to be surrounded by the barbarians. The only direction for a man of faith to go was where there might be a priest to hear a last confession and to perform last rites. He began crawling toward the mission along the banks of the river in the thickets, out of sight of any hostiles.

After several hours, he reached the clearing between the river and the burning stockade. He tried to crawl out unnoticed, but it didn't take long for a pair of warriors to spot him. They let out a war cry and dashed toward him, but Vasquez had no weapon, or the strength to resist. He was certain they would scalp and torture him on the spot, but they had a more horrific end in mind as they stripped him of his armor. One grabbed his legs, the other his arms. Vasquez realized as they carried him to what remained of the fort's wooden stockade that they intended to burn him alive. He screamed as they flung him into the inferno.

But they threw him too hard.

Vasquez cleared the blaze and landed with a thud on the other side of the wall of fire. Flames had licked his hand and side, but he lay otherwise unharmed on a patch of dirt. He closed his eyes to feign death in case the Indians came around. But they didn't.

He slowly opened one eye and saw that there were shots being fired at the attackers from slots within the head priest's living quarters. He watched the battle for a few minutes, lying as still as possible. One of the Indians rushed the building and was cut down by a musket ball. His fellow warriors ran up to grab him. As they turned to drag him to safety, Vasquez realized that he might not have another chance. He arose and with every last bit of energy in his being stumbled up to the door. "Please," he begged. "Let me in. I must give my last confession."

The door swung open and he was ushered inside. The survivors covered him up and gave him water. Left for dead twice by the invaders, he was fortunate to still be alive. Yet he now found himself in an equally dire situation. One of the three friars,

Father Molina, sat in a corner, severely wounded. The loopholes were being manned by two stewards and a corporal. With them were a boy, some of the servants, and a couple of the mission Indians' wives.

Father Terreros was dead, they reported. One of the corporals Colonel Parrilla left behind had foolishly convinced the mission president that the tribes had come in peace. He recognized some of the Tejas Indians, a tribe that had never made war against the Spanish, so he opened the gates for them. The warriors flooded inside the stockade and for a while made a show of accepting the father's gifts, claiming they were looking only for Apaches and meant the others no harm. Meanwhile, out of view, other Indians were piling brush against the stockade wall in preparation for lighting it. Soon enough, the charade was over and the slaughter began. Father Terreros was the first to wear the crown of martyrdom.

Some tried to flee to safety but didn't make it. The smart ones had seen through the ruse and holed up in the buildings in anticipation of the inevitable. They had been there the whole day fighting off the Indians when Corporal Vasquez knocked on the door.

Eventually, the attackers set the residence on fire. As flames crept over the roof, the Indians turned their attention to the warehouse, which others were busy looting for valuables. The survivors dashed out of the burning building and made it to the friars' residence next to the church. There, they found a small number of others hiding from the attack. Soon the Indians discovered them and set that building on fire as well. The final refuge was the church itself, where by nightfall some thirty survivors had gathered.

The Indians had come there earlier in the day and found Father Santiesteban praying. A pool of blood was found in front of the altar, but his body was nowhere to be found. The attackers had made a point of smashing the statues of the saints.

One of the corporals had brought a small cannon with him. There were ten muskets and enough able-bodied men and ammunition to keep the horde at bay for the time being, at least until one of the marauders managed to set the church on fire. The licking flames of the other buildings reminded Vasquez and the others that the Comanches held a terrible fate in store for them.

In the middle of the night, the Indians erupted in alarm. The mission dogs began howling at some unseen intruders, and the warriors grabbed their weapons and ran to the line of trees. Father Molina, Corporal Vasquez, and the others suspected that Colonel Parrilla had ordered some kind of counterattack. Whatever the case, this was their chance to escape. Finding the east side of the mission unguarded, they all managed to slip over the dying embers of the stockade.

Sergeant Flores and a small party of soldiers and mission Indians had indeed tried to covertly reach the fort, but the dogs gave them away. The fires from the burning buildings were giving off too much light for them to step out into the clearing. When the Indians rushed toward them they were forced to retreat. Flores had no way of knowing that his furtive attempt to rescue survivors indirectly led to their escape.

The following day, the Comanches turned their attention to the fort. The attackers surrounded it, lit brush fires, and took potshots at the soldiers. They did everything they could to lure the Spanish from the relative safety of the stockade to fight, but Colonel Parrilla was not about to fall for any of those old tricks.

On the third morning of the assault, the invading force returned north. They had failed to destroy the presidio, but the Comanche Empire had delivered the intended message: this was their territory and they would accept no encroachment.

Father Molina, Corporal Vasquez, and the mission survivors took the safest and most circuitous route possible to avoid being captured or killed. They didn't make it back to the presidio for almost two days.

I drive through what remains of Menard's downtown. As I've seen in many small towns on Highway 83, some of the buildings are closed forever. The first Texans to settle here after the Civil War reportedly used stones from the presidio ruins to construct a few of the first buildings. If the historians are right, Corporal Vasquez was wounded somewhere near the town center.

I take Farm to Market Road 2092 east in search of the spot where, after some thirty years of searching, archaeologists finally discovered the mission site. The San Sabá is a meandering, untamed river that shifted course over the years and has deposited layers of silt over the victims' graves. No one knows where they are buried.

I find a white granite marker sitting on the north side of the road in front of a green pasture. It reads: "Sacked and left in ruins by the Comanches in 1758 * * Here perished Padres Alonso Giraldo De Terreros and Jose Santiesteban Martyrs to the Christian Cause."

It was called a "massacre," although the death toll was only eight men, which isn't a lot by today's massacre standards, but it certainly could have been a lot worse. The Comanches wouldn't have hesitated to slaughter every last one of the survivors holed up in the church.

Colonel Parrilla gathered up a force of Spanish soldiers, Apache warriors, and a ragtag bunch of untrained volunteers to go teach the northern tribes a lesson and to seek vengeance. He had one victory against a camp of Tonkawas who had participated in the San Sabá attack, and took more than a hundred prisoners. Not yet satisfied, he pressed on to look for the Comanches. He found them among a camp of Wichitas. The villagers were armed with modern French muskets and were well trained in how to use them. The two sides fought to a standstill. The volunteer militiamen, who had little or no training, did not acquit themselves well. They, along with the Apaches, deserted in droves. The Comanches captured two cannons. It wasn't a rout, nor was it a victory.

It was now certain that the Spanish could never muster a force large enough to take on the Comanche Empire and its allies. And the Apaches, observing the stalemate, no longer considered the Spanish a powerful ally.

The presidio stayed in its location for ten more years, a lonely, poorly supplied post constantly harassed by hostiles. In 1772, King Charles III of Spain issued a decree pulling the Spanish out of East Texas, which included the San Sabá Valley. The wilderness posts and missions were abandoned and all personnel pulled back to San Antonio.

The power and influence of the Comanche Empire hadn't even reached its zenith yet. It would rule the northern reaches of Texas for another century until the Red River War of 1874–75 abruptly brought it all to an end.

As for Spain, and later Mexico, they would lay claim to the land along what would be Highway 83 south of here for several more decades. How it all became part of the United States is a story that will be revealed farther down the road.

Junction was so named because it was settled at the confluence of two rivers, the North and the South Llano. It's now the junction of Highway 83 and Interstate 10, the two longest roads in Texas. After traveling the Great Plains on Highway 83 from the North Dakota border to this spot, the hills look more like honest-to-God mountains to me, looming over the town, gray silhouettes in the early morning light. I'm driving the Protegé into a radically different landscape.

But first, breakfast. I blew out of Menard that morning without eating. The diner I find along one of the town's main drags is packed, and I'm lucky to find a seat at the counter. I order a standard morning meal for me: eggs sunny side up, hash browns, sausage, and wheat toast. In grade school, I was taught that breakfast is the most important meal of the day. It

Cafe in Junction, Texas. March, 1940. Farm Services Administration and Office of War Information collection (Library of Congress). Taken by Russell Lee.

was one of the few things I learned there—along with looking both ways before crossing—that has stuck with me my whole life. The cashier is a young woman, probably in high school, and I hesitate to even ask her. Does she know where the book and movie *The Junction Boys* took place? She did indeed—and gave me clear directions to the spot.

I had one goal before arriving in town, and that was to see the practice field where the legendary coach Paul "Bear" Bryant put more than a hundred young football players through a practice camp that its survivors called a living hell. I'm not actually a big football fan, but this is Texas, after all. When someone here says, "The Canadian team was state champs two years running in 2007 and 2008," I don't need to ask, "In what sport?"

I follow the road south of town in search of some sports history. But if I were to keep going another seventeen miles or so, I would catch up with Bonnie and Clyde, who stopped at a nearby ranch house one Sunday afternoon to look for a place to hide.

Not ten minutes before there was a knock on the door, Marge Livingston had been reading an article in the *San Antonio Express* about the notorious Clyde Barrow, Bonnie Parker, their gang, and the fifteen lives they had taken during their crime spree.

She looked up and saw her husband, J.M., talking with the young man pictured right there on the front page of the paper! She sat there stunned, barely able to move or speak. Clyde, his hat in hand, was respectfully asking if he could camp on their land for a night. Her husband, utterly clueless as to whom he was addressing, firmly said "no." His policy was to let only family and close friends camp there, but he suggested another spot by Seven Hundred Springs, the source of the South Llano River.

The visitor then asked if he could buy some butter and eggs. Marge found the courage to go to the icebox and retrieve them. At the door, looking over Clyde's shoulder, she spied Bonnie waiting in the car. The Red River accident had left her nearly unable to walk.

For a moment, Marge's eyes locked with Clyde's. She saw in them not the cold eyes of a killer but those of a frightened, lost boy. He pulled out a wad of bills, but she insisted that he take the eggs and butter without charge. He sincerely thanked her and said it was one of the kindest things anyone had done for him.

After they drove off, she grabbed the paper and, and showed it to her husband. "Don't you know who that was!"

They didn't have a phone, so they jumped in their car and drove to Junction, where they found the county sheriff and reported everything that had happened, including the spot where they thought the pair might be camping. The sheriff didn't seem to want any part of it. He said he would contact the state police, but that was it.

Over Marge's objections, J.M. drove past the campsite to see if the fugitives were there. Indeed, they were. They had lit a campfire and were cooking her eggs. It was obvious they didn't want to be spotted. They had taken pains to cover their license plates in front and back with towels. The pair by that time was so well known, they could no longer check into motor court motels. Their lives had been reduced to one long chase.

Marge couldn't understand why her husband was looking for trouble. After dropping her off, he insisted on finding his brother and taking another look-see. But by the time they returned, nothing remained but the warm embers of a campfire.

It wasn't long after that Marge picked up the newspaper again and read that a former Texas Ranger and a group of other men had killed Clyde Barrow and Bonnie Parker in an ambush in Louisiana. The hellhound had caught up with them.

All she could think about was that look in Clyde's eyes. And she wept.

Bear Bryant, in his first year as the Aggies' head coach, wanted to escape the media, naysayers, and other interlopers back at Texas A&M, so he took two buses full of players and coaches 200 miles west of College Station for a training camp. He sure found the perfect spot. The small campus, now part of Texas Tech, isn't even walking distance to town. This was back in 1954, long before Interstate 10 connected Junction to the rest of Texas.

The small campus—as I drive in a circle looking for some kind of historical marker—is green now. But what passed as the playing field then was dirt, rocks, and prickly pear. In the middle of a drought, temperatures reached 100 degrees every day of the ten-day camp. Bryant wanted to toughen his players up and weed out the weaklings. He drilled them all day and didn't allow water breaks. There were two wet towels, one for the offense and one for the defense, to cool themselves off.

I finally find a couple rows of what look like barracks—short, squat buildings—along with a man walking across the road.

I ask him if that was where the team in *The Junction Boys* practiced.

"I believe it is. These are the buildings where they slept," he said.

I'm incredulous that such flimsy buildings are still standing some fifty-five years later. They have large windows and screens and fit the description in Jim Dent's book. They look like chicken coops.

The only relief for the players was the spring-fed South Llano River, which flows next to the field and doesn't dry up. The boys walked into the channel next to the practice field with their gear on, a brief respite before they had to attend hours of team meetings. Most quit. They either snuck off in the middle of the night, called home for their parents to fetch them, or took the Greyhound to San Antonio.

They could be called quitters, but it was a dangerous game Bryant was playing. They might have very well saved their own lives. One boy collapsed. When Bryant saw him lying on the ground, he walked up and kicked him. Assistants helped turn him over and saw that he was turning blue. He was rushed to a local doctor and barely lived. Not long after, Bryant ended the camp. The survivors—numbering only thirty-six—filled only a half a bus.

The Aggies' record that year was 1-9.

As I head out of Junction, I search for the legacy road—Highway 83 before it was replaced by the interstate. The map says I have to drive on Interstate 10 for a few miles, but I have found that the old road usually remains. I get twisted around and accidentally turn onto 10's on-ramp. I'm just about to floor the Protegé to climb the biggest hill I've encountered on the road so far, when I spot the old man hitching a ride by the side of the road. He is dressed from head to toe in black, including his cowboy hat.

He doesn't have his thumb out, he just smiles and waves. So instead of gunning it, I slow down, stop and roll down the window. He pokes his head in. He says he is going to San Antonio. I tell him I'm only going as far as Uvalde that day.

"That's okay. There's a bus there to San Antonio," he says in a thick Spanish accent.

The passenger seat is full of crap: business cards, an atlas, travel brochures, a half-eaten bag of cashews, CD sleeves, a camera and two lenses. Whenever I have to come to an abrupt stop to take a picture, half of this goes flying onto the floor mat. I start tossing all of the accumulated stuff in the back of the car.

"You have a lot of CDs," he remarks.

He introduces himself as Salvadore Garza. We shake hands and off we go, climbing into the heart of Hill Country.

I was a hitchhiker myself once. The summer between my junior and senior years of high school in Omaha, I was bored and couldn't find a job, so I took what little money I had and left for a "life on the road." The whole adventure lasted only two weeks, but I made it as far as Niagara Falls before turning back. More than a few of my rides that summer were older gentlemen driving in nice, air-conditioned Buicks who had once been forced to hitchhike or ride the rails themselves during the Great Depression. Three decades later, they were repaying strangers' assistance by giving me a ride. A couple of them insisted I take a few dollars to buy a meal.

I pick up hitchhikers when I can to repay the kindness shown to me in the summer of 1980, which isn't very often because thumbing rides has almost become a thing of the past. Salvadore is the first hitchhiker I've encountered since leaving the Canadian border.

It is overcast as we turn off the interstate and return to 83, heading south along a ridge. Many hitchers feel they must keep the driver entertained or answer any questions they might have. It's part of the price of the free ride. He points to a couple of ranches where he tells me told me he broke horses as a young man. We pass some cattle that are sitting down in a bunch. "That means it's going to rain."

Salvadore proceeds to tell me his life story as the car continues upward. He's eighty years old. He was a construction worker most of his life, moving from town to town with the jobs. He had a long-lasting stint in Wyoming. Following his stories is difficult because of his broken English. I gather that he has three adult children—a daughter who lives near his house in Menard, where he departed from that morning—and another in San Antonio

Salvadore Garza, May 2010

who is raising some of his grandchildren. He has a son, but he avoids talking about him.

His wife, Alexandra, passed away "a long time ago" shortly after his mother died.

Salvadore is not hitchhiking because he is broke. It's "because they won't let me drive anymore."

To entertain me, he tells me two long stories, both of which I have a hard time following. The first is about some trial. The central character is a "colored man." I couldn't understand the beginning and middle of the anecdote, but it ended with the judge sentencing the man to prison.

I look over while he is telling the story and notice for the first time that he has vivid blue eyes. He occasionally takes a silver crucifix adorned with a blue stone out from under his shirt and rubs it between his fingers.

Another story is about a boss of his in Wyoming when he was working in construction, a house he was trying to acquire and two men named Martine and Poncho. I couldn't follow this one either, but it had a lesson at the end: "Buy your house before you get married," he tells me earnestly.

I warned him before he got into the car that I might be stopping frequently to take pictures because I was working on a book. After a long climb into the hills, we reach an overlook, and he seems just as delighted as I am to get out of the car and gaze into the valley below. He's not in any hurry to make it to San Antonio. I can see tennis courts and campgrounds. It is still a gray day, and cool enough for us to both have light jackets. Wildflowers, purple and yellow, bloom along the road. My old friend the turkey buzzard is here, circling on top of the thermals. I can just make out the bend of a river in the valley.

The Texas Hill Country comprises 5,400 square miles and rises up to 2,300 feet above sea level at some peaks. In recorded history, it was Lipan Apache territory until the Comanches booted them out and claimed the land as their own after the San Sabá massacre.

Further back in time—way further—20 million years ago in the Cretaceous Period, the eastern side of what would be Texas began to sink. And when that land, now known as the Coastal Plain, slipped toward the Gulf of Mexico, the west side of the state began to bulge. The leverage point was a line known as the Balcones Fault Zone. The Edwards Plateau, including these hills, rose up, but they were covered in sediment from a dried-up inland sea. When it rained, the water washed off the loose amalgam of sand, fossils, and gravel until the mountains and valleys emerged.

And the water continues to flow, cutting into the limestone and karst, forming caves, collecting water into a vast underground sponge known as the Edwards Aquifer, which supplies water to more than a million residents in cities such as San Antonio. There was never much soil here. Junipers, mesquite and grass hold on to a thin layer of dirt, and when I look closely at the nearby mountains, they are not thick with pines like the Rockies, but stubbled and patchy.

We reach the mountain town of Leakey, and on the outskirts, there is an antiques store. Salvadore is just as excited as I am to look around. On a table in back he finds a snow globe that still has its original box. He grabs that and a picture of the Last Supper, not the DaVinci version, but another I don't recognize. The snow globe is a present for his lady friend in San Antonio. The picture is for his church. He talks the owner down a few dollars and gets the pair for twenty bucks. He takes out a big wad of cash to pay.

Leakey has the feel of a forested mountain town. I remember what Brent Jackson told me back in Lubbock about this area being a favorite for bikers. Indeed, we pass several small groups out for a Saturday afternoon ride.

Salvadore doesn't act like he's pressed for time at all, yet I feel obligated to get him to Uvalde, so I rush through. We make only one more stop at a convenience store to hit the restroom and buy some cold drinks. He insists on buying my Coke.

Sitting beside the cash register is a self-published book, *The Boy Captives* by Clinton L. Smith, which I snap up. It's the account of two brothers, Clint and Jeff Smith, who were captured by the Comanches. The narrator, Clint, was adopted by a chief of the tribe, while Jeff was sold to Geronimo, according to the cover, which features a photo of the two brothers as old men. It was originally published in 1927 and the family has kept the copyright updated ever since, preserving their ancestors' story for people like me to randomly discover in a roadside convenience store. I'm already familiar with their story. It was recounted in a more recent book I read, *The Captured: A True Story of Abduction by the Indians on the Texas Frontier* by Scott Zesch. Like the red-headed Kiowa captive Tehan, many of these captive children became fiercely loyal to their adopted tribes.

As we head south, we pass Garner State Park without stopping. The park was named after one of Uvalde's most famous residents, FDR's vice president John Nance "Cactus Jack" Garner, who famously said that the role of the VP "wasn't worth a bucket of warm piss."

The hills abruptly give way to flat farmland. Just like that I'm back on the flatlands. I look for some beehives, for I've known since long before leaving on the trip that Uvalde is the self-proclaimed "Honey Capital of the World," but I don't see a single one. I realize I haven't seen one sheep, either, despite seeing wool warehouses from Eden to Junction. Maybe I need to explore the side roads some more.

A sign on the outskirts of town advertises one-stop shopping: "Liquor/Guns." And then I spot the LoneStar Saloon: a real Texas roadhouse from the looks of it, and according to the sign, there's a live band that night.

I'm starting to get worried about Salvadore. Is there really a bus to San Antonio? I thought inter-city bus travel out in these small towns was a thing of the past. I have yet to encounter a Greyhound on my Highway 83 travels. What if the bus is long out of service and he is remembering a line that went out of business years ago?

We come to the intersection of Highway 83 and 90 at the beautiful town square. Salvadore tells me to take a left at the light. We travel past the supermarkets, motels, and fast-food joints, and then he spots the depot. Not only is it in business, it is clean and modern. I jump out and find a schedule posted. He's going to have to wait a couple of hours.

He takes the black bag, the Last Supper picture, and the snow globe out of the car, and gives me a smile and a hug.

"I hope you get your book," he says. Once again, I'm traveling alone. I miss him as soon as I pull away.

Another motel room in West Texas, another long conversation with my wife, who is sitting alone in our dinky condo back in Arlington. It's a little better this time. We're beginning to heal a bit.

I prefer to stay in motels on Highway 83 if I can. In Uvalde's case, they are all on Highway 90. Outside my room, I hear the big trucks rumbling east to San Antonio or west to El Paso.

We talk about a life together without children. We can travel. See the world and do the things others who have taken on the responsibility of raising children can't. We talk about a trip to Italy. I have a friend who operates a treehouse hotel in Costa Rica. We can go there in the fall.

I do bring up adoption. I remind her of Grace, a neighbor girl of ours adopted from Korea. She's a cute, bright, funny kid, brimming with personality. There are a lot of other children out there who need parents, I remind her. She hasn't come around to the adoption idea yet. I believe she will one day. Now isn't the time to push the idea.

We talk for an hour as the sun fades outside the motel room window. There are no tears this time. We finally say our good-byes and I love yous, and I feel that we're in a better place. But as I walk out to the car, I have an almost indescribable feeling deep down in my guts. It's not relief. I'm definitely not happy. Yet it's not the despondence I experienced at Wellington. It's something in between. Not contentment. Not yet anyway. Life will go on, and I don't know what path ours will take, but I suppose there will always be a little bit of sorrow buried deep down, a little smidgen of it like how I feel as I drive off.

Normally, I take every opportunity I can to explore Highway 83, but tonight I'm emotionally drained from the long conversation. I find a movie theater and watch a British film about Robin Hood before he became known as Robin Hood. Sometimes you just need to escape your thoughts for awhile.

After supper, I make my way north to the outskirts of town where I'd seen the roadhouse. By the time I arrive at the LoneStar Saloon, the parking lot is full. Inside, the dancers are already circling the floor to the music of a Mexican band called Yahari. The exterior of the building is corrugated steel, the inside all hardwood. I've grown used to cramped blues bars and rock clubs on the East Coast. This joint is as big as a warehouse. Everything is bigger in Texas, especially the local watering holes.

I find Kathy Martinez, who co-owns the saloon with her husband, Joe, tending bar, grabbing longnecks from the cooler. She's petite with long brown hair, and if she weren't married, would probably be breaking a lot of hearts. I ask permission to take photos.

"No problem," she says, and pours me a complementary Coke.

There is a line of single men with their backs to the bar, scanning the dance floor for the single ladies, I presume. About half of them sport either a black moustache, a white cowboy hat, or both. I appear to be the only non-Hispanic person in the whole place.

"You should have been here last night," she shouts over the music. "Randy Rogers was here. I had to turn away 500 people."

"'You should have been here last night.' That's the story of my life," I reply.

The Martinezes have owned the LoneStar for about ten years. They were living the life of an upwardly mobile couple in San Antonio, Joe working as a phone company executive, when they grew tired of the rat race and decided to move to a ranch outside of Uvalde. The roadhouse was just a fun, weekend business at first, but now it's turned into a full-time job for both of them. Joe is in the back going through receipts.

They have a tried-and-true formula: country-western on Friday nights; Tejano music on Saturdays. As much as I would have like to have seen an up-and-coming honky-tonk band, it sounds as though I wouldn't have made it in the door.

I set my camera up on a rail alongside the floor and try to take low-light pictures of the dancers. The couples glide in a counterclockwise circle as the band plays a mix of modern and traditional conjunto music. The men sling their right arm over their partner's shoulder; his left holding hers in front of the waist, they are mostly doing variations of the Texas ten-step, or the two-step, which ends with a twirl, but never with the couple breaking stride. It's a good dance if you're wearing stiff cowboy boots.

I'm glad I'm married, or I would be quite miserable and alone—not knowing how to dance in this style, yet feeling that I

should walk up to a woman who is otherwise a complete stranger and ask her to dance. I do not envy the line of single men with their backs to the bar looking wistfully out at the crowd, which does include a number of attractive women.

On the other hand, I miss my wife, who speaks fluent Spanish and would enjoy the music and the people watching even though she has never set foot in Texas and has no knowledge of the two-step. It would be a lot more fun with her. Other than Kathy and Joe, the only other person I interact with all night is a roadie who comes around to sell the band's CD for ten dollars apiece. I buy one as a souvenir to remember my night at a Texas roadhouse.

After leaving Hill Country, the land flattens out and becomes "the Great Mesquite Forest of Texas." This little-known natural wonder stretches south of Uvalde and extends some 130 miles to the Rio Grande at Laredo.

Motorists will not see any signs to tell them that they are entering the Great Mesquite Forest of Texas. Nor will they find it on any road atlas. There is no Great Mesquite Forest National Park, or even a state park. I pretty much make it all up as I drive from Uvalde on my way to Laredo.

That's not to say that there isn't plenty of mesquite north of the Hill Country and that I won't encounter any south of Laredo. It's just that here, it's a bit overwhelming. I love traveling the wide open spaces, the Great Plains and the desert lands of America. I have always said that mountains are overrated. I have loved the topography of every stretch of Highway 83 so far. But my love is being challenged here with a decidedly flat landscape and a gnarly twelve-foot mesquite tree every few feet blocking the view. As always, my faithful turkey buzzard friend is circling about a football field ahead of the car this morning. There is a pattern: miles of the gnarly trees just beyond the barbed wire with some prickly pear cacti and soapweed for garnish, an iron gate denoting the entrance to a ranch, then repeat.

"Hey," I want to call up to my old friend the buzzard. "Can you see anything out there other than mesquite?"

Highway 83 crosses the famous Nueces River once, then it hugs it to the west for some forty-five miles. It's out there somewhere, according to my map. It is a natural and historic boundary. The land between it and the Rio Grande is a region known to early explorers as the Wild Horse Desert. Mexico claimed after the Texas Revolution that its boundary stopped at the Nueces, while the new republic and later the United States asserted that it was the Rio Grande.

The small town of La Pryor breaks up the uniformity of the forest for a bit. I stop to take the obligatory picture of its downtown along with a man selling watermelons from the back of his pickup.

So why shouldn't Texas put a charming face on this wall of mesquite? Throw up a giant sign: "Now Entering the Great Mesquite Forest of Texas." Build an informational traveler's kiosk that explains the natural history and the wonders of the mesquite tree. Make some postcards! Print T-shirts. Sell bags of mesquite beans.

There is another important feature that lies beneath the road—a vast reservoir of water trapped in sand and gravel called the Carrizo-Wilcox Aquifer—a formation that stretches hundreds of miles from the border of Mexico northeast to Louisiana. But here in Zavala and Dimmit counties, pressure from below pushes the water close to the surface creating artesian wells. The nearby town names speak to their origin: Carrizo Springs, Crystal City, Big Wells, with Valley Wells and Artesia Wells just over the county line to the east.

I drive past a small penitentiary, where a stern sign warns me not to pick up hitchhikers. A guard tower sits next to the highway in a spot carefully selected to keep track of traffic. A second sign surrounded by wild sunflowers is more comforting: "Welcome to

Crystal City: Birthplace of the Texas Vietnam Veterans Memorial Highway." This is where the veteran Pablo Aguillon lives.

Here, nestled in the Great Mesquite Forest of Texas, is the so-called "Winter Garden" of the United States, where easy-to-tap groundwater and fertile soil are found far enough south to grow spinach and other legumes when snow covers the ground up north. It was rangeland at first: cows, sheep, and horses. Then in 1907, an enterprising rancher busted up his land holdings into ten-acre plots and sold them to farmers. He set aside another piece of land for a town and named it Crystal City for its pure water.

I drive through the town of some 7,000 residents when everyone is buttoned up in their churches for Sunday services. There is hardly another car on the streets. The Mexican-Americans call the town "Cristal." Even the Anglos, the white folks, drop the "City" when referring to the town.

Statue of Popeye, Crystal City, March 1939. Farm Services Administration and Office of War Information collection (Library of Congress) Taken by Russell Lee.

Crystal has proclaimed itself the Spinach Capital of the World. It has a big festival every year, and a Del Monte plant is located nearby. The bulging forearms and pipe of the spinach-devouring cartoon character Popeye are featured on the water tower and on the town's main street, where a statue of the sailor man stands between a wide street lined with a hodge-podge of businesses, many of them permanently shuttered. I'm sure it's more lively around here on weekdays.

But the town has another claim to fame. It's not on any

signs out on Highway 83, and it would be tough to portray it on the water tower. There is one more item besides, water, soil and warm sunshine required to grow veggies: and it is found near here in abundance as well. And that is labor. Those first farmers needed help harvesting their crops, and they found it just a few miles to the east in Mexico. The town's population jumped up in the winter, then decreased in the summer when the migrants either returned to Mexico or headed north to work other harvests. Many families ended up staying year-round and putting down roots. While the vast majority of towns on Highway 83 owe their existence to a railroad, Crystal began its life as a de facto labor camp. And as with any camp, there are those in charge and those who are subservient.

For the first half century of its existence, the wealthy Anglo landowners ran the town and the Mexicans and Mexican Americans were treated like blacks in the Jim Crow–era South. But as other civil rights movements began to take hold in the 1960s, the paradigm began to change. The community became a battleground. One scholar even called it "The Cradle of the Chicano Movement."

Now that would make a pretty cool sign for Highway 83.

THE INGRATE

José Angel Gutiérrez and some of his friends were heading south on Highway 83, returning to their hometown on an inter-city bus. It glided down the final hill past the scattered gas stations and restaurants and pulled into the town at West Zavala Street. The nineteen-year-old junior college freshman had spent the short trip from Uvalde talking and joking with his college pals. At last, he had found a clique he fit in with. The five of them were pursuing college degrees, a rarity for the few Mexican-Americans who graduated from the Cristal's high school. The small group returned home almost every weekend to take part in the revolt. It wasn't a violent revolt. But it was an organized rebellion against those in power nonetheless.

The Teamsters union and the Political Association of Spanish Speaking Organizations (PASSO), both based in San Antonio, looked at Crystal City and saw an opportunity to make history. The population was overwhelmingly Mexican, but the city council and city management, school board, and county government were run by a few elite whites, and had been since the town's founding.

The two organizations came to Cristal in 1963 with experts in grass-roots activism ready to advise the locals on how to change the paradigm. They put together a slate of five local Mexican Americans—known as Los Cincos—to run against the Anglo city council members, some of whom had served for decades. The establishment's strategy was the poll tax. City residents wishing to vote had to pay $1.75. The system was cooked up by Southern Democrats such as Uvalde's John Nance Garner as a means to suppress the votes of the poor and minorities.

Gutiérrez was among the best and brightest the town had produced. In another day, he would have been tapped for a scholarship to attend an elite school in the East, or at least at the University of Texas in Austin, but he had to content himself with a community college in Uvalde, where he could barely afford the tuition. He and his pals volunteered to help potential voters pay their poll taxes. They held fund-raisers that would go toward the fee and knocked on doors to convince neighbors to participate in the next election. Gutiérrez spoke passionately about the movement at rallies held in a public park, and had gone so far as to publish—along with his friends—an anonymous mimeographed scandal sheet that exposed the town's racism and hypocrisies. It named names.

The bus arrived at its usual stop, the ice cream stand on the corner of Zavala and Crocket. As soon as he stepped off, a car skidded to a halt in front of him. Local businessman Raul Tapia pointed a pistol at Gutiérrez and told him to get in. He had no choice but to comply. As Tapia pulled out, Gutiérrez looked back at his friends, who stood there frozen.

Tapia smelled of booze. He was a big bear of a man, more than 200 pounds, mostly muscle, and probably didn't need a gun to intimidate. But he kept his hand on the trigger anyway, laying it across his lap with his left hand and driving with his right.

Where was Tapia taking him? He knew his kidnapper was in league with the Anglo elites, but would he really shoot him?

"You're gonna pay," is all Tapia said.

The boy was the product of two worlds.

His father, Angel Gutiérrez Crespo, was a doctor who had learned medicine after being conscripted into Pancho Villa's army in Mexico. After Villa's death and the end of the revolution, he became involved in politics and served as the mayor of Torreón, a Mexican city about 300 miles to the southwest of Laredo. When he found himself at odds with a military strongman, he was forced to flee to the United States, and ended up in Cristal, a refugee who wanted more than anything to return to his homeland.

He was by then a middle-aged man with grown children back in Torreón. After setting up a practice in Cristal, he became smitten by one of his friend's daughters, sixteen-year-old Concepción Fuentes. He made an arrangement with the young woman's father: Angel would take care of her mother and siblings if anything should happen to him.

Concepción was born in Crystal City and had split her formative years between there and San Antonio. Unlike Angel, she spoke English well, but she had quit school because the Anglo kids harassed her so badly on the school bus. Not long after they married, her father died, which sealed Angel's fate. Making good on his vow to take care of Concepción's family meant he would not return to Mexico to live.

Angel and Concepción were married ten years before their only child, José, was born. Angel made sure his son understood Spanish and learned about the literature and history of Mexico.

Meanwhile, his mother knew that her only child had to learn English to make a better life for himself. As soon as he was old enough, they arranged for him to take English lessons.

The local school district simply ignored legal doctrine that called for the segregated schools to be separate but equal. There was a white elementary school and a Mexican elementary school, with the bulk of resources going toward the white school. A minority child attempting to attend the Anglo school had to pass a language test. Few did. Many Mexican parents and students followed the harvests up north and arrived back in town late in the fall. The high school rarely graduated Mexican students, for most never made it past the eighth grade.

José himself spent little time in the segregated elementary school. His mother insisted that the white school test his English, which proved good enough to have him placed in the second grade.

José's family was among the town's small Mexican middle class. His father was an intellectual, well read and educated. That did not mean he was treated with respect by the white establishment. He couldn't practice at the local hospital. The boy saw how the sheriffs would dump injured Mexican prisoners off at their house without any indication that his father would be paid for patching them up. The white farmers often did the same with injured day laborers.

His father taught him about the Mexican revolution and the Mexican-American War, but from a different perspective. The heroes of the Alamo were not Davy Crocket, Jim Bowie, and William Travis. It was President General Antonio López de Santa Anna, the man who fought to hold onto land that was rightfully Mexico's. When the boy brought this up in his history classes, the white teachers and students didn't appreciate his opinion one bit.

There was only one junior high in town, but the classrooms were segregated, and José was put in the same rooms as the Spanish-speaking Mexicans. When his mother complained, he was allowed to attend the white classes, but was disappointed.

The Mexican kids were much smarter. Many of the white kids seemed rather dim.

It was about this time when his father passed away. Overnight, his life changed. Without the steady income that his father had provided, his mother fell into poverty. The stores that were once happy to extend credit cut them off. José found himself accompanying Concepción to do field work. All this came as he wrestled with the grief of losing his father.

By the time José entered high school, enough Mexican students were making it in to change the student body from white to brown. Yet the school authorities ensured that the status quo would remain. Teachers and administrators made sure the student leaders were white; that also went for cheerleaders, football captains and homecoming queens. Arbitrary rules that skewed in favor of the Anglos suddenly appeared on the books. The students once chose their homecoming queen based on a popular vote. Now it was the white teachers who chose. The Anglo students took college-prep classes, the Mexicans shop class and vocational education. José Gutiérrez persevered and took the academically challenging classes. He honed his public speaking skills as part of the debate team. He was also the first Mexican-American to win the state championship in public speaking.

A year after Gutiérrez graduated, the Teamsters and PASSO were running an effective campaign to change Cristal. But the white establishment was not taking any of this lying down. They goaded management at the Del Monte plant, the town's biggest employer, to fire supporters of Los Cincos. The Teamsters, with the help of boss Jimmy Hoffa, managed to have their dismissals reversed. They began a divide-and-conquer campaign by recruiting the Mexican middle class to their side.

Raul Tapia was one of them. The gas station owner took Gutiérrez to his home, where he sat him in front of a small group of white officeholders that included the county sheriff, along with another Mexican-American, Jesus Rodriguez, the owner of a grocery store. Sitting across from him was the influential Texas Ranger Captain Alfred Allee. He was a stocky man, half a head shorter than Gutiérrez, sported a potbelly, smoked cigars, and carried pearl-handled pistols.

Gutiérrez, like many Mexican-Americans in Texas, feared the Rangers. For most Texans, and many throughout the United States, the Rangers symbolized a romantic part of the Old West. With their roots going back to 1823, long before statehood, they were one of the few forces that stood between the settlers and the Comanches. They had chased bandits and tracked down bank robbers and cattle rustlers. The fictional Lone Ranger and his sidekick Tonto were a model of interracial harmony, fighting for justice on the prairie.

But as the organization entered the twentieth century, its history became more checkered. It was called upon to stop incursions by Mexican revolutionaries along the Rio Grande Valley. Mexican-Americans became caught up in the violence as the Rangers' ranks swelled and it allowed some unsavory characters to join its ranks and engage in a dirty war. The local population complained of extrajudicial killings. To many on the border, the Rangers weren't romantic heroes of the West—they were the cattle barons' lackies and agents of repression. And that was exactly why the white citizens of Crystal City had contacted the Rangers and asked them to send help.

It arrived in the form of Captain Allee and some of his hand-picked lawmen. Allee knew Crystal City well. He was a third-generation ranger who was born in nearby La Salle County, and he had begun his law enforcement career as a game warden and deputy sheriff in Zavala County. Like his namesake grandfather Alfred Y. Allee, he'd spent most of his career in the borderlands. And like his grandfather, he had a reputation for doling out rough justice with little regard for due process. Charges of misconduct and lawsuits followed the fifty-eight-year-old Allee wherever he went.

The captain set a tape recorder on a table in front of Gutiérrez. He pressed the record button and began grilling him on PASSO and the Teamsters. He wanted Gutiérrez to admit that the organizations were paying him, but they weren't, so he kept denying it. He wanted him to say he was a communist—also not true. Gutiérrez was shaking with fear but kept his hands tucked under his thighs so the ranger wouldn't know it. The white men reminded him about all the good people who drove him to debate tournaments in high school. This was how he repaid their kindness? He was an ingrate. Eventually, Allee placed a blank piece of paper and a pen on the table and instructed Gutiérrez to write a confession.

Gutiérrez kept his hands firmly tucked under his legs. The interrogation went on for hours. The whole time he wondered if they were going to take him out in the country and shoot him. At one point, Gutiérrez realized that the men, all older, meaner and tougher than him, were scared, too. They weren't afraid of him, but they were afraid nevertheless. That's why they were there.

In time they gave up. Tapias escorted him outside, drove him to a hamburger stand, and bought him dinner to show that there were "no hard feelings." He even complimented him on his bravery.

Gutiérrez didn't feel brave at all. But the lesson he learned that night would stick with him for the rest of his life. They were afraid.

It was 1969 when José Angel Gutiérrez returned to his hometown to fight the second battle for control of Cristal. A lot had happened to him by then. He had kicked around several schools until finally obtaining a bachelor's degree at Texas A&M University–Kingsville. He spent a year in law school, then some time in the corporate world. He ended up back to college in San Antonio, where he co-founded the Mexican American Youth Organization. MAYO spread to other colleges around the state. Influenced by the tactics of the black Civil Rights movement, they protested the biases that minority students faced. They organized walkouts at high schools where Anglo school boards ruled, and even picketed in front of the venerated Alamo.

At a press conference he said the organization would "eliminate the gringo." His definition of a gringo was lost on the public and he elaborated that they would only do so in self-defense. His detractors would accuse him of inciting racial hatred and violence.

His thesis was about the prospects for political revolution in Zavala County, a topic that would become more than an academic exercise before long. It was while pursing his graduate degree when he married his wife, Luz, and had his first child, Adrian.

The Civil Rights Act of 1964 had gone into effect, but the war for racial equality wasn't over. In California, Cesar Chavez and the National Farm Workers Association were struggling for the rights of the mostly Mexican-American field laborers. Protests were becoming commonplace as opposition to the Vietnam War heated up. While studying for his PhD in Austin, he joined the Army Reserve to avoid being drafted, and completed basic training. When the Army released him from service, he decided to go back to Cristal, but not before traveling to California to meet Chavez.

A lot had happened to Crystal City in the previous six years as well. Los Cincos had won in a landslide. It was the first instance of Mexican-Americans wresting control of a Texas town from the Anglos. The victory made headlines throughout the world. Reporters came to interview the new mayor and city council members. The Texas newspaper editors called it the state's second most significant news story of 1963 after the Kennedy assassination in Dallas.

But it all quickly unraveled. The town's Anglo elite fought back. The white bureaucrats quit, leaving the town in control of the inexperienced city council and mayor. In retaliation, one councilman had his hours at his job halved. Another had passed some bad checks. Captain Allee, who had stuck around a few more years, threatened to arrest him if he didn't turn against the others. Within a few years, the Anglos had managed to reverse the results of the 1963 election.

By the time Gutiérrez returned home, he had solved the question of what he was. He was a Chicano. Not Mexican. Not a white American, but something in between. Like the pejorative—*pacho*—but spoken with pride. He had also added another term to the lexicon he used in speeches: "gringo." The pejorative was not meant for every single white, just the rednecks, racists, and other Anglo elites who were doing their best to keep the Mexicans down.

He found Crystal City firmly back in control of the Anglos. The surnames of most of the council members and the mayor were Hispanic, but these were men like Tapias and Rodriguez, business owners who hated the "leftist radicals." The poll tax no longer existed, but the former Los Cincos supporters became cynical and many didn't bother to vote.

Gutiérrez knew the conditions he and Luz would find in Cristal. They hadn't returned because he was homesick. He had a plan to permanently wrest control of local governing bodies from the gringos, not only in Crystal City, but the whole region. He called the campaign the Winter Garden Project.

Gutiérrez and Luz didn't have much money or prospects for good jobs, but they did have advanced degrees, writing skills, and a strong work ethic. They set about writing proposals to far away benefactors for grant money, and it soon began rolling in. They administered the town's first Head Start preschool and kicked off several other programs to help uplift the town's Mexican population. The foundation money allowed them to be economically independent of the Anglos, who controlled the well-paying jobs in town.

Captain Allee, by the time Gutiérrez returned, had finally left the area. When Cesar Chavez's organization came to the Rio Grande Valley in 1967 to organize a series of farm worker strikes, Allee decided that he was needed there instead, to protect the wealthy and bully the downtrodden.

The second Chicano revolution in Crystal City began over the matter of cheerleaders. For Gutiérrez, the high school was the perfect institution to confront first. Chicano pride was strong in the hallways, where a cadre of white teachers and administrators were doing their best to hold onto the old days despite the fact that the school population was overwhelmingly Mexican. There were bright young students he could work with, who were much like himself when he was in the school. They had already led some minor classroom walkouts when teachers made particularly offensive comments.

In the spring of 1969, only a few months before Gutiérrez had returned to do battle, the students were up in arms over the selection of an Anglo girl for cheerleader. The committee's informal quota system gave one of the four cheerleader positions to a Mexican, and the remaining three to Anglos. Two Anglo cheerleaders were graduating. When a clearly inferior Anglo student was chosen over a more popular Mexican, the unfair quota system was laid bare in the students' minds. A group of young activists first went to the principal. He dismissed their allegations out of hand. They then went to the superintendent with the cheerleader issue and several other demands including more bilingual education, and found him more reasonable. He promised to institute a formal quota system with three cheerleaders for each race and to look into the other matters. It was a mixed bag for the students, who felt they had no leverage with the school year coming to an end. Protests could result in some of them not graduating, or flunking their classes.

Over the summer, when most of the students were away working in the fields with their families, the Anglo parents and teachers forced the superintendent to reverse everything he had promised, little as it was.

In the fall, when the Anglos hatched a thinly veneered scheme to ensure that the school's homecoming royalty would represent the beauty of the white race and no one else, the fight was on. Gutiérrez decided he would stay in the background as much as possible and dampen the fiery rhetoric that had made him a household name in South Texas. He could play the part of Machiavelli as well as any of the town's smartest Anglos. He was sharp, was well-educated in the history and methodology of social protest, and had dozens of case studies to draw upon.

His first act was to meet with the students. He instructed them to go to their parents and tell them what was happening in the school, and to get their blessings before they took any action. It was a crucial first step, but one that wasn't hard to accomplish. Their mothers and fathers had firsthand experience in the school system.

The town's Mexican community was far from monolithic. There was a growing middle class, and not all of its members sympathized with the students. Like their Anglo counterparts, they were conservative in their politics and had done their best to assimilate. They hated radicals and "hippies" like Gutiérrez, and believed he was fostering hatred between the races. They thought the doctor's son, far from bettering their people, was turning the clock back on the progress they had made. The Anglos allowed a few such men—never any women—to take places on the city council. Two of them served on the school board.

The first confrontation came at the November school board meeting. More than 100 students and their parents came to file a list of grievances. One of the Anglos' tricks to keep the Mexican and Anglo students socially separated was to make some events outside affairs. Therefore, dances were not official "school dances;" they were private parties held at the country club. The homecoming queens weren't selected by teachers; that was done by the Ex Students Association. They had naturally selected a lily-white queen and her court, who would be presented at the homecoming football game halftime. The students and parents spoke out against the practice, but the board members wouldn't back down. Finally, Gutiérrez stood up to speak. If the queen and her court were presented at halftime, there would be a "disruption," he vowed. What that would be, he left to the board members' imagination. "There will be no coronation," he said.

The board voted to deny the Ex Students Association the right to hold its ceremony on the field. As for the numerous other demands, they punted them to the next meeting in December.

For the Chicano students, it was a clear victory, showing that the board would cave into their demands. Gutiérrez and the student leaders spent the next month preparing for the inevitable boycott. The Anglos in town spent the same time seething and tossing recriminations at everyone from the school board to Gutiérrez. They called him a communist, a "disturbed young man," and said he was really half white, a "spreader of racial hate." They had equal vitriol for the board members and the superintendent.

The December board meeting was decidedly short and rancorous. Having spent a month being criticized for appeasing the Chicano students, the members denied all demands, passed the buck to the school administrators, and allowed a shouting match to ensue.

The walkout began the next morning.

Two hundred high school students of a student body of 673—along with some of their parents—gathered on the lawn with their picket signs and refused to enter the school. As the day wore on, more students trickled out of the building, adding several hundred more. The administration let it be known that it planned to enforce a policy of two points off total grades for every absent day, plus zeroes for any missed tests.

The parents were there not only to lend emotional support, but to make sure nothing got out of hand. Lawyers from the Mexican American Legal Defense Fund observed and were there in case the police showed up.

For Gutiérrez, everything was going as planned. He wanted a peaceful protest that would grow in numbers by the day. He arranged for the junior high school kids to join the boycott the second day, and the numbers swelled.

It was no accident that the media caught wind and began arriving in town. A protest without newspaper reporters and television crews was like the proverbial tree falling in the forest with no one around to hear it. Gutiérrez let the students and the parents speak for their side and remained in the background.

To their credit, the school board and superintendent did not call in the Texas Rangers, but rather representatives of the administrative services division of the Texas Education Agency to mediate. Yet the town's leaders didn't want to make any meaningful concessions or take any of the agency's recommendations such as closing down the school for the winter break early to diffuse tensions. By the third day, 416 of 673 students in the high school were boycotting.

All along, the school board refused to meet with any group that included students. It refused under any circumstances to wipe away the penalties for missing classes; not only was it critical to prevent students to be seen as their equals in negotiations, but they wanted to punish students for rebelling. The students were equally stubborn, insisting that since they were the aggrieved party, they should have a seat at the table.

The boycott dragged on to the winter break. By that time almost two-thirds of the student body were participating in the walkout. The state government began to express concern about so many students missing classes, and the Texas Education Agency sent signals that the district's funding might be drastically reduced if such low attendance persisted.

After Justice Department mediators arrived, the school board finally said it would meet with the students as long as their parents were present. For several days, the Justice representatives, the students, and the board argued. In the end, the school board acquiesced to all the demands. The students would return to school with no punishment. Twirlers and drum majors would be selected by band members, not faculty. Students, not faculty, would select cheerleaders. There would be new uniforms for band members, a paved parking lot, new showers, and no more dress codes. There were also deeper changes ahead: professional consultants would be brought in to evaluate the tests and eliminate biases; ethnic isolation would end; a position for a Mexican-American counselor would be created; and the school system would recognize the Spanish language as equal in importance to English and would provide bilingual and bicultural programs. A grievance committee composed of parents would look into allegations of teachers acting improperly.

When the Anglo community found out about the agreement, there was an uproar. They were as outraged as the Chicanos were elated. Not only would the boycotters go unpunished for the walkout, they now had real power in the school district. No students in Texas had ever won such a victory over the Anglos. For Gutiérrez, it was a great achievement, but only one battle in a longer war to come.

José Angel Gutiérrez's plan to radically alter the politics of the Winter Garden region would ultimately succeed, although it took several more years and several more election cycles. School boards and city councils had staggered their elections so the 1963 debacle wouldn't be repeated; only two positions would be open in any election. It took time, but soon the Anglos were out of power and the majority ruled.

He founded La Raza Unida, the United Race Party, which spread throughout Texas and to other Southwest states. He eventually was elected to the school board, and for a time, served as an administrative judge in town before eventually departing. He would go on to obtain a law degree and settle in as a professor at the University of Texas at Arlington. He is today considered to be one of the four most important Chicano leaders emerging from the Civil Rights Movement.

Scholars who have studied the two Crystal City revolts consider them pivotal moments in Mexican-American social history. And the 1969 walkout was a turning point within the turning point. John Staples Shockley, in his book *Chicano Revolt in a Texas Town*, said of the town's Anglos after the student's victory: "All the tactics that had worked for them before—and everything they had thought they had learned from the 1963 revolt—now suddenly no longer sustained them. Frightened by the loss of power and unsure of what retribution would mean, they found their right to rule and their invincibility had been shattered simultaneously. Their legitimacy and their authority had crumbled."

The self-service car wash in Carrizo Springs is majestic. Painted royal blue and trimmed in golden yellow, it sits on a prime spot on the corner of Highway 83 and West Nopal Street amidst the gas stations, fast-food joints, and motels with their plastic signs. It's a castle surrounded by a moat of architectural mediocrity.

A self-service car wash—four or five bays built out of cinder blocks and some high-pressure hoses—is seldom anything to behold, but the Mr. B. Car Wash beckons vehicle owners with seven spiraling flagpoles, each with a fake flag unfurled to spell C-A-R W-A-S-H. A cartoon portraying who I can only assume is Mr. B. himself bows to welcome those who have come to make what is dirty, shiny and new again.

Give me your dusty, your muddy, your rivulets of bird poop streaking down the side of your car. For a handful of quarters, you may enter here and blast the grime and bug juice away with world-renown pure crystal water gushing straight from ancient artesian wells.

Or pull into bay five, sit back and relax as the automatic car wash does it all for you. At the end of the wash, pull up to the shaded finishing area where our super-sucker vacuum cleaners will rid your carpets of dirt, sand, cockleburs, and the French fries dropped while wolfing down lunch at the nearby Stars Drive-in.

For only a few dollars, purchase one of our chamois to wipe your car or truck clean.

If my 1999 Mazda Protégé could talk, it would probably tell me to put down my camera and stop taking pictures of this fabulous mid-century–style car wash and to give it a little love with a quick bath, but I like the "Dead Bugs of the Southern Plains" collection on the front bumper, and I have a few more miles to cover before I stop for the day in Laredo.

Approaching it from the north, the Catarina Hotel is seemingly sitting out in the middle of the Great Mesquite Forest of Texas. A sign tells me that there a historical marker ahead, but I would have pulled over anyway to investigate this once grand-looking hotel. The two-story, red-brick building looks like it predates the heyday of the 1950s motels. I spot the first palm trees of my trip in the courtyard, which opens up to the highway. It looks empty now, with yellow caution tape strung around its doors. Window a/c units list perilously outside several windows. The historical marker is across the road and isn't for the hotel, which is too bad. I wonder who built this, and when? A picture above the side door is a painting of a much older, wood structure and says "Built 1924." After poking around on the internet later I discover that the building was derelict from the 1950s until 1997, when it was restored to serve as a hotel again. That article was written in 2005.

Despite my impression, it is not sitting by the road seemingly in the middle of nowhere. There was once a thriving town to the south of here. Catarina, Texas, boasted thousands of residents until its artesian wells went dry at the worst possible time: the Dust Bowl years of the 1930s.

After snapping a few pictures, I turn my attention to the roadside marker across Highway 83.

As I walk to it, a young man, dark complexion and black sunglasses, not much bigger than me, is coming up from the south on the shoulder, also with a camera dangling around his neck. We arrive at the small, knee-high rough-cut red granite marker at the same time. Hello, fellow history buff!

We strike up a conversation about the incongruous hotel and the marker, which reads:

Kings Highway
Camino Real
Old San Antonio Road
Marked by the Daughters of the American Revolution
And the State of Texas A.D. 1918

Next to the D.A.R. marker is a larger, modern interpretive kiosk that explains more. We're standing at a real crossroads: The modern Route 83 and a system of east-to-west Indian trails that date back to before the Spanish colonial era.

I tell him about my travels down U.S. 83. His name is Noel, and he and his father, sitting in a pickup truck a few yards away, have taken off for the day to explore the backroads of Texas.

"You're my kind of people," I say. He brings me back to meet Noel Benavides Sr., who, once discovering that I am traveling the length of 83, invites me to stop in at their business, a Western wear store that sits right on the highway in Roma, Texas, in the Rio Grande Valley. It will be a few days before I get there, but I promise to pay a visit.

As I continue the drive south, I see that the hotel wasn't truly out in the middle of the road, but was part of a small town. President William Taft's bother once owned a ranch nearby. Like Asherton, a town I passed through on the way here, there isn't much left of Catarina other than the Catarina One Stop gas station/convenience store.

I'm at the tail end of my Great Plains adventure. I can see on my map that Highway 83 will soon merge into Interstate 35, which will funnel me to the borderlands and the Rio Grande Valley. Until then, it's mesquite, mesquite, mesquite, gate to a ranch, more mesquite, more mesquite, more mesquite, gate to another ranch, repeat.

But suddenly there is a change. The barbed wire is replaced by an eight-foot-tall fence. The next gate is closed. On either side are the metal silhouettes of deer with impressive sets of antlers, not the predictable longhorn cattle. Private deer hunting is big here. The fences and gates aren't designed to keep interlopers out; they are designed to keep trophy bucks in. A couple strings of barbed wire is enough to control cattle, but that doesn't work for deer. Dimmit and Webb counties are part of the so-called Golden Triangle, a region prized for its trophy bucks. Landowners charge anywhere from $4,000 to $10,000 for lodging, meals, a guide, and the right to kill a whitetail with a bow or rifle. And while there are somewhere around 25 million deer in the United States, well-heeled hunters fly to Laredo or San Antonio and drive to this remote area to hunt them. The unique mineral content of the red soil is absorbed by the vegetation, which is in turn eaten by the deer. This supposedly helps the bucks grow impressive racks. And the endless mesquite forest provides the cover to make it challenging for the hunters.

I'm about to meet Interstate 35. I hate those mind-numbing four-lane roads, and if I have the time and there is an old highway available as an alternative, I try to avoid them. The main reason for my disdain is freedom, or lack thereof. I want to stop and explore, but the interstates just want to shuffle drivers off as quickly and efficiently as possible. If I have to take them, I try to do so at night. I'm hoping I can take a legacy road all the way to Laredo.

"JERKY!"

Whoa, what's this?

"DEER"

A series of crudely painted signs planted on the right shoulder slows me down.

ALLIGATOR.

I spot the roadside stand off to the left.

BUFFALO.

It is a roadside stand with American and Texas flags flapping in the wind and JERKY in giant red letters across the top, in case there was any doubt about what was for sale there.

ELK.

I pull over where a stocky man in a muscle shirt is helping a customer.

OPEN, reads another sign. No doubt about that, either.

GREAT GIFT, LEMON PEPPER, ELK-BEEF-BUFFALO signs are posted on the side. "Fried Peanuts" are an alternative. If the signs weren't enough to grab drivers' attention, a human-sized stuffed Mickey Mouse dressed as a superhero with his chest puffed out hangs on the side of the trailer. When he's through with the customer, we strike up a conversation as I look through the various dried meats hanging on pegs.

His name is Russ Carlson, and the business is Jody's Jerky. He sits there all day long watching the traffic on Highway 83 go by, listening to the radio, selling the jerky he has prepared himself for about ten bucks a package.

He's not a Texan. He's actually from Council Bluffs, Iowa, the town across the river from Omaha, where I grew up. He was the manager of a Dairy Queen there and sold Christmas trees before he and his wife decided to move south. He's got the type-A personality of a salesman, and as such, has the gift of gab. We talk about Omaha and Council Bluffs and the vagaries of the roadside jerky business for quite some time before I pull myself away. We strike a barter deal: Three packages of buffalo jerky for a signed copy of my latest book.

I gnaw on a dried piece of bison jerky as I head south to test my theory that the tires of my Protegé never have to touch an interstate when traveling Highway 83. On the west side, there is a frontage road, and believing that it must go all the way to Laredo, I think I have it made. It takes me to a massive travel plaza where dozens of semis are parked, then continues south.

Suddenly I'm in a warehouse parking lot and the road abruptly ends. Now, if I had taken even a few minutes to consult

Google Maps before setting out or had a GPS this would not have been a surprise to me. As it is, I have no choice but to turn back and find an on ramp to Interstate 35.

Defeat! (Google maps would prove later that I could have taken a series of side streets until reaching the city.) After a few short minutes on the detested interstate, I exit onto Laredo's Santa Maria Avenue, also known as Business 83.

There was a time before the intestate when Laredo was considered the gateway to Old Mexico for tourists and snowbirds escaping cold northern winters. They called the city "Fiesta Land." That was back when popping over the border to drink cheap beers and experience a different culture was a cinch.

Routes 81 and 83 funneled the travelers south, where they found a string of moderately priced accommodations: Las Palmas Court, Pan American Courts, the Evelyn Motor Inn, the Ranch Motel, El Cortez Motel, Graf's, Land's Court, and the Haynes Motel. The street was lined with basket and pottery shops.

Mexican food wasn't as ubiquitous as it is today, so they treated themselves to an exotic meal at the Cactus Gardens Café, sitting strategically where 81 and 83 converged with U.S.

3502 San Bernardo Ave.   LAS PALMAS COURT   LAREDO
"LOOK FOR THE FLAGS"   TEXAS

Route 59 coming west from Houston. Open 6 a.m. to 10 p.m., it advertised that it was "centrally located among tourist courts." Along with broiled streaks, fried chicken, and Mexican food.

Its "Pre Columbian Museum" boasted "Pretty maids of Mexico made of mud, 1,000 years ago. Come to see them. Cactus Gardens is proud of its collection of thousands of items." There was a rock collection and arrowheads. The waitresses wore traditional Mexican dresses. And cacti grown in its nursery were available for purchase, of course.

The U.S. & Canada Highway 83 Association held its annual meeting here in 1963 back when the organization was going strong. This was the golden age of motor travel. Kids piled into the back of station wagons and were driven cross-country to Disneyland, Disney World, or in my family's case, the Black Hills in South Dakota. Few middle-class families considered flying back then, even if it did take three days to make it to their vacationlands by car.

A full-service gas station and garage, Limon's Texaco, helped motorists traveling on 83 continue on their way. Mexican automobile insurance and pesos could be purchased at Humble Mexico Travel Service, Cavazos, and Sanborn's. "Yankee Spoken," the latter's sign declared.

"Visiting Nuevo Laredo, our sister city, across the Rio Grande requires no passports, visas, or other governmental restrictions," explained a tourist brochure. "You are free to come and go as you wish, except that you must stop at designated entry lanes to acknowledge your American citizenship."

Many of the old motels still stand, but with the exception of the Evelyn they look run-down now. Cactus Gardens Café is gone, knocked down and replaced by an AutoZone. There are a couple gaudy-looking pottery and basket stores remaining, although they appear to be wholesalers. This onetime gateway is a mix of old and new today, with the post-war motor hotels mixed in with the familiar chain stores. To wit, I'd gone online

U.S. Highway 83 in Texas, Laredo to Brownsville

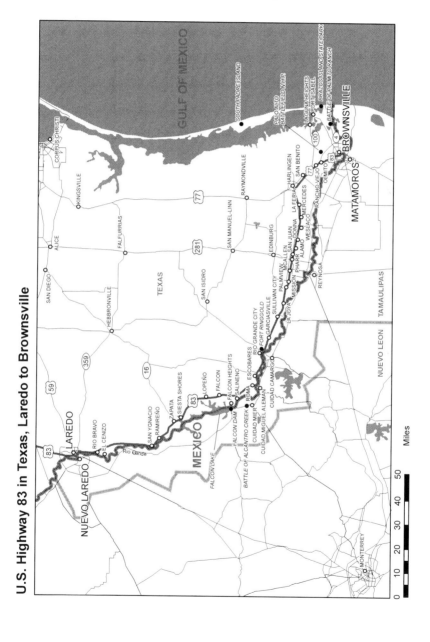

and booked myself into a Super 8 several days ago. Highway 83 still caters to travelers, but the throngs of tourists who once made their way here in the winters have disappeared.

Fear grows out in concentric circles. The farther those with no firsthand experience reside away from an area such as this, the easier it is for them to inflate the danger in their minds. Fed by second-hand knowledge, neighborhoods or cities become scary places. Several times since arriving in Perryton a week ago, I have had conversations with Anglos about the Rio Grande Valley. "Be careful when you get down there," they would say. In their minds, I should be wearing a bulletproof vest. There are running battles with drug gangs and police, they say, and there is a fair chance I will be in mortal danger.

I'm not a neophyte to the borderlands. In my day job covering defense and homeland security, I have been on ride-alongs with the Border Patrol in Arizona and California and with the Coast Guard south of San Diego. I even had the opportunity to explore an abandoned drug smuggler's tunnel. I've been to El Paso, Juarez, and Tijuana, and on one epic trip traveled by inter-city buses from Los Angeles to Mexico, Belize, and Guatemala and all the way back to Nebraska. I was a reporter overseas, where I covered a coup d'état and riots. When I was warned away from the Valley, I politely nodded my head and said I would watch my back, and left it at that.

I arrive at the corner where I can take a left and drive Business 83 south, go right into Laredo's historic district, or continue straight and cross the bridge into Mexico. In case there is any doubt as to where the road ahead leads, the largest flag I have ever seen slowly undulates in the wind. The green, red, and white banner must be a mile away, but sits atop what must be the world's highest flagpole.

I opt for the historic district.

I would like to have my first glimpse of the Rio Grande before the evening light fades, and I figure the best way to do so is to park my car and walk so I don't take some kind of wrong turn and end up on a bridge leading to Nuevo Laredo. I park the Protegé and wander the streets for a while. I haven't caught on yet, but I'll read in a tourist brochure later that Laredo is known as the "City of Saints and Generals" because the north-south streets are named after martyrs and east-west streets after military leaders. As I stroll around, poking my head in shops, taking pictures of the old buildings, I have a song stuck in my head.

As I walked out on the streets of Laredo.
As I walked out on Laredo one day.
I spied a poor cowboy wrapped in white linen,
Wrapped in white linen as cold as the clay.

I'm singing the Johnny Cash version of "The Streets of Laredo." And in my mind, I have a rich, deep baritone just like Cash's—although nothing could be further from the truth.

Laredo's downtown seems to be suffering as much as any of the West Texas small towns I encountered. There are blocks of empty or underused buildings, a closed movie theater. The once posh New Plaza Hotel, a ten-story building where the well-heeled once stayed, is gone. Its rival, the twelve-story Hamilton, has been converted to apartments.

But there are plenty of pedestrians around. Those crossing into the United States on foot over the nearby Gateway to the Americas Bridge stream into the neighborhood—a real river of humanity. Some carry small suitcases, others nothing at all. There is a line of shops catering to them along Convent Avenue. Every storefront is occupied on this stretch of road, but a block or two away stand many forlorn buildings, beautiful and old, but empty.

In the hour I spend wandering, I don't see a single white face or hear a word of English. And that's a good thing. There are two cities in America where every time I visit, I feel like I'm visiting a different country: New Orleans and Las Vegas—the French Quarter and the Strip. They are two extremely different places, of course. One old, one new. One genuine, one fake. And I love visiting both of them because I feel like I've escaped my everyday life. As I walk the streets of Laredo, I add its historic district to my list. The architecture, the people, and the vibe it puts out make this a singular city in America. I'm out of my element, and I love it. Isn't that what traveling is all about?

Convent Avenue is where I first see the Rio Grande and Mexico. Across, I see the hazy silhouettes of Nuevo Laredo's buildings. Locals call these U.S. and Mexican urban areas separated only by the river "twins." The channel funnels between the two cities with steep banks on either side. The Rio Grande begins in Colorado at the Continental Divide and travels 1,896 miles before emptying into the Gulf of Mexico. Highway 83 is just short of that at 1,885 miles. The Rio Bravo de Norte, as it is known in Mexico, has been the official boundary between the two nations since 1848, and I will be hugging it to the north for the next 200 miles until I reach Brownsville.

Laredo-based author Ken Bowden addressed the two names in his book about biking, rafting, and canoeing the length of the river, *The Tecate Journals: Seventy Days on the Rio Grande*.

The Rio Bravo, as the Mexicans call the Rio Grande, is often mistakenly translated as 'Brave River,' but in Mexico *bravo* suggests 'angry' rather than brave. 'Brave' River, however would be a more accurate translation than 'Large' or 'Great' River. Except during a flood, no single section of the Rio Grande as it forms the Texas-Mexico border is even moderately large. Brave, however, it is. Considering the systematic abuse man has delivered to this desert waterway through pollution, excessive irrigation, agricultural runoff and the importation of salt cedar, the fact that river remains as pristine as it does is a miracle of nature. For the Mexicans to name it 'Angry River' seems to portend how the river feels about its mistreatment centuries later.

I retreat back to the historic district where I stumble on San Agustin Plaza. The cathedral of the same name towers above the town square, which is full of occupied benches, statues, historical markers, and people who are looking anxiously at the street for someone to pick them up, or perhaps a city bus.

On the same block as La Posada Hotel I find the Republic of the Rio Grande Museum, unfortunately closed for the evening. Outside its flat façade fly seven flags: Spain, France, Mexico, the Republic of Texas, the United States, and the Confederate States of America are the first of the well-known "Six Flags over Texas." There is a seventh for Laredo, black, white, and red with three stars. The building has been here since 1830, and is believed to have once been the capitol of the Republic of the Rio Grande. The historical evidence linking the building to the republic is thin. Yet it tells a story of a time when men could attempt to carve out a nation from this remote and inhospitable land—or die trying.

From Laredo to Brownsville, the history found along Highway 83 is marked by war, unrest, and conflict, almost all of it intertwined with the story of Mexico. There is the Mexican War of Independence from Spain in 1821, the Texas Revolution of 1836, the Mexican-American War of 1846, the U.S. Civil War, and the Mexican Revolution beginning in 1910. Toss in World War I as well, since it was widely believed that the Germans wanted Mexico to distract the United States by attacking it on its southern border. This building reportedly had a role in perhaps one of the least known and strangest conflicts of them all.

THE RIVER REPUBLIC

Antonio Zapata, Antonio Canales, Jésus Cárdenas, and a handful of other men gathered in the sandstone and adobe building underneath the shadow of San Agustin Church on a cool February day in 1840.

Five weeks had passed since January 1, when the men had declared independence from Mexico and named Laredo the capital of the newly created Republic of the Rio Grande, but this was the first time since that day that they'd set foot in the town. This austere, one-story building would have to serve as its capitol for the time being.

The three men came from different walks of life but had a singular goal—to escape the tyranny of the central government in Mexico City and carve out their own nation, just as the Texans had done four years earlier.

They made their declaration of independence about forty miles south on the north bank of the river, across from the town of Guerrero, Mexico, Zapata's hometown. They wanted the Mexican states of Nuevo Leon, Coahuila, and Tamaulipas as their own, and created a flag with three stars to symbolize the new federation.

Antonio Canales

Canales was the instigator. A well-educated lawyer and politician, he had served in the Tamaulipas state legislature, and like many citizens in the far-flung provinces, bristled at the rule of the heavy-handed central government. Mexico fought the Spanish crown for its independence in 1821, and by 1824 it had created what most believed was an acceptable constitution. But after Antonio

López de Santa Anna was elected in 1833, he ripped up the document and settled in as a dictator. Several states rose up in rebellion, not the least of which was Texas, by then occupied by a sizeable Anglo population. After his brother-in-law failed to pacify the northern state, Santa Anna took charge of the army himself, routing the rebels at the Alamo, but was then soundly defeated at the Battle of San Jacinto in 1836. Despite the defeat, Mexico continued to lay claim to the borderlands between the Nueces River and the Rio Grande and stationed troops along the Rio Grande's southern bank.

Canales saw what the Texans had accomplished and wanted that for his own people. Law did not interest him as much as war. He found a willing ally in Zapata, a mixed-race Mexican with African blood who had been born into poverty as a sheepherder. He had risen above his station and grown wealthy by accumulating large herds. He had also distinguished himself as an Indian fighter, taking on the Apaches and learning some military tactics. At the time of the rebellion, he owned a large swath of land north of the river across from Guerrero. But that was all he had left. Once the proud owner of a flock of 90,000 sheep, he'd found himself impoverished when the Mexican army during the Texas rebellion helped itself to his livestock and all they could carry away. He was left bereft, and it was all Mexico's fault. Along with his landholdings, he still had the respect of the people. That earned him a spot at the side of Canales.

Before the republic was formed on New Year's Day, the pair had spent more than a year making war against the centralists. They had even found a group of battle hardened Anglos, about 180 Texans under the leadership of Colonel Samuel Jordan, who were still anxious to fight. Recruits to the cause were promised twenty-five dollars a month, a share of any loot, and a nice chunk of land.

Jordan was also a man who lived to do battle. He served as a corporal in the Texas Revolution and later joined the Rangers to fight the Cherokees in the eastern part of the republic. Life was probably too quiet for the adventurer when he encountered

Canales in San Antonio. The Mexican offered to make him a lieutenant colonel in the federalist army, and more importantly, the opportunity to join a war again. When Canales left San Antonio, he had Jordan, another seasoned Anglo officer, Captain Reuben Ross, and the Texans under his command.

Along with the Anglos and Mexicans, about sixty Native Americans joined the interracial army, which was 600 men strong when left to push the centralists out of the three states.

Their first order of business was to oust a garrison of some 500 centralists occupying Zapata's hometown. It was meant to be a surprise attack, but the commander in charge found out that they were coming and fled toward Monterrey. Canales's army, which included the Texans, soon caught up with them, and scored its first major victory at the Battle of Alcantro Creek. The federalists not only defeated the centralists, they captured four pieces of artillery and about 350 of the soldiers who surrendered switched sides to join their cause. News of the victory spread up and down the valley and gave Canales instant credibility. Men rallied to his cause and the army swelled to more than 1,000 mounted and dismounted troops.

Canales set his sights on the strategically important town of Matamoros, which sat a few miles west of the mouth of the Rio Grande. The army of irregulars traveled 165 miles in twenty-eight days and found a well-fortified city with 1,500 men and eighteen cannons there to defend it.

Colonel Zapata scored the first victory by leading a small force of Texans and Mexicans against an outpost, overrunning it and killing a dozen centralist troops. That prompted the city's commanding general to order the troops manning the outposts to abandon them and withdraw into the city to prepare for a siege.

Canales wanted them to come out and meet on a battlefield, but the general refused. If they wanted the city, the rebels would have to come and take it. Much to the chagrin of the Texans, Canales announced that he would abandon the Matamoros campaign and attack Monterrey instead. Jordan was livid. They had just traveled a month from that direction. Now they were turning around and heading back? But Canales said he didn't want to harm the innocent civilians of Matamoros. Jordan and Ross said if Canales didn't want to invade the city, the Texans would. But Canales wouldn't back down. A few dozen Texans, including Ross, slipped away, expressing disgust, and returned north.

Monterrey was an even bigger fiasco. It was said that only 400 men garrisoned it and there were vast stores of weapons and ammunition there for the taking. In fact, by the time the Rio Grande army arrived near Christmastime, the centralists had been reinforced with more soldiers and a skilled leader, General Mariano Arista, was there to command them.

Arista was a battle-hardened officer who had joined the Spanish colonial Army then fought on the side for independence. It was said that politically, he leaned more toward the liberal, federalist cause, but after the serving with distinction during the Texas

General Mariano Arista

revolution, Santa Anna appointed him commander of the army of the north. It was his duty to crush the rebels.

Arista met the invading force outside the city in a spot that gave his troops some protection. Unlike the general in Matamoros, Arista was more than willing to engage the Rio Grande army head on. On the first day, the two sides exchanged artillery fire and fought several skirmishes. Canales was outmaneuvered by Arista's cavalry, and they fought to a stalemate.

The second day brought another series of questionable moves on the part of Canales, who again appeared overly cautious, unlike Zapata, who charged at the centralists and fought with valor, breaking Arista's lines. Canales failed to take advantage of Zapata's victory and ordered the men to start digging trenches on the outskirts of the city. When night fell, the two armies retreated to their camps.

Arista sent agents behind the rebels' lines, where the infiltrators found their opponents huddled around campfires. They bribed the Mexican troops to switch sides—or in the case of the 350 men who had surrendered at the Battle of Alcantro—to switch back. For the most part, the agents were successful. By morning's light, Canales and Zapata discovered that 700 of their troops had deserted. They had no choice but to retreat to the borderlands with Arista's now much larger army on their heels.

Despite the defeat, Canales took this time to reveal his intentions. He declared the formation of the Republic of the Rio Grande. He called for delegates to gather in Laredo, its capital. They designed the flag and wrote a constitution that was almost identical to the Mexican Constitution of 1824. Men were appointed to various government positions: Canales the lawyer declared himself commander-in-chief of the army, which barely existed. Zapata was named second in command. Cardenas was the president. They published a newspaper to help spread the word. One reason the newly formed government remained in Guerrero was that it had a printing press, but when word arrived that Arista was planning to invade the town, they had to leave for Laredo, where the new republic had a great deal of support. The sandstone-adobe building was where they conducted their business. But they couldn't rest there long.

The ragtag army of irregulars by February was depleted, with only a few dozen Texans remaining. Even the stalwart Colonel Jordan had left for the north. Canales's only excursion that month resulted in another defeat at the hands of Arista. There simply would be no Republic of the Rio Grande until its army broke the back of the centralist forces.

President Cardenas and Canales went north to recruit more Texans to the cause. Texas's president, Mirabeau Lamar, refused to recognize the self-declared republic and would offer no material support. Some believed that Canales wanted to eventually create an alliance or a federation with the Republic of Texas, which would extend the newly formed country's influence as far south as the Sierra Madre mountains. The two leaders, meanwhile, found more than 400 Anglos ready to fight, again promising them a salary, all the loot they could carry, and a swath of land if they stayed throughout the whole campaign. Among them was Jordan, who couldn't resist the call of battle.

An equal number of Mexicans from north and south of the river—mostly untrained cowboys or men with few prospects—joined them. Canales and Zapata had an army to lead again.

In the summer, they split their forces. Colonel Jordan was paired with two Mexican captains, Lopez and Molano, who led several hundred men southwest along the river. In every town they swept into, the people greeted the multiracial army as liberators. They women waved, the children followed along. They danced, drank, feasted—at the expense of the townspeople—and encountered no resistance. Lopez and Molano told Jordan that they had received orders from Canales to proceed due south to take the strategically important town of Saltillo.

It was more of the same as the force made its way there. Victoria, the capital of Tamaulipas, fell easily, and the leaders installed a state government there. The Texans and Mexicans looted the town, but there was little to be taken except a cache of fine cigars.

Next would be the most important prize, Saltillo, but Lopez and Molano began taking a circuitous route. It was about this time when Jordan received an anonymous letter from an informant stating that the two Mexican officers were leading the Texans into a trap. He confronted the pair, but they swore to their maker, and all that was holy, that this was one of General Arista's tricks to divide the force.

On an October day, the Republic of the Rio Grande's forces lined up about three miles outside of Saltillo for the deciding battle. They faced about 1,000 troops who were dug in for the fight. The town's citizens—men, women, children—lined up on the rooftops of their adobe homes to see who would prevail and ultimately rule their town.

What they witnessed was the mounted Texans beginning to gallop toward a gorge, then abruptly stop. Lopez had ordered Jordan to take his men and swing through a gorge to the west to outflank the centralist army. Jordan gave the order to proceed, but one of his captains rode up to him and told him he was insane. Word of the possible betrayal had spread through the Texan ranks, and if Jordan had been blinded by the Mexican's words, the men had not. Jordan was so eager for a fight that he couldn't see what every other Texan could. His captain told him if they went into the gorge, none of them would ever return. It finally dawned on Jordan that this was the trap and the letter was legitimate. He turned his men around just in time to hear Lopez yell, "Long live the Supreme government!" And with that, he and all the Mexicans dashed over to the centralist lines, and joined them in firing on the Texans.

Whether Lopez was a centralist infiltrator from the beginning, or had just cut a deal the night before to betray the cause, was unknown. Jordan and his men could only beat a hasty retreat for the border. Lopez and the army followed them right up to the river. Jordan only lost five men, but he was finally through with this new republic. The Texans returned north and quit the fight for good.

Zapata's army fared even worse. Arista had invaded Laredo and found it undefended. Zapata's army was in a town to the north, Santa Rita de Morelos, and that is where he chose to make his stand against the superior force. The siege lasted for several days, but the new republic's army couldn't hold out. When he was down to twenty-two men, he was forced to surrender. Zapata strode up to the skirmish line, broke his sword over his thigh, and threw it on the ground.

Arista told Zapata if he would join the federalist forces, he would arrange for a pardon. Zapata steadfastly refused. Arista made him a second offer. If he swore to never again take up arms against Mexico, he would spare his life and those of his men. Zapata again refused. He demanded that they be treated like prisoners of war from another sovereign nation, rather than rebels.

Arista's answer was to put Zapata in front of a firing squad.

Highway 83 in Laredo heads west through several old neighborhoods, then takes a sudden turn south where it begins to resemble the suburban commercial strips of many American cities with chain restaurants, strip malls, and such. The one variation on the Everytown, USA, theme are the drive-thru liquor stores where motorists pull into a tunnel-like edifice, tell the cashier what they want, and emerge with their libations without having to step out of their car.

I do my best to patronize the businesses on Highway 83, and that means staying in motels along the road. The Super 8 tested my determination, though. My first-floor room, which was just a few dozen yards from a stoplight on San Bernardo Avenue, featured the "sounds of Highway 83" all night. I could record a lovely CD with that name. It could feature the symphony of birds I experienced at the Audubon National Wildlife Refuge in North Dakota, the wind rustling though the buffalo grass at the Fort Pierre National Grasslands, and the water trickling underneath the Canadian River bridge. Last night, I was treated to the screeching of brakes, the revving of engines, and the thumping of car stereos as drivers waited for the light to turn green. I had a rough night in the hotel, but a better morning doing some research at the central library learning about the Republic of the Rio Grande. I'm departing after the lunch hour, but I don't intend to go far. The town of Zapata and nearby Falcon Lake are a short sixty miles south. It's not long before I've left the Laredo outskirts and enter mesquite country.

There he is! My old friend the turkey buzzard, circling and circling, as if he were waiting there all morning to escort me south.

I'm cruising on a four-lane stretch of road, stopping only for a few minutes to take some snapshots of the town of Rio Bravo and at a scenic overlook of the river, but it all ends when I reach the county line.

The comfortable four-laner abruptly funnels vehicle onto a two-lane road that seems a bit too narrow. I've been warned. As far away as Kansas, I was told about the dangerous stretch of road south of Laredo. Truck traffic and fast-moving cars combine to make a deadly mix.

That's not me. I'm perpetually stopping to take pictures or explore some roadside attraction, and I have rarely hit the gas pedal hard on this trip.

I heard some late-night talk-show comedian years ago describe everyone on the road as either an "asshole" or an "idiot." When the drivers go too fast and pass you at break-neck speeds, you mumble "asshole" under your breath. When they cause you to slow down, they're an "idiot." I'm the idiot in this equation. There is a custom in Texas that I have experienced nowhere else. Slowpokes such as myself pull over onto the shoulder as much as they can to allow the faster drivers to pass. That's how to "Drive Friendly, the Texas Way," as the signs say.

Maps dating back to the Spanish colonial era show a road just to the north of the river stretching from Laredo down to through the Valley. Highway 83 doesn't follow its path precisely, but travelers have been following the riverbanks by foot, horseback, buggy, and car for centuries.

For me, 83 is a road of beauty, a unique strip of blacktop that takes me to places of natural wonders and historic sites. For others, it's a place of heartbreak. I'm reminded of this when I pull over to investigate six wooden crosses adorned with plastic flowers on a dusty incline on the east side of the highway. They sit just above a creek.

Informal roadside memorials marking the last place on Earth where a loved one was alive are not unique to the Rio Grande Valley. I have seen them from the Canadian border to here, and more than a few on Highway 83 in southern Kansas. The State of South Dakota has permanent markers, diamond-shaped metal signs with the word "Think" and a giant red X to "mark the spot" wherever someone died in a vehicle accident when alcohol or lack of a seatbelt was a factor. They place a sign for each death—with the family's permission—so a particularly horrific night will result in a sad cluster.

Such is the case here, a family of four, wiped out February 27, 2005, a little more than five years ago. All I have to go on is the names and dates on the cross. Clemente Sr., age forty, the mother, Maria, age forty-two, their son Clemente Jr., just turned ten, and little brother Emmanuel, age seven. A fifth cross with a flat piece of wood for some kind of sign indicates that there was once more information here, but it was most likely paper and has long since weathered away. The plastic flowers are tipped over and beginning to fade.

A few feet away is another cross. This one has a much larger bunch of plastic flowers piled high, as if someone had been along recently to arrange them. At first, I thought this was the same accident, but that isn't the case. Juan Jose Ortiz, age forty-one, lost his life here two and a half years later, on July 26, 2007. Is it the dip in the road leading to the creek that makes this such a deadly spot?

I will discover in a *Laredo Morning Times* article that the first accident was even more devastating than the roadside memorial suggests. The fifth unmarked cross may have been placed there for Jose Villarreal II, the twenty-year-old driver of a Mercury Grand Marquis. He was a friend of the family and had been pressed into making a late-night drive to Donna, Texas, to visit Maria De la Paz Roja's sister and to attend morning mass at the nearby

Lady of San Juan del Valle basilica. It was said Maria and her common-law husband, Aaron Martinez—identified as Clemente Sr. on the marker—preferred making the trip at night to avoid traffic. Villarreal—while attempting to pass another vehicle at 1:30 a.m.—slammed into a 1998 Ford Winstar, killing two of its four passengers, Alicia Luna Arellano, age fifty-five, and Maria Elena Arellano, age seventy, both from Nuevo Laredo. Two other passengers in the Ford survived, but with serious injuries. All of the victims were pronounced dead at the scene. They were just seven of the 43,510 U.S. motor vehicle deaths recorded in 2005.

But they were more than numbers.

The boys liked to ride bikes, and Maria regularly brought them to the local parks where they played catch and ran around the swing sets. This was Maria's second family. She had left behind four children in Atlanta, Georgia. The article portrayed a large, extended family of modest means who were struggling with both the shock and grief and finding a way to pay for the funeral expenses. The students and teachers at Leyendecker Elementary School in Laredo were provided with grief counselors. It turned out that Alicia Arellano was the grandmother of a second-grader at the same school.

Death came for all of them in an instant. I imagine and hope that the boys were asleep, sprawled out in the back of the Grand Marquis, not knowing, not feeling. The adults, spared what would have been a lifetime of endless grief, would never have to second-guess their fateful decisions. This is clearly not a spot to pass another vehicle.

I take pictures of the fading plastic flowers as I found them, then tip them up and blow off the Texas dust.

The town of San Ygnacio doesn't look like much more than a wide spot on the road. Fortunately, I take a right turn into its narrow streets and discover that it's so much more. The entire

town, from Highway 83 to the Rio Grande, is in the National Register of Historic Places.

I follow Business 83 through winding streets with low-slung white stucco buildings made of sandstone. Except for its paved streets it's a mid–nineteenth-century border town frozen in time. The town square is a small, shady plaza with a gazebo, concrete benches, and a few historical markers. Among them is a granite memorial for Petty Officer 2nd Class Alfredo Salinas, a sailor who served on the USS *Indianapolis* in World War II. After being struck by Japanese torpedoes, the heavy cruiser sank in twelve minutes with 300 men aboard. The surviving 879 men floated in the sea for four days, most perishing of exposure, seawater poisoning and shark attacks. It is considered one of the worst disasters in U.S. Navy history. The marker doesn't specify whether Salinas died aboard the ship or in the harrowing days at sea—only that his body was never recovered.

Founded in 1830, San Ygnacio was a meeting point for Canales and Zapata when they were organizing the Republic of the Rio Grande. Over the years, it was invaded by Comanches, Mexican revolutionaries, and one Hollywood film crew. But the most important event in the town's history is something that didn't happen. San Ygnacio was not emptied out and subsequently flooded in the name of progress.

While some of the history I've discovered along Highway 83 I owe to serendipity, this is not the case here. Long before I departed on the trip, I had cast my eye on the Texas map and spotted Falcon Lake and its dam. I had done extensive research on two other dams near Highway 83 in North and South Dakota that created Lakes Sacagawea and Oahe.

It was the 1940s and the mighty Missouri River was periodically doing what it had for hundreds of thousands of years, flooding in the spring and inundating the river valleys. Riverine peoples such as the Mandans, Arikaras, and Hidatsus had learned to live with these natural cycles and take advantage of what the river offered them. In 1944, Congress passed the Pick-Sloan Flood Control Act, a plan that had emerged from two agencies, the Army Corps of Engineers and the Bureau of Reclamation. It called for a series of dams on the Missouri and its tributaries that would control flooding, create reservoirs for irrigation, and generate hydroelectricity for the cities. It was a great day for the residents of big cities downstream, but upstream it was a disaster for the tribes. No one had consulted them. They had lived there for thousands of years—and suddenly the U.S. government came and snatched away their livelihoods. In a time before the Civil Rights and environmental movements, they fought the law as best they could, but lost everything in the end. Their homes and villages were flooded. Self-sufficient farmers were suddenly made dependents. The dams destroyed their way of life.

So what happened here?

Take Native Americans with little political power or say over their lives, and substitute Mexican-Americans. Is it the same story?

I know that in this case, the dam uprooted people in two nations. The residents of San Ygnacio had to put up a fight back in the late 1940s. The Texas Historical Commission marker on the plaza credits the town's salvation to a committee of citizens headed by Mercurio Martinez. They prevailed. But five villages along Highway 83 didn't, and are today underwater. As I drive south of San Ygnacio, I come across historical markers for two of the five lost towns of Highway 83: Ramireño and Uribeño.

I pull into Zapata, which sits on a ridge above the man-made lake. The town and the county are named after the Republic of the Rio Grande's second in command, Antonio Zapata, who once owned most of the land I'm driving on. After General Arista executed him, he chopped off his head, preserved it in a glass jar with brandy, and placed it on a pole in Guerrero's town square for the residents and his family to see.

I can catch glimpses of the lake from the road. Somewhere out there underwater is Old Zapata, and a few hundred yards farther is Old Guerrero. I follow a sign search for the town library, where I hope to prove a theory.

The friendly librarian, Aida Garcia, brings out the folders for me to look through. I find a table and start leafing through the loose pieces of paper. Someone has already done the painstaking work of collecting newspaper clips and any material having to do with the building of the dam, which will save me loads of time. But the library closes in a couple hours, so I dig in. For an amateur historian like myself, looking through a pile of unorganized documents, articles, and ephemera is like a food critic sitting down to sample a meal at a five-star restaurant.

The date, the name of the newspaper, and on which page articles appeared is vitally important to professional historians. Happily, I'm not one of them. I'm not big on little numbers floating around at the end of sentences. The clippings and other documents are not in any particular order. Some articles have the dates, but not the newspaper. Some have the periodical name and the author, but no date. I have been doing research like this on the fly in small-town libraries for some 1,600 miles.

"Photocopy first, read later," is my motto. Here, I want to slow it down a bit so I understand what happened as I finish the remainder of my journey.

And this is what I learned from that file.

The Lower Rio Grande Valley is not a valley at all. It's a delta collecting sediments washed down through the millennia. As such it is slightly elevated from the land around it—a situation that makes it especially prone to flooding. Those who wanted to take advantage of this rich soil had to accept the fact that every few years they needed to run for higher ground.

The first Spanish colonists dealt with this reality, but they also wanted to irrigate in the dry years. Not hard if the farm was right next to the river, but much harder for lands farther out. In this endeavor, they had varying degrees of success.

Fast forward to the first half of the twentieth century. The United States and Mexico have put their troubles stemming from a series of Mexican rebellions and one notable war behind them. They begin to cooperate in matters of mutual interest, such as building bridges over the river. They form the International Boundary Commission—later known as the International Boundary and Water Commission—to hammer out treaties.

The International Water Treaty of 1944 paved the way for three dams on the Rio Grande. Congress followed suit in 1950 by ratifying the treaty and funding a series of projects, including what would be the Falcon Dam.

This background I learned from a typed press release written by a Brad Smith of Weslaco, Texas, on behalf of the Lower Rio Grande Valley Chamber of Commerce and included in the "Welcome Amigos" press kit distributed to the White House press corps upon the arrival of President Dwight D. Eisenhower for the dam's dedication ceremony.

The next item I find is a newspaper clipping from May 3, 1953. "RAW DEAL CHARGED: Zapata Protests Land Value Set by U.S. Agents."

The clipping does not include the name of the paper. Staff Writer Clarence J. LaRoche reports that property owners are unhappy with the amount of money being offered for their land and homes. In the town of Guerrero the Mexican government is offering 100 percent replacement value for property, including an equal amount of land as well as a modern home. The U.S. agents were declaring homes obsolete, using depreciation tables and whatever they could to whittle the value of a house built fifty years ago for $3,000 down to $1,200. That would barely buy a shack in 1953. Owners of irrigable lands were being forced to relocate onto non-irrigable lands. Such property along the river bottom could fetch $1,550 per acre, while dryland farms went for $55 per acre.

"When you take away a man's property for the public good, the practice is to replace it on as equal a basis as possible," one unnamed Zapata resident declared.

In an undated clipping, the roving editor of the *Valley Evening Monitor*, Don Hinga, writes a sympathetic, although patronizing, account of the "Mexicans'" plight: "In many of these homes, several generations have been born to live out quiet lives in the sleepy atmosphere of the border. They have raised children, seen them grow to manhood. They have laid their loved ones to rest in cemeteries that always seem to have fresh flowers on hoary gravestones.

"Mexicans, who comprise the greater part of the population of Zapata are deeply sentimental. Homes to them are not just mere dwelling places. Into these thick-walled cottages they have built the greater part of their lives. Each stone and timber has a meaning.

Now as the prices of progress, they are to have their roots torn up, their homes buried beneath the waters, their memories deep beneath the waves," Hinga writes.

Ben Spruell owned a gas station and a half dozen tourist cabins for twenty-six years, the article says. Once Highway 83 came through, the business took off. He will have to find a new spot on the relocated road, the article said.

Every article mentions San Ygnacio as one of the towns that would be flooded. Nine-tenths of the homes in Zapata County will be underwater. There is nothing in the clips about San Ygancio's fight to be spared. But as residents of a town on what would have been the northern end of the lake, the committee spearheaded by Mercurio Martinez probably made a case that the town should be given a reprieve. That is apparently what happened. If it were located three or four miles to the south, it probably would have shared the same fate.

Several pages later, I find clippings of two photos that were apparently published with the story. One is of Spruell. He's a gaunt, hatchet-faced man, holding an oil can, wearing a Humble gas cap.

And then I find a three-page self-published article printed in cursive script and written by Janie Martinez and Jo Emma Quezada in 2002: "Uribeño: The Forgotten Town." I had never seen it on any old highway maps, and didn't know it existed, until I stopped earlier in the day at the historical marker that overlooked the site on the lake where it now sits.

Most of the residents of the hamlet near Highway 83 were descendants of José Nicolas Clemente Gutiérrez, who was awarded a land grant by the Spanish crown for his service in the Spanish Army in 1803. Despite the royalists' generosity, the family members were known as rebels, first siding against Spain in the War for Independence. One of Gutiérrez's nephews was executed by a firing squad in the conflict. A couple generations later, a grandson joined a short-lived borderland uprising in 1890 against the Mexican strongman President Porfirio Diaz.

Uribeño never reached the size of the other Zapata County towns. It peaked at some 150 residents in the 1800s. When the Falcon Dam plan came into fruition, it had a schoolhouse, a grocery store, and a cemetery. The residents of the other four towns, Zapata, Falcon, Ramireño, and Lopeño opted to move

A historical marker for Uribeño, north of Falcon Lake.

their communities to higher ground. The Uribeño families chose to leave. They scattered to other towns in the county or bigger cities, insisting only that the graves of their loved ones be moved.

The cemetery sits on Highway 83 north of Zapata.

And then I find *The Town of Old Zapata* Volumes I, II and III—a compilation of pictures taken by the federal government of every building that was destroyed. I'm completely floored. I never came across anything like this researching the Dakota dams. Jo Emma Quezada, coauthor of the Uribeño article, apparently took the time to compile the pictures into the books. Each building had a hand-painted and numbered sign set in front so the bureaucrats could keep their records straight.

I find Ed Spreull's Humble gas station, "B-Y-7," on a sign stuck between two gas pumps. I can just make out where the tourist cabins are in back. There is a side view picture with a little piece of Route 83 running along it. Residents, seemingly going about their business, are in the doorways and walking on the drive. With a map, one could recreate the entire town in the mind's eye.

Also, on Highway 83: T-W-5, the Conoco Café, festooned with Royal Crown Cola, 7up and Coca-Cola signs. The Hill Top Café, B-W-10, owned by one Alejandro Saenz, also primarily decorated with porcelain soda-pop signs. I go through pages and pages of modest homes, nothing resembling a mansion, many looking like what I saw with my own eyes earlier in San Ygnacio. Thanks to a bureaucrat with a camera and the efforts of a local historian, a bit of Old Zapata lives in the new town's library on in these pages.

There were a dozen newspaper articles in the file devoted to the October 19, 1953, dedication ceremony. The Texas Highway Patrol closed off one lane of Highway 83 to allow the VIPs' motorcades to speed through. Organizers paved a parking area just to accommodate all the vehicles. A special platform was constructed so the 550 invited guests and members of the media could see the leaders of the two nations deliver their speeches at the boundary line in the middle of the dam. It wasn't every day that a sitting U.S. president visited the humble towns of the Lower Rio Grande Valley. Quezada, in her introduction to the compilation of pictures wrote: "The Valley prepared for the celebration and President Eisenhower's visit for months, while Zapata County residents, many living in tents, were trying to survive the chaos left by the reservoir's murky waters."

The San Antonio Express printed the complete speeches delivered that day by Eisenhower and Mexican President Adolfo Ruiz Cortines. There were plenty of platitudes about the friendship between the two nations, the fight against totalitarianism, and so on, but not a single word from either man acknowledging or thanking the uprooted citizens for their sacrifices.

There are a few more clippings from the 1950s. They tout the new fishing mecca of South Texas. New Zapata was slowly taking on a role as a tourist destination. The hotels and restaurants that I see today on Highway 83 as it cuts through town catered to these new visitors.

Aida, the librarian, tells me that when the water is low the old Highway 83 bridge emerges from the lake and anglers boat out to it and fish from atop its still intact concrete. Fish love to congregate among the pilings. I drive out to a park after supper where families are congregating and look for it. I ask a teenager walking up the boat ramp with a fishing pole and a fat bass on a string about the bridge. He points it out. I can barely out make a narrow strip of gray underneath the waters. Old Highway 83 sleeps with the fishes.

On my way out of Zapata the next day, I set out to find the ruins of a gas station that was once on Highway 83 before the Falcon Dam inundated the Valley.

A souvenir-store owner had tipped me off about the building, which he said was near an old fishing camp about five miles west of 83. He gave me detailed directions on how to find it, so after driving a few miles I left the safety of the highway and took off on a gravel road, getting lost for a bit, but eventually righting myself until I come across the fishing camp.

I can't find anything resembling an old gas station, so I start to drive through the ramshackle collection of aging campers and mobile homes shaded by gnarly old trees. It's not long before an old man in a red pickup truck intercepts me near a boat ramp. He rolls down the window.

"What ya looking for?" he asks. He looks a little miffed, and I realize that maybe I shouldn't be here.

I tell him my story and he listens carefully as we both step out of our vehicles. He sizes me up and decides I'm not a threat. They have been having all sorts of problems with drug smugglers, and for all he knew, I could have been someone here to meet a boatful of dope coming over the lake, he explains. The local cartel has been known to fly helicopters overhead to see if the coast is clear.

"People round here sleep with their guns loaded by their beds," he says.

His name in Jack Cox Jr., and his father once owned the fishing camp, which has been here for some fifty years. The old gas station is just a few yards past the camp entrance and over a fence. It's marked "No Trespassing," but it shouldn't be a problem if I just want to hop over and snap a few pictures, he tells me.

Jack Cox Jr.

Since I introduced myself as an author, he wants to know what I've written. It just so happens I have copies of my first book in the trunk, and he wants to buy one.

"There ain't much to do out here except read," he says.

There are only three full-time residents in the camp, and he's one of them. He sold the property four years ago, but part of the deal with the new owner was that he could stay there five years rent-free.

He invites me back to his house for a cup of coffee.

Out front of the white mobile home, I'm greeted by a shaggy white dog and a friendly cat, who has just brought Jack a dead bird as a present. Inside, the mobile home is not what I expected. It is decorated with African art: masks, textiles, carvings.

"I managed a hunting camp in Somalia on the Jubba River for five years," he declares.

"You did *what*, now?"

I'm glad I grabbed my notebook.

Jack takes a seat in a chair, while I sit on his sofa and fumble for a pen. He's eighty-one years old, he tells me. I would expect an elderly widower's mobile home to be a mess. The room is cluttered, but clean. His coffee table is covered in magazines: *The Weekly Standard, National Geographic, Smithsonian*. Fox News is on mute. He tries to peg me as a liberal, Washington, D.C.– based journalist. I tell him I'm a radical centrist. That seems to confuse him.

"It means I'm in the middle and I get to argue with everybody."

Fortunately, the conversation turns away from politics and to his days as a big game guide.

"I was an elephant hunter and a safari guide," he continues, first giving me a quick version of his life story.

He grew up in Midland, Texas, where he was a friend of Larry L. King, who would go on to be a journalist and author and the co-writer of *The Best Little Whorehouse in Texas*.

Like many in that region, Jack was drawn into the oil business and worked for Rogers Exploration as a "seismic man." The company sent him to Australia, Tanzania, Brazil, and Bolivia for years-long stints.

He married twice, both times to Australian women. His second wife died fifteen years ago. He is still in contact with his first. Back when he was a young man in Midland, he was in love with a high school classmate. But a fighter pilot from the nearby Air Force base stole her away. A lifetime later, the Air Force officer passed away, and Jack and his long-lost love are at last together. She lives in Sweetwater, Texas, and he travels there quite a bit to see her. She hates the fishing camp.

"I got her in the end," he says with a smile.

He doesn't mention any children, and I forget to ask. Some kind of journalist I am.

He was in Tanzania working for the oil company when the opportunity to run the hunting camp in Somalia presented itself.

He pushes himself up from the chair, walks to another room, and returns with a photo album. Inside is a plain white envelope, and inside the envelope is a perfectly preserved brochure for the camp. It's fifty years old, but it looks like it was printed yesterday. He was there from the late 1950s to the early 1960s—back when well-heeled men could live out their Hemingway fantasies—for a price.

He shows me black-and-white pictures of the kills.

"My first lion," is written in pen on the edges of one. Jack and some other fellow is squatting and smiling next to a lioness, holding her mouth open. Jack is young, his black hair slicked back, with a broad, handsome face. It's startling to see him as a young man.

"Those were good times," he said, showing me another picture of two guests he identifies as members of the Kennedy administration.

"And the women…" he trails off. Smiles. I can see that he's remembering one of them, maybe more. I don't dare interrupt his reverie.

"I closed up many bars in Nairobi," he continues as I look at a series of pictures of dead elephants, gazelles, and such. That was back when the Italians ran Somalia. Once the colonialists left, the "whole country went to shit," he says. That was the end of the hunting lodge on the Jubba River. He went back to being a seismic man for the oil companies, although he did spend a couple years trying to grow cotton in Australia.

"Money never was the thing, you see. But I wish I had saved just a little bit more of it."

He's heading up to Sweetwater that day to see his "lady friend," as he calls her, so it's time for me to go. He really wants me to see the old gas station before I leave. So we head back outside where he lets me take a few pictures of him as the cat curls around his leg.

"It's been a good life. I'm not a religious man, but I wonder what the adventure is on the other side."

US PROPERTY
NO
TRESPASSING

WARNING: YOU ARE ENTERING FEDERAL
PROPERTY. DO NOT ENTER. NO WEAPONS
ALLOWED. VIOLATORS WILL BE PROSECUTED.
I.B.W.C.

Well, Jack said, it's no problem. So I climb over the fence where the signs are hung and walk a few feet back to find what remains of old Highway 83 and a gas station.

The filling station is a pink shell. It looks like the waters have come up several times to wash away everything but its walls. The roof is gone, but a beam that once held up the canopy to keep the sun and rain off motorists filling up at the pumps still stands. Someone else has ignored the sign and taken potshots at the beam, leaving a half-dozen bullet holes in the concrete. Mesquite and prickly pear are growing around it.

The old road itself is gravel; it disappears into the vegetation. I poke around for any relics from the old days, an old bottle, a sign. There's nothing but pieces of corrugated steel. A cluster of cactus bulbs has somehow taken hold on top of the wall. I wonder how it can do that.

I imagine the gas station in its heyday. If it ever had one. It was unattached to a town—a good ten miles away from any of the now submerged villages. I see the cars pulling up for gas and water on hot days, parents yanking Coke bottles out of a machine for their kids, the attendant wiping the dust and bug juice off the windshields.

Included in the $47 million the federal government spent to construct the Falcon Dam was $3.5 million allocated to improve fifty-five miles of Highway 83, and to relocate several miles of it to the north. The Texas Department of Transportation did the work. The unflooded sections of the road and bridges were widened from eighteen to twenty-four feet and graded to eliminate the "rollercoaster effect," as one newspaper described it. Care was taken to construct the new sections far to the north, beyond where the lake was expected to rise. Work was finished before the dam was dedicated in 1953. Slowly, the Rio Grande waters swallowed up the villages and the old highway. I wonder if they left any of those old federal shield signs standing. I can picture bass swimming around one now.

One of the first dry spells after the dam was built exposed the abandoned villages and their buildings. The U.S. feds decided that the structures were hazardous and it bulldozed them, leaving nothing but foundations. Yet the gas station sitting out here survived the destruction. The Mexicans didn't bother, and the buildings of Old Guerrero make an occasional appearance in times of drought.

Taking a picture of the highway as it emerges from the mesquite, I notice there are car tracks in the gravel. I doubt they were left there by the ghosts of old U.S. Route 83, so I'm not going to push my luck with the Border Patrol, a drug smuggler, or whoever has been driving back here. I don't linger.

Lopeño sits atop a ridge on the east side Falcon Lake. This is "new" Lopeño. Old Lopeño is beneath the waters. The town today is a collection of fairly plain looking mid-century homes.

As I slowly drive up and down the streets, the town is full of activity. If canines count anyway. I don't actually see any humans about. The dogs are all alerting each other to my presence. Do they know I'm from out of town? Can they spot a Virginia license plate? A couple of loose mutts nip at the Protégé's wheels. I shake them off in time to stop at a park, where the town keeps its historical markers. Two other dogs across the street behind a chain-link fence continue the cacophony.

The first sentence of the Texas Historical Commission's marker reads: "Development of this area began about 1749 when Col. José de Escandón began bringing colonists to establish permanent settlements along Mexico's northern frontier."

Escandón. He is not as well remembered as Coronado, but he was the one who succeeded.

It took almost 200 years after the conquistador's ill-fated 1540–1542 expedition for the colonialist powers in Mexico to establish permanent settlements in what would be Texas.

Occupying the Wild Horse Desert between the River of the North—soon to be known as the Rio Grande—and the Neuces would provide a buffer against British and French intentions. The Spaniards had long since given up on the prospects of cities of gold. The real wealth would be found in what the settlers could raise in terms of crops and livestock, and what taxes could be excised. The idea to gain a foothold in the region had been bandied about for decades, but would-be pioneers needed the right kind of man to lead the effort. The land there was prone to blazing hot summers and chilly winter temperatures. And, of course, it was already occupied by dozens of different tribes, some of whom would not be happy about new neighbors. The church would provide spiritual help, for what that was worth, in exchange for the requirement that the clergymen be taken care of and provided with a place of worship.

Escandón was the man for the job.

THE DREAM OF NEW SANTANDER

José de Escandón landed on the shores of the Yucatán Peninsula in 1715 to find his fortune in the New World. With few prospects, but a good family name, the fifteen-year-old boy was accepted into an elite cavalry unit, Los Caballeros Encomenderos. The horsemen's name was derived from the word *encomienda*, a system of extracting tributes from various native tribes. Whether it was gold, food, or labor, the Indians of the Yucatan were required to render goods and services to Spain. When they resisted, Los Caballeros came riding in. Escandón spent six years as a cadet making war on the tribes before being promoted to lieutenant. He married into a wealthy noble family and rose a notch on the social ladder.

As he grew older and was promoted to lieutenant general, he learned to pacify warring tribes with diplomacy rather than a heavy hand. He studied how the Romans conquered most of Europe by allowing native peoples to be absorbed into the Roman way of life. He would do the same, but with missionaries to help him. The idea was to transform societies rather than conquer them. His reputation as both a military leader and skilled negotiator grew.

José de Escandón

For the better part of the 1730s, leaders in Spain and Mexico were conferring on a plan to expand the empire to the east of Santa Fe. Vast regions along the eastern coast all the way up to Texas were unsettled, and prone to French and English encroachment.

Correspondence between the colony and Europe took months, and the Spanish bureaucracy moved at a deliberate pace, but after years of squabbling a plan to settle the north was approved. Now, to find a leader. There were many who wanted the job—at least one of them wanted to return to the old days of enslaving and killing off the natives—but the church wasn't about to allow that. After two centuries, the days of Cortez and Coronado's bloodthirsty, gold-crazed conquests had passed, although this would still be an *entrada*, an invasion. Nomadic "savages" roaming the plains to the north posed a threat. The mission required a man of unique skills, and Escandón possessed them.

At the age of forty-five, he was named "Knight of the Order of St. James, Regiment Colonel of the city of Querétaro, Lieutenant Captain General of Sierra Gorda, its Missions, Fortresses, and Frontiers, and Lieutenant of his Excellency the Viceroy of New Spain." In short, he was the man in charge. The success or failure of the endeavor rested on his shoulders.

He took two full years to plan the mission and recruit an army. Unlike with the Coronado entrada, the governments of Spain and New Spain were now willing to cover a certain amount of expenses. They knew by then that there was little in terms of mineral wealth in the region. If the leaders wanted a buffer against French and English influence, they had to invest some of the crown's money. Yet Escandón still had to come up with half of the funds.

During that time, he devised a unique plan. Unlike Coronado, who cared little for the exploration part of his mission, Escandón's goal was to gain a full understanding of this land being called New Nuevo Santander, after a region in Spain. He decided to split his forces into seven columns. Each would have a little more than 750 troops, including Indian allies, missionaries, and skilled servants. The seven groups spread out in seven directions with orders to survey and map as much as the region as they could before converging at the mouth of the Rio Grande, the Rio del Norte, as they called it then, on or before mid-February 1747. They were ordered to not provoke the region's natives, and to fight only in self-defense. Payment for the participants would be all they could pack on their burros from the region's reported deposits of salt—a vital commodity then that was just about worth its weight in gold.

There is no record of what the Native Americans thought of this invasion, only that there were no skirmishes and no lives lost. The occupants of the land either fled in the face of the superior force, or made peace overtures. Escandón reported that most tribes were nomadic, yet had a very definite belief that the land was theirs. He estimated some 2,500 village dwellers lived near the mouth of the river. Interestingly, there was a tribe of mixed-race African-Indians near the shore who were apparently the descendants of a wrecked slave ship.

The ninety-day excursion was a great success. He returned to his home in Mexico, where he began to sort through the reports from the seven columns. Ultimately, he settled on a plan to create fourteen settlements along the Rio Grande, and abandoned the idea to settle the lands near the Neuces.

There would be twelve colonies on the south bank and two to the north. Each would be expected to be self-sufficient. There would be some soldiers left behind, but no presidios. The citizens would be have to organize their own defenses against the natives in case of attack, as well as provide a church and sustenance for the missionaries.

Excitement for the plan grew throughout Mexico, especially as Escandón revealed the incentives. There would be free land grants, up to 200 pesos to cover travel expenses and the first year of settlement, and no taxes for ten years. Escandón publicized the fertile soil, the abundant grass, the proximity to the river and salt. The crown would provide some military protection—about ten soldiers for each settlement. It also gave the priests and missionaries an allowance.

In December 1748, two years after the first expedition, Escandón and some 700 families departed for their new lives. In choosing the first wave of settlers, Escandón wanted to avoid the pitfalls of the past, when colonists were either wealthy or nobility and didn't posses the basic skills needed to survive on the frontier. He didn't care about pure blood: Spaniards, mixed-race Indians, mixed-race blacks, it didn't matter as long as they were hearty souls who could withstand the vagaries of life on the edge of the empire. For political expediency, he had to allow some of the upper class to join. A few weeks after departing the comforts of their homes, several made excuses and turned back, just as Escandón predicted they would.

Escandón oversaw the establishment of each settlement. The first order of business was to plot out a town square, where the church would sit. Streets would radiate out and eventually give way to farmland, and then pastures. He named captains to be in charge of defenses, and moved on to settle the next town. No natives were to be booted off their lands. There also would be no colonies near the mouth of the river, where the tribes resided. Although they were not in the original plan, he permitted two more settlements to be established, Laredo and Dolores, which would never amount to much more than a ranch hacienda. The former he named himself after a town in Spain he once visited.

After five years, he had successfully settled more than 1,300 families. While there were raids by some of the warlike nomadic tribes such as the Lipan Apaches, thousands of Indians had converted to Christianity. Most important for the crown, there wasn't a Frenchman in sight. The king and viceroy rewarded Escandón handsomely for his work. He retired to begin writing his personal history of the settlements. In his final report, he recommended that the soldiers be dismissed from service, as most had married into local families, but that the missions continue to receive financial support. He recommended for the time being that there be no land grants—there were already too many people and it would only serve to anger the have-nots. No one was capable of sorting out who should get what.

Twelve years after Escandón founded the first town along the Rio Grande, Captain Parrilla arrived in the San Saba Valley to build the presidio and expand Spain's influence even farther north.

Escandón, meanwhile, had one more piece of advice for the crown: maintain vigilant control of New Santander, or the colonists were likely to revolt.

The Benavides' western wear store is right where they said it would be in Roma, back when I met the Noel Senior and Junior three days ago across from the Catarina Hotel.

"J. C. Ramirez Co." is painted on the side of the building facing oncoming traffic from Highway 83. "Wrangler * Levis * Justin * Tony Lama"

"Remember Dad. Best Gifts here," says a moveable letters sign. Thanks for reminding me, I think.

As I park the car, I realize what a prime location this is for the family business. It occupies the corner of Highway 83 and the short street that leads to the bridge to Mexico. Neither Roma, nor the town's twin across the Rio Grande, are major cities. Ciudad Miguel Alemán has a mere 27,000 residents, and until the suspension bridge was built in 1950, was a relatively small village. Yet there seem to be quite a few people walking to and from the crossing.

An electronic bell announces my arrival.

The store is what one would expect: racks and racks of western-style shirts, stacks of blue jeans, and posters of attractive cowboys and cowgirls modeling the attire in rustic settings.

Noel Senior emerges from the back.

"We were wondering about you," he says.

Noel Benavides Jr. looking into Ciudad Miguel Alemán.

His wife, Cecilia, rises from a desk where she has apparently been adding up the accounts, and introduces herself. Noel Junior is in town somewhere and expected soon. She gets on the phone to hurry him up.

We chat about my travels on the road for awhile, and it turns out Cecilia has something for me: a story that involves Highway 83.

Back in 1934, her grandparents Pablo and Claudia Ramirez departed Roma in their car to visit family in Laredo. It was a long, ninety-mile journey on the dusty, gravel Texas Highway 4 back then. About a half hour into the trip, Pablo seized up. The car swerved and skidded. His last act was to safely guide the car into a ditch. Claudia shook him, yelled his name, and pulled him over to listen for a heartbeat.

There was nothing. He was dead. All she could do was sob. She didn't know how to drive, so she just sat there, staring off into the wall of mesquite.

After a while, someone tapped on the car window. It was a man she knew, a traveling salesmen who often stopped at the store to sell a line of clothing. He managed to coax her out of the car. She would have never gone off with a stranger. It was the only good fortune on that tragic day that someone she knew had come along. He drove Claudia back to Roma and returned later with a coroner and her son Javier.

"I remember that story because it was right after that my dad took charge of the store—not this building but the third building, because this is the fourth building," Cecilia says.

Her father, Javier, took over the family business at age twenty-nine, representing the third generation. By that time, the family had already been doing trade in Roma for eighty-six years.

It began when a merchant, Pablo Ramirez, married into the Garcia Saenz family. The Saenzes had founded the town in 1821 under a Spanish land grant that includes much of the property that Roma lies in today. The couple opened their first general store in 1848 on the plaza just after the signing of the Treaty of Guadalupe Hidalgo, which ended the Mexican-American War. Roma was a bustling town then. It was the terminus point for steamboats, which couldn't navigate the Rio Grande any farther. Anything going inland had to be unloaded here and taken the rest of the way by wagon.

When the Mexican government in the 1850s imposed onerous import duties on foreign goods, Roma—and Rio Grande City just to the south—thrived as smuggling centers. The two towns' merchants grew rich and were wealthy enough to hire the German architect Heinrich Portscheller, who designed and constructed many of the towns' buildings for the wealthy merchants, including Pablo Ramirez and members of the Saenz families. He added a New Orleans flair with cast-iron balconies and molded bricks. Roma grew, survived an assault by the forces of Mexican warlord Juan Cortina in 1861, then endured the tumultuous Civil War years, when the town again became a smuggling center for the South. Trains replaced the steamboats, although the vessels continued to ply the Rio Grande until 1907, long after their heyday was over up north. The Ramirezes' store had three locations up until 1953, when Javier moved it to its current spot along Highway 83.

"There are lots of ghosts around here," Cecilia says. The most famous is a nanny who accidentally dropped a baby off one of the Portscheller-designed balconies. "People see her crying."

"The baby?"

"No, the nanny. She's so sad, you see, for what she did."

I want more details, but Noel Junior finally arrives.

"We were talking about ghosts," she says.

"Supposedly, the Burger King here is haunted," he adds.

Noel Junior wants to give me a tour of the town, so we walk up to the plaza. The entire neighborhood has been placed in the National Register of Historic Places. Most of the old buildings aren't occupied. Some on the side streets aren't doing well. They are eroding away. As I saw in San Ygnacio, the bricks are covered in a thin stucco veneer. Once the first layer comes off, they are exposed to the elements.

The Church of Our Lady of Refuge of Sinners is atop the plaza, as one would expect. Noel brings me to an overlook where I can see the Rio Grande emerging from the trees to the north after it has been released by the Falcon Dam. Directly across, Cuidad Miguel Alemán looks peaceful. The sound of dogs barking and roosters crowing carries over the waters.

To the south, a suspension bridge linking the two towns adds to the charm. It's also the perfect spot to make a run over the border. It's quiet now, but the river is shallow here, with plenty of cover for smugglers or those seeking a better way of life in the north. If the river-crossers can dodge the Border Patrol for a few blocks and hop into a car, they can blend in with the Highway 83 traffic.

We walk back to the plaza, where Noel takes me inside one of the old buildings he has just finished restoring. He has done a wonderful job. I can see he has an eye for detail. He plans on renting it out for weddings and other events. Its back door overlooks the river and the bridge.

The entire plaza was used as a backdrop for the movie ¡*Viva Zapata!*, which arrived in movie theaters about the same time Javier Ramirez moved the store to Highway 83. John Steinbeck penned the screenplay and Elia Kazan directed. He cast two young theater actors, Marlon Brando and Anthony Quinn, to play the revolutionaries Emiliano Zapata and his hotheaded brother Eufemio, who rebelled against the Diaz regime during the Mexican Revolution of 1910–1920. Brando at the time had only appeared in a non-starring part in one movie. He was well known on Broadway for playing Stanley Kowalski in *A Streetcar Named Desire*, but movie audiences knew little about him. Quinn had replaced Brando as Kowalski on Broadway and in a road version of the play. Kazan directed the film version of *Streetcar*, then cast Brando as the revolutionary. While ¡*Viva Zapata!* was being filmed, the movie version of *Streetcar* hit the screens, and Brando became a movie star overnight.

Kazan manipulated the pair into thinking they didn't like each other in order to create some dramatic tension. It worked. Quinn and Brando were at odds during the entire film shoot. Quinn, who was half Mexican, was a veteran of films and had been playing bit roles in movies for years, mostly as ethnic characters.

Before filming began, Brando traveled to Zapata's homeland south of Mexico City to learn the customs and mannerisms of the locals and to speak with some of those who knew the leader. While the producers cast mostly white actors, he insisted that the makeup artist at least attempt to make him look Mexican.

Adding to the tension were the conditions. Mexico had refused permission for Kazan to shoot the film in the country. Roma was the best they could do on short notice. Not wanting the studio to find an excuse to pull out of the film, the director began filming as soon as he could, which happened to be in the middle of summer. Most of the cast and crew stayed in a hotel in McAllen and had to make the fifty-five-mile trip on Highway 83 in un-airconditioned station wagons every morning, wearing their costumes. Even worse was when they shot a few scenes in San Ygnacio, which required even more travel.

The movie almost didn't get made. Anti-Communist sentiment was running high, and here was a movie based on a revolutionary land reformist. Zapata and Pancho Villa were two commanders leading a rebellion against the Diaz regime. Zapata's war took place south of Mexico City, but Roma's old buildings provided the perfect backdrop. In real life, Roma and all the towns in the Valley felt the spillover effects of the decade-long revolution. After Diaz was overthrown, the war degenerated into conflict between would-be military strongmen and their supporters, who often fled to Texas as refugees, or to stage attacks on their rivals. Violence spilled over from El Paso down to Brownsville and would serve to polarize the Anglo and Tejano communities.

Noel and I walk back to the store through the side streets, past crumbling old buildings. Being in the National Register of Historic places is no guarantee that the elements won't destroy some of these century-old buildings.

Before I depart, Noel Senior sends me off with a copy of the 1994 book, *A Shared Experience: The History, Architecture and Historic Designations of the Rio Grande Heritage Corridor*, compiled by the Texas Historical Commission. He was an advisor for the Roma section of the book. It will prove invaluable for my research.

There was one last stop I had to make in Roma: The haunted Burger King. As soon as I pull up I can see why the rumors started. It sits next to the town's oldest graveyard. I'm not hungry, but I could use a Coke. Inside, a tallish teenage Mexican-American gal greets me with a forced smile and takes my order. As I hand her a five-dollar bill, I broach the subject in a lighthearted way.

"I hear this place is haunted. Have you ever seen a ghost?"

Her smile suddenly disappears. She gives me an almost imperceptible nod but doesn't say a word. I see real fear in her eyes. I take my Coke and leave it at that.

Rio Grande City is every bit as charming as, if not a little busier than, Roma. The town rises from the banks of the river and climbs up to the hills overlooking the valley. Highway 83 splits into two one-way streets here, running as East Main to the southeast and West Second back to Laredo to the north. In between are stately historic buildings, some of which Portscheller designed.

It was at a spot near the present-day town where the Republic of the Rio Grande came to its end. Canales, the commander in chief of the army and driving force behind the hopeful republic, surrendered to General Arista here in November 1840.

"The Republic of the Rio Grande was dead, never again to be revived. It had lasted 283 violent, tumultuous days," wrote historian Jerry D. Thompson in the book Noel Senior had given me as a gift.

Unlike his comrade Zapata, Canales readily accepted Arista's terms and was soon appointed an officer in the centralist army. Overnight he became one of Santa Anna's most fiercely loyal officers and a tenacious foe to the fledgling Republic of Texas.

Rio Grande City has one sight that sets it apart, Fort Ringgold. I drive right past the fort several times before giving up and

Highway 83 Through Rio Grande City, 1948. LL Cook Company Collection. Prints and photographs collection. Texas State Library and Archives Commission.

phoning the museum for directions. The call instead goes to the local school district. It purchased the fort and its grounds from the federal government decades ago, a nice lady explains. The museum isn't open that day, but I can drive inside and see some of the buildings. The fort is found through a gate across from the Burger King, she tells me (again, a Burger King).

A friendly guard at the gate directs me to the main fort area and soon I'm parked beside the Robert E. Lee House, a one-story white home perched on an incline with a wraparound porch—a perfect spot to cool off on hot summer nights. The house has apparently been here about 155 years, and the soon-to-be commanding general of the Confederate States of America only occupied it for about two or three weeks in 1860 when he was a mere colonel, but that's long enough for it to be forever known as the Lee House.

Canales, Arista, Juan Cortina, Robert E. Lee, General John J. Pershing, and the Texas Ranger John Salmon "Rip" Ford are just a few of the names associated with Rio Grande City, or Rancho Davis, as the Mexicans called it.

The U.S. Army established the fort in 1848, and it stands as a reminder of the bloodshed here as Mexicans, Apaches, Anglos, Confederates, and Unionists fought for control of the Valley. The name Ringgold itself conjures up one of the most horrific battles in the history of the region, the Battle of Palo Alto, which took place just five miles west of present-day Highway 83 and just north of Brownsville.

It could be said that Major Samuel Ringgold literally wrote the book on Army artillery, or at least rewrote it. A West Point graduate and the son of a Maryland congressman, he had an idea for what he called "flying artillery." Instead of large, cumbersome cannons, he would take lighter cannons and make them more mobile. He trained the men under his command to quickly move the artillery pieces and ammunition around the battlefield as needed.

The inauguration of President James K. Polk in 1845 set in motion the war that would ultimately bring the Rio Grande Valley, and the entire Southwest, under the control of the United States. Running on a platform that embraced Manifest Destiny—the belief that God intended white men to occupy America from sea to shining sea—Polk wasted little time implementing what many believed was the plan all along for the Republic of Texas, which was for it to be annexed by the United States. Mexico, along with many Americans, opposed the plan. Mexico believed it had a deal in place with the Texans for the republic to remain independent. Pacifists, and especially abolitionists, didn't want to see a war. Texas would be admitted to the Union as a slave state. But Polk believed his election was a mandate. The deal to admit Texas was in place by the end of the year. Polk dispatched General Zachary Taylor to the lands between the Neuces and Rio Grande Rivers to provoke Mexico. The Nueces Strip had been in dispute for the ten years of the republic's existence. Mexico had never relinquished its claims, so from its leaders' point of view, U.S. troops were on Mexican soil. Taylor and his Army, which included a young Lieutenant Ulysses S. Grant and Major Ringgold, landed in Corpus Christi then traveled by land to the bank north of Matamoros, where, on March 28, 1846, they raised the U.S. flag for all the Mexicans on the other side to see. Taylor established Fort Texas where Brownsville sits today. The Americans spent several weeks giving General Arista and his troops the stinkeye from across the river as both sides fortified their positions for the fight to come. It was never a matter of if, but when and where.

Both Arista and Taylor dispatched companies into the brush to report on each other's movements. On April 24, Polk and Taylor got what they wanted. A force of 500 Mexicans attacked two of Taylor's companies north of Matamoros, causing more than sixty U.S. casualties. American blood had been shed on American soil, Polk said. He could now declare war. The ultimate prize wouldn't be this borderland backwater, but all the lands to the west, including California.

Word reached Taylor that Point Isabel, a spot at the river's mouth where his supply ships unloaded, was under attack. He departed with 2,200 men to defend it, but after a thirty-six hour march the Army discovered that the attack was a rumor, or perhaps deliberately planted misinformation. Indeed, the morning after the force arrived there, the bombardment on Fort Texas began. The rumbling cannon fire reached Taylor's ears some twenty-six miles away. He was in the wrong place at the wrong time, and Fort Texas had only 500 men to defend it.

Taylor gathered up his men, loaded up a wagon train with new supplies, and ordered everyone to march back. It was on a wide, flat meadow on the road back to Matamoros where Arista revealed his plan. Taylor found the chessboard all set up as the column waded into the shoulder-high grass near a watering hole surrounded by towering trees. The Mexican general had spread out his 3,200-man infantry, dragoons, and artillery in a mile-long line he dared Taylor to break. The sun was directly overhead and the humidity unbearable.

"They stood ready to receive us. . . their horses neighing, pennons fluttering, and music playing," one American junior officer wrote in his memoir.

Taylor immediately dispatched Ringgold and his flying artillery to his right flank as his troops formed its own battle array. Seven hundred yards separated the two lines, but Arista had at least a thousand more men than Taylor.

The Mexican general rode down the length of his line shouting "liberty or death" before giving the final order for the cannons to fire their first volleys.

General Taylor, sitting atop his white horse, concluded that the Mexican line was drawn so thin that a bayonet charge would be ineffective. He watched as the large Mexican cannons in their fixed positions failed to hit their targets. Some of cannon balls rolled harmlessly at the U.S. troops' feet.

Meanwhile, Ringgold's previously untested artillery tactics were tearing holes in Arista's lines. In addition to the light artillery, Taylor had brought several eighteen-pounders. For every Mexican artillery volley, the Americans were firing four. The cannon balls stuffed with grapeshot ripped into man and horseflesh. One slammed into Arista's band, stopping the inspirational music for good.

Arista, despite witnessing the destruction being visited upon his men, put into action his original plan, which was to outflank the Americans on both sides. He sent his best cavalry officer and two four-pounder cannons to his left flank. As the Mexicans' artillery got bogged down in mud, the American infantry set up a line along with two of Ringgold's light cannons. The horsemen were met with devastating musket fire, and just as one of the Mexican cannons was about to be lit, one of the flying artillery pieces scored a direct hit, wrecking the four-pounder and killing everyone near it.

A prairie fire set off by the explosions sent a gray smoke over the battlefield, and burned to death any wounded man unable to remove himself from its path. The wounded cried out for water as the sun took its own toll.

When the smoke cleared the fight continued, although it remained mostly an artillery duel. The Mexicans, while they

"Death of Major Ringgold." Engraving by G. White. Undated. Prints and photographs collection. Texas State Library and Archives Commission.

couldn't match the frequency and mobility of the U.S. cannons, grew more accurate with their fire as the battle wore on.

Arista surmised that the day was lost and ordered a retreat. One of the final Mexican volleys tore into Major Ringgold and his horse, nearly taking off his legs. The man whose tactics helped win the day fell to the ground mortally wounded. He was the first officer killed in action during the Mexican-American War.

Another historic name associated with Fort Ringgold is the legendary John Salmon Ford, better known as "Rip" Ford. He was perhaps the most famous Texas Ranger in the institution's first eighty years of existence, although he was much more than that—lawmaker, doctor, explorer, newspaper publisher, Confederate colonel. Ford wore many hats.

He arrived in the republic from Tennessee a few months too late to participate in the Texas Revolution, but he had his hand in every major conflict that took place between the Neuces and Rio Grande thereafter.

He was a medical doctor by training, and served in the Texas army. After being elected to the legislature, he became a strong advocate for annexation to the United States. He would have the opportunity to help make that happen when he served in the Second Regiment of Texas Mounted Rifles as an adjutant and medical officer in the Mexican-American War.

As the U.S. Army drove deeper into Mexico, it was his duty to draw up the list of those who lost their lives. He wrote "Rest in Peace" after every name. As the casualties mounted, he was began abbreviating "R.I.P." Soon, the men began calling him "Old Rip."

He joined the rangers back when they were more of a state militia than a law enforcement agency. Most of the men who signed up were a rough and tumble lot. But he believed in discipline and training. Men under his command were expected to take part in drills. This professional approach to soldiering paid off with many high-profile victories against the Comanches, and soon he became a favorite of governors who called upon him time and time again whenever trouble broke out, especially in the wild borderlands along the Rio Grande. And he was intimately familiar with Ringgold Barracks and Rio Grande City.

A few years before the Civil War, a wealthy Mexican rancher Juan Cortina put together a private army and fought a series of battles against Texas and the U.S. government along the Rio Grande. Cortina despised Americans and resented the annexation of Mexican territory after the Mexican-American War ended in 1848.

The Treaty of Guadalupe Hidalgo guaranteed that the land claims of Mexican landowners would be honored, but in reality, there were many Anglos ready and willing to take advantage of the situation. If the Tejanos didn't have the proper documentation to prove their claims, there were men willing to use the legal system to snatch the land away from them. A group of well-connected judges and lawyers in Brownsville conspired to wrest land away

Colonel John Salmon "Rip" Ford, circa 1865.

from the Mexican aristocracy and had managed to grab some of Cortina's mother's ranch six miles upriver from the town.

Cortina became a folk hero after he witnessed a white city marshal brutalizing a Mexican in the town of Brownsville. Cortina shot the officer in the shoulder and rode away with the victim. Ten weeks later, he returned with a force of sixty men and shot up the town, seeking the lawyers and judges who were defrauding the Tejanos. Most escaped, although two on his hit list lost their lives. Federal troops had only recently abandoned the newly named Fort Brown, leaving the region without any protection. Cortina occupied the town for several days.

Cortina inspired downtrodden Mexicans and Tejanos to join his army, which was based at his ranch on the U.S. side. They repulsed a militia formed of men from Brownsville, and then beat back a company of ill-trained and poorly equipped Texas Rangers.

In the wake of these defeats, the governor called on Ford to take care of Cortina. By December, he was leading a well disciplined company of fifty-three rangers along with a force of some 120 federal troops. The combined army pushed Cortina up the river, as he robbed and looted along the way.

The two forces clashed at Rio Grande City on December 27, 1859. It began when Ford's cavalry charged into a heavy fog and cut a swath into Cortina's defenses. Unfortunately, the commander of the U.S. troops didn't know this, and Ford's men initially were on their own. Soon enough, the U.S. Army joined the fray, and Cortina was in retreat. They chased him all the way to Roma before what remained of his army fled into Mexico.

It was shortly after this battle when Lee and a contingent of U.S. troops arrived at Fort Ringgold to help pacify the region. He succeeded, although it would not be the last time Texans had to contend with Cortina.

The Protegé idles at a stoplight at the town of Palmview.

Ahead of me is the ramp to Expressway 83 to the right Business 83. Tourism promoters once called the old highway the "Longest Main Street in America." There are still some locals who call the old highway "Main Street." There is no question as to which way I will initially drive.

I plan on spending two days exploring these towns. I will make a short detour to see the Museum of South Texas History in Edinburg, probably spend several hours doing research in local libraries, and I definitely plan on stopping at the last drive-in movie theater on Highway 83 at Mercedes.

There were about 300,000 residents living here when the finishing touches were put on the Expressway in the late 1960s. The Valley is today one of the fastest-growing regions in the United States. The 1,300 families Escandón settled in the region has swelled to 1.5 million people living in Laredo and the five counties that Highway 83 passes through on its way to Brownsville. That comes to 10 million when adding the twins in Mexico. The part of my trip that featured long, lonely stretches of highway is over. My friend the turkey buzzard is gone. I will probably not see him again.

Palmview, Mission, Pharr, San Juan, McAllen, Alamo, Donna, Weslaco, Mercedes, La Feria, Harlingen, San Benito, Rancho Viejo: the chain of towns ahead of me didn't exist before 1904. How they popped up almost overnight and transformed the region is a story seldom told.

The light turns green as I begin the last leg of my long journey.

One of the most pleasurable parts of traveling in the Lower Rio Grande Valley on old 83 is the hand-painted buildings that serve as signs. When a new business opens, the owner doesn't call a sign company—he calls a painter, who transforms the stucco exteriors into a giant advertisement. A yellow-orange piñata store in Mission festooned with cartoon characters is one spot where I pull over to take a picture. This expertise translates to mural painting, and the block-long homage to the town's favorite son, Tom Landry, takes him from his days as a star quarterback on the Mission High School team through college and onto fame as the Dallas Cowboys head coach. Business 83 as it splits into a one-way street going north is named after him.

Mission quickly melds into Pharr. Collision 83 Autoparts is another must-stop to take a picture, and then I find one of the most extreme examples, the VFW Post in Pharr. The whole building is painted as an American flag. There is a for sale sign in the window, so I wonder how long this stunning work of folk art will remain before it is painted over, or the whole building is knocked down.

I have lunch at the appropriately named Junction Café, which sits at the corner of U.S. Highways 83 and 281. The

building has been here since the town was founded, first as a grocery store and now a restaurant. When the American Association of State Highway Officials came up with the numbered highway system in 1926, three-numbered roads were meant to be of less importance. For example, 183 was of less importance than 83 and therefore less deserving of funding allocations. Therefore, Highways 283 and 383 were given an even lower priority. But here is 281, which has grown into a vital way north for the residents of the valley. It takes travelers straight up to San Antonio.

A look at the map shows that the Valley got the short shrift in 1956 when the Eisenhower Interstate System was created. The closest four-laner is I-35 connecting Laredo to San Antonio. The only other major road north other than 281 is U.S. Highway 77, which takes drivers to Corpus Christi. Valley residents have been clamoring for an interstate to end their isolation for decades, but their calls have gone unanswered.

On the Great Plains, there are towns so tiny they say "if you blink, you'll miss 'em." Here, if you blink, you will miss the "Welcome to" sign. As I drive, Pharr has melded into San Juan, which I didn't realize until I pull over at the San Juan Hotel. I spot a familiar Texas Historical Commission plate in front and pull over to investigate. The hotel is two stories, a block long, constructed in the Spanish revival style, and appears to be in good shape even though it is empty. It's reportedly one of the oldest buildings in the Valley, and it joins dozens of other abandoned, forlorn hotels I have come across in my travels on 83 that are too beautiful to tear down. Attempting to do so garners the wrath of preservationists. Yet no one has the deep pockets to restore them to their former glory. Some are refurbished as offices or apartments. The San Juan awaits its fate.

Normally when there's a historical marker next to a grand old hotel, it's there to explain a bit about the building. Surprisingly, the marker is actually about one of its residents, the legendary lawman Tom Mayfield, who spent his twilight years here as a full-time resident, living free rent in exchange for keeping an eye on things. The marker alludes to his most famous arrest.

PLAN DE SAN DIEGO

Tom Mayfield and the customs inspector found the man they had been waiting for, Basilio Ramos Jr., on the steps of a general store in McAllen on a cool January day in 1915. Standing six-foot-three, slim, with deep brown eyes and jet black hair, the Hidalgo County deputy sheriff looked down at the Mexican with suspicion. Mayfield had already served fourteen years as a lawman in the area, and as such, he knew who the outsiders were. He could look a man in the eye and see if he were up to no good. He also had an advantage afforded few other peace officers in the Valley: he spoke and read Spanish fluently, a skill he had picked up from the laborers on his parents' cotton farm in Gonzalez County.

He arrived in the Valley at the turn of the century as a stagecoach conductor and guard, just as the St. Louis, Brownsville and Mexico Railway was making its way south to connect the isolated region with the rest of the nation. He then hired on as the manager of a plantation where the town of San Juan now sits. He married a teacher, Denley Edwards, and began to raise a family. His ability to handle a gun, coupled with his Spanish fluency, caught the attention of the local sheriff, who convinced him to change careers.

Early on, he was called in to investigate an unusual occurrence. Two of the new horseless carriages had somehow managed to run into each other. It was the first recorded traffic accident between two automobiles in the Valley.

Meanwhile, there was plenty of intrigue, and reasons to be suspicious of outsiders. The Mexican Revolution was underway, and the violence already spilling over the border as Pancho Villa stirred up trouble. Mayfield was among those in the Valley who believed that there was more to the story. He had traveled to Detroit the year before to testify before a commission and to present evidence he had gathered suggesting that German agents were behind the scenes. He brought German-made weapons, ammunition, and other intriguing items he had found on the persons of Mexican soldiers and bandits. Germany was in the middle of a war in Europe but seemed to be cultivating friends and allies in Mexico. But to what end?

After asking a few questions, Mayfield searched Ramos's valise and found some loose papers. A quick read of the pages confirmed that the man was more than he claimed to be.

Basilio Ramos Jr., whose family name was actually Garcia, was a twenty-four-year-old supporter of General Victoriano Huerta, whose supporters had only enjoyed a year in power before the would-be strong man was ousted by the government of José Carranza. Huerta and his supporters had no love for the United States, which had refused to recognize and support the general. The same year Huerta got on a boat to Jamaica to escape his enemies, Garcia slipped over the border to flee political persecution. He wound up working in San Diego, a small town about 100 miles north of the Valley, at a brewery with some fellow Hueristas. After work, the young men plotted another revolution, but this one would take place north of the border. Life north of the Rio Grande for Mexicans and Tejanos was now one of political repression. Most of the old Mexican families—the descendants of Escandón's settlers—had lost their land, and therefore their power, within a couple of short years. Land prices grew so quickly, they couldn't pay the taxes and were evicted from their properties. The time was right to start a new revolution here in Texas.

After compiling some debt he couldn't pay, Garcia fled San Diego and returned to Mexico. That was a big mistake. He was promptly arrested for being a Huerta supporter and tossed into a

Monterrey prison. It was there where he refined the idea. He and some other inmates composed the "Plan de San Diego," a fifteen-point manifesto.

Garcia escaped prison with a copy of the plan in his pocket and made his way back over the border to implement it. To gather support, he had to share it with possible supporters. At least one of them was alarmed enough by its contents to tip off the customs inspector, who in turn told Mayfield. The informant arranged a meeting with Garcia at the store.

Mayfield took a quick look at the document, which was signed by eight men. In brief, it called for the extermination of all "North Americans" over the age of sixteen in Southern Texas, New Mexico, Colorado, Arizona, and California, and the creation of independent, racially pure states populated by Mexicans, blacks, and Indians. Native Americans would have their lands returned. Blacks would select six states to populate and serve as a buffer between the Anglos and the newly independent republic.

On February 20, 1915, at 2 p.m., the slaughter would begin.

Mayfield took Garcia to jail in the nearby town of Edinburg. He was later transferred to Brownsville and held under a $5,000 bond. The news garnered little interest at first; the notice of the arrest appeared in a few Texas newspapers, but it was not even the top story. A judge in Brownsville lowered Garcia's bond to $100 and said he was more in need of a doctor—to have his head examined—than anything. It was, after all, a preposterous plan. Garcia, a.k.a. Ramos, promptly skipped out on his bail, crossed the Rio Grande, was not seen nor heard from again.

But the document he left behind would serve as a ticking time bomb.

I've spent the day exploring Business 83, so now it's time to experience the expressway. It's night and I'm not stopping to take any pictures, so I go with the flow of the local traffic, which is moving at a breakneck speed. "Breakneck." It's a cliché, and I know it, but it fits here because everyone is traveling at least ten miles beyond the already liberal speed limit. If I crash on the expressway, I will in all likelihood break my neck and many other bones.

The expressway is a necessary evil, and despite my misgivings about interstates in general, I can see why work began on building it in the late 1950s. It was obvious by then that the Valley's population—along with truck traffic associated with border trade—was booming. Without a new road, Highway 83 and the surrounding through-streets would be parking lots. "The Longest Main Street in America" sounded quaint in the tourist brochures, but the road had one of the highest traffic accident death rates in the state. The Texas legislature allocated the money for two expressways, one traveling north from Brownsville and the other going east and west from McAllen to Harlingen. The towns squabbled over its route. It seemed no matter where its proposed path went, there was an old cemetery in the way, or strong opposition from citizens. Some wanted it north of U.S. Route 83 and some south. Eventually, it would swoop south of Business 83 in Mission and McAllen to pass near the airport, then go north of the legacy road after Pharr.

The real estate agents had a field day—literally. The citrus growers and onion farmers who owned fields near the new road cashed in as the new expressway transformed where residents did business. The expressway's construction coincided with the advent of shopping malls and chain stores. The forty-six mile stretch from Mission to Harlingen was mostly completed by 1964, although the interchange connecting it to the Brownsville-Harlingen 83-77 expressway wasn't finished until 1971.

The expressway lifts up to climb over the main thoroughfares where the national chain stores and restaurants are clustered. The glowing plastic business signs on either side of me are perched on tall poles to ensure they are seen, like eager students with their hands up, begging to picked: MacDonald's, Pizza Hut, Luby's,

Cracker Barrel Old Country Store, Target, Office Depot, Whataburger, CVS, Walmart Supercenter, Taco Palenque, Taco Bell, Taco Bueno, car dealerships of every make, motels: La Quinta, Best Western, then repeat. It's all nationally affiliated or regional chains here with the occasional suggestive name that denotes a strip bar. Billboards fill in the empty spaces to urge consumers to pull into the next exit. After driving as far as La Feria, I turn back to McAllen and begin searching for a place to eat supper.

fotos & facts about **McALLEN** **TEXAS**

EARLY ORANGES

IN THE LOWER RIO GRANDE VALLEY

● CITRUS FRUIT
● VEGETABLES
● COTTON
● OIL
● TOURISTS

McALLEN is a soundly growing city of about 30,000 contented, reasonably prosperous people.

Cover of a tourist brochure, late 1950s

I have reached a point where I can't look at another burrito, and a complimentary basket of chips with salsa has lost its charm. My diet has consisted of breakfast food, Mexican food, burgers, and the occasional Asian buffet ever since I left Interstate 70 two weeks ago. And so I exit at a promising-looking commercial strip in McAllen and start hunting for something different. I do not want to eat at a chain restaurant, so my search continues for quite some time among the strip malls and standalone fast-food and casual dining restaurants. No chain. No Mexican. No Chinese. With these criteria, I may starve in this land of plenty.

Suddenly, sushi!

It's tucked away in a strip mall, along with the usual collection of businesses. I wasn't looking for it. I didn't expect it. But now that I have found it, that sounds pretty good. And although I have been traveling on the cheap, I think I'm ready to splurge on a big plate of raw fish.

Inside, the shop is clean, nicely decorated with somber colors and dim lights. The waiter takes my order, a whopping thirty-six piece sashimi-sushi combo, hold the octopus, I tell him. I see the chef at his station begin to put my order together as the waiter brings me a bowl of miso soup. I think I know decent sushi when I taste it—I lived in Japan on and off for five years—so the chef will have to impress me.

And then something happens that really shakes me up. A black man walks in. He ordered ahead, apparently. He pays the cashier, takes his bag, and leaves. Wow. A black person. I don't think I have seen a black person since ... Abilene? And then it dawns on me. The whole restaurant staff is Latino. The waiters, the chef. The other customers. I try to think back to the last time I saw another white person. It was Jack Cox, back at the fishing camp. I'm the oddity here!

My daily life back home is racially diverse: my office is populated by whites, blacks, Asians, Persians, and that is normal in Arlington, Virginia, and the greater Washington, D.C., area. It probably should be more surprising when I suddenly find myself in a racially monolithic area. Maybe it wasn't jarring because the change was gradual. Garden City and Liberal, Kansas, were the first two towns with noticeable populations of Latinos. The Texas Panhandle towns, each had a sizeable minority, but most folks I encountered were white. By Uvalde, it was nearly fifty-fifty, and then Crystal City, all Tejano. Ever since Angel Gutiérrez's hometown, just about everyone I have encountered has been Mexican-American. The Lower Rio Grand Valley is truly a region like no other in Texas, and Highway 83 is the ribbon of asphalt that connects it to the rest of the state.

I remember back at the beginning of the trip when I stopped by the *Perryton Herald* and met its publisher Jim Hudson. He invited me into his office to chat about my project. He was the quintessential newspaperman, with a paunch from too many years sitting behind typewriters, then computers, notes and papers spread out along his desk along with a full ashtray. He was among the first to warn me about traveling in the Valley. But he also sang the praises of 83. He printed out a copy of an editorial he had written for the August 16, 2009 edition, "83 turns 83." He repeats a story that was also in the article.

"One time I was leading a Panhandle Day delegation at the Capitol in Austin. Our job was to talk issues with a selected group of state representatives.

On my list was a Democrat legislator from the Valley. As I was walking to his office the only thought in my mind was, 'What in the world will a gringo, Republican from the Panhandle find to talk about with a Hispanic, Democrat from the southern border of Texas?'

After the introductions, we discussed a few areas then settled on highway funding. 'What is the major highway in your county?' the legislator asked.

'U.S. 83,' was my reply.

With that answer, the legislator and I became fast friends. We talked about how the highway department in Austin just ignored the far ends of U.S. 83. At the end we were both pounding his desk cussing and discussing the failings of the highway bureaucracy."

A highway can bring people together, Hudson wrote. It connects two very different parts of this great state. And that is perhaps the best thing about U.S. Route 83 in Texas. Its potential is much more than an efficient conveyance of travelers and goods. It can bring together two peoples, who have an oftentimes anguished, but shared, history.

The combination sushi-sashimi plate comes out, and I dig in. Lower Rio Grande Valley sushi is not bad. No doubt I will be back to burgers and burritos tomorrow.

McAllen looks like a city. Maybe because its skyline as seen from Business 83 features two "skyscrapers," the Chase Texas Tower and the Bentsen Tower. Highway 83 here has a tropical vibe, as palm trees line its sidewalks. I take a right and drive into the dense downtown. I spend an hour walking its streets, shopping for a gift for my wife, knowing that my trip would soon be coming to an end. As in many central business districts, its tree-lined blocks are a mixed bag architecturally, with tiny open-air hamburger stands in the shadows of the towering buildings, coin-operated parking meters, and businesses that are hanging on here despite the malls out on the expressway. I encounter only a handful of fellow shoppers.

From 1790 to 1904, the land I'm standing on—the Santa Anita land grant—belonged to the same family. The ranch they began eight generations ago is still in operation beyond the urban sprawl and onion fields in the northern part of the county. In 1916, when James B. McAllen, the son of the man for whom this town was named, died relatively young at age fifty-four, much of the family lore and stories went with him. His widow knew almost nothing about the family she had married into, and his children were too young to have remembered much.

Years later, one of James B. McAllen's daughters, Margaret, took it upon herself to piece together the 200-year-long story of the land grant using a box of old papers and photos she inherited after her mother's death. In an old ranch house, another family treasure was uncovered. Unbeknownst to anyone, John McAllen, the Irish-Scotch immigrant who had married into the Mexican family, had written a memoir of his early life. While Margaret was unable to finish her work, her daughter, Mary Margaret McAllen Amberson, with a master's degree in history in hand, completed the task, publishing, in 2003, *I Would Rather Sleep in Texas: A History of the Lower Rio Grande Valley and the People of the Santa Anita Land Grant*.

In it, she wrote of her grandmother, who knew so little of the family history.

"In some ways, the same story is true for many of the Valley's inhabitants who are not aware of the secrets the landscape conceals. The Rio Grande's now tranquil, dam-controlled waters belie its tumultuous and fascinating history."

MCALLEN

John McAllen had spent eight months sharing an open-air courtyard with dozens of other prisoners, languishing in the filth of a makeshift Mexican jail in Matamoros, awaiting his fate.

He was twenty-one years old, a Scotsman who had fled the devastating potato famine in Ireland, where he was born. He was six feet tall, with dark hair and vivid blue eyes, and rail-thin. After months in captivity, he was wasting away. He had escaped the prison of indentured servitude in the Old World only to find himself in a literal prison two years later.

English landowners had brought his forefathers to Ireland to work as tenant farmers. Always in debt to their masters, the Scots in Ireland were the poorest of the poor. His parents died when he was a small boy, but when he was nineteen and the blight was causing mass starvation, the uncle who raised him gave him the small fortune needed to book passage on a ship to America. He had broken loose of the economic chains.

It was a rainy June day when the Mexican soldiers and a marching band came to the courtyard. The federalist troops forced the prisoners into wagons as the band struck up a death march. If they didn't know already, the somber music should have revealed what was to come: they were going to be executed for taking part in an ill-fated rebellion. The prisoners, a mix of Mexicans, Americans, and recent immigrants such as McAllen, were paraded through the city streets as the citizens silently watched them pass by, the men doffing their caps in respect.

McAllen had always maintained his innocence. He had been convicted of taking part in the insurrection after a dozen Mexican officers testified that they had seen him taking part in the fighting, but he had yet to be sentenced. He had written the British consul in town for help, but to no avail.

Soon the wagons left the walled city and arrived in a muddy, untilled field. The Mexican general in charge of the city's defense, Francisco Avalos, was there. A short, vindictive man, he had ignored all pleas for mercy and was determined to go ahead with the executions. When the wagons stopped, the soldiers separated the prisoners into two groups. The unsentenced, such as McAllen, were placed alongside the convicted. It was an act of apparent cruelty to put McAllen and the others next to the doomed men. Avalos lined up the firing squad in such a manner that it appeared that both groups would be executed. The music stopped, and the general screamed "Fire!"

For eons, the river was just a river and not a border. That was still the case for the people Escandón left behind, who lived north and south of its banks. Like that of many pioneers, life was tough and unforgiving. It was subsistence living at first. Settlers raised cattle and sheep, grew beans and a few vegetables such as corn and squash in small gardens. They hunted game, fished, gathered mesquite beans, all while keeping a wary eye out for Apaches, Comanches, and a dozen smaller Indian nations, some friendly, others not. Those who lived on the settlements' outskirts bore the brunt of the attacks. Meanwhile, the townspeople were expected to fend for themselves as the thinly spread Spanish army was sent north to expand Spain's sphere of influence in spots such as the Presidio at San Sabá.

The well-to-do built nicer homes in the town centers where it was safer, while others in the outskirts settled for adobe and thatched roofs. The friendlier, sedentary Indians, numbering about 14,000 when Escandón arrived, helped the colonists learn about local flora and fauna. Within a few generations, though, their cultures and languages had all but vanished. They had either died of disease, been captured as slaves by the Comanches, or intermarried with the Spanish.

Escandón, after he declared his work completed in 1755, actually left a mess behind in New Santander. Many came expecting land grants, but he left that task for others to sort out. It was not an easy process. It involved officials coming to conduct a survey of the property to ensure that the settler had made the proper investments, compiling a detailed list of assets and measurements, and marking boundaries. Those who wanted a land grant had to pay for all this, so only the wealthy could afford it. Other families gained their land through connections to the royal family or by performing some service. Escandón's original vision was to leave the bluebloods and privileged behind because he didn't think they had what it took to survive in this rough frontier. But a class system did develop. Soon three main clans emerged—the Ballís, the Hinojosas, and the De la Garzas. The families intermarried, making them wealthier and more powerful.

Reynosa, which sits across from present-day McAllen, was the region's center. The well-to-do preferred to stay in the bigger town and let their workers maintain the ranches north of the river.

One settler who endured the application process was José Manuel Gomez, who arrived as a relatively wealthy merchant in 1777. He married a widow with two sons from the Ballí family. He applied for his grant in 1790 but didn't receive the paperwork proving that the land was his until November 27, 1801. Until that point, the land was his to work on, but it still belonged to the crown. It was no ordinary day. The signing of the paperwork was a cause of ceremony and celebration. A big fiesta was in order.

Gomez and his descendents would own a plot known as the Santa Anita land grant across from Reynosa. But Gomez didn't live long. He died two years later, and the land would eventually go to his stepsons. Also not lasting much longer was Spanish rule over Mexico. By 1821, Mexico was an independent nation.

In the years leading up to the Mexican-American War, European and American entrepreneurs flooded the town of Matamoros to take advantage of its vitally important spot at the mouth of the Rio Grande. Goods coming by steamship had to be distributed upriver or taken overland into Mexico. The merchants grew rich, and unrest only served to bolster their profits, as they shipped guns and ammunition south. Wool, cowhides and bones, and later cotton, left on these ships as they returned north.

One of these merchants was a rapacious businessman named John Young, who seemed bent on buying up every piece of property between the Rio Grande and Neuces Rivers that became available, as well as businesses and steamboats. He had his hand in about everything.

After the Mexican-American War, those who held land grants north of the Rio Grande had a choice: remain there and become citizens of the United States, or pack up their possessions and move south. Those of Mexican decent who remained became known as Tejanos.

The Ballí-De la Garza family living on the Santa Anita land grant chose to stay put. Salomé Ballí de la Garza was a woman of vision. At age twenty-five she married the fifty-one year-old John Young at the behest of her father, who insisted that his daughters marry into this new wave of European and American traders. Salomé proved every bit as adept as her husband in acquiring land. Even before the marriage, she had set her sights on the Santa Anita land grant, which by that time had already been subdivided among several heirs. And with her husband's purchasing power, she managed to bring almost all of the property back under her ownership. Spanish custom and law allowed women equal property rights, so powerful matriarchs such as Salomé emerged along the borderlands.

Meanwhile, seeking the protection of the United States, the Anglo and European businessmen of Matamoros founded the town of Brownsville across the river. Another motivation was to escape the outlandishly high tariffs Mexico was imposing on goods flowing into the republic. Even though the merchants grew rich off smuggling, they went so far as to start their own conflict in hopes of wresting control of the territory from Mexico. They bankrolled the so-called Merchants War, which found a Mexican sympathizer, one José Maria Jésus Carvajal, who formed a small army of Mexicans and Anglos and started raiding centralist posts in Northern Mexico. The San Antonio–born self-proclaimed general fancied himself the George Washington of his people. It was called a second attempt at a Republic of the Rio Grande. And like the first effort, this one also involved the mercurial General Antonio Canales, but this time with his brother José. Both were leading their own armies. Canales had pledged his allegiance to the centralist cause during the Mexican-American War, but here he was again in the federalist camp. Two of his sons were serving as lieutenants for Carvajal. Also throwing his weight behind the cause was Colonel Rip Ford, who came with thirty well-armed and well-trained rangers. The merchants began a propaganda campaign, called Carvajal a visionary, and sent his army over the border. Starting in Guerrero, the Anglos, Tejanos, and Mexicans swept down the Valley, liberating the border towns from the tyranny of Mexico's sparsely staffed customhouses. To the joy of the merchants, the goods began flowing south again, without the onerous taxes.

But Matamoros was another matter. Walled, well defended, and strategically important, Matamoros had to be conquered for the alliance to succeed. The conflict was a nine-day battle and a bloodbath. General Avalos put up a strong defense, demonstrating no qualms about using his cannons inside the city despite the civilians living there. Carvajal fought to a stalemate as he and Ford waited for reinforcements. They believed that Canales and the 1,000 men under his command were on their way.

Canales was actually not far from the city, waiting to see which way the wind blew. After Carvajal floundered, Canales declared himself a centralist again, and helped Avalos send the merchants' army packing.

John McAllen landed in New York at a time when the city was choking on Irish refugees. He spent one year there and another working as a laborer in Boston before signing on as a cabin boy and cook on merchant ships. In 1849 he quit life on the sea to make his way to California, where the Gold Rush was luring in young men such as himself. He found himself in Matamoros in the tumultuous years shortly after the Mexican-American War. He spent his savings to equip himself for the long overland journey through Mexico to California. This route was not only shorter, but would hopefully be southerly enough to avoid Apaches and other hostile Indians. McAllen joined a mule train and left the border town dreaming of riches. It wasn't Indians who foiled him, but centralist Mexican troops. They stopped the train and confiscated the mules and equipment. They probably didn't have the right to do so, but the result was the same: McAllen was left bereft.

Back in Matamoros, he found work as a clerk for one of the wealthy traders. He was definitely in the wrong place at the wrong time when the Merchants War broke out. As soon as the smoke began to clear, Avalos's men began rounding up and imprisoning any white face they could find. McAllen was caught in the dragnet and sent to the makeshift jail, where he was sure he would soon be released. Eight months later, when he was shoved in the wagon to be taken to the muddy field, he thought this was the end of the road.

The firing squad cut down the twelve convicted men, but that was all for the day. McAllen and the others were taken to a regular prison, where he was placed alone in a cell. He was there for another year and three months until the opportunity to escape presented itself. He slipped out of the walled city and swam the Rio Grande to Brownsville and freedom.

McAllen stayed in Brownsville and eventually landed a job as a clerk with John Young, who took McAllen under his wing. He worked for him for seven years, all the while growing closer to the Ballí family. He eventually saved enough money to buy a small parcel of land north of the river. The orphan born into indentured servitude was now a landowner.

Young died at age fifty-seven, leaving his thirty-year-old widow Salomé half of his vast holdings and his five-year-old son the other half. She named McAllen manager of the Brownsville-Matamoros businesses, as she continued to buy out her relatives and neighbors' properties. Two years later, in 1861, shortly before the Civil War began and after an appropriate mourning period, Solomé married McAllen, and they settled in Brownsville. A year later she gave birth to McAllen's first child, James.

Neither McAllen, who had been born into de facto slavery, nor Salomé, wanted to sign the loyalty oath the Confederacy demanded, so they, along with many other

John McAllen and Salomé Ballí de la Garza

Brownsville merchants, moved back to Matamoros during the Civil War. And while they did not support the South's pro-slavery agenda, they were happy to help move the Confederacy's cotton over the river to avoid northern blockades. The border town merchants made immense profits during the war. McAllen grew and ginned his own cotton, cutting out the middlemen and maximizing his profits. He then became a pioneer in growing sugar cane. He was also the first to bring modern ranching practices—including barbed wire—to the Valley. The price of cotton, meanwhile, soared, as the South depended on the commodity to fund the war. For the next forty years the couple continued to prosper, the only major change being John Young Jr. taking possession of his half of his father's properties after coming of age.

By the turn of the twentieth century, the Lower Rio Grande Valley remained a remote and insular part of the United States. The descendants of those Escandón relocated lived as workers on ranches, in cities like Laredo, or in small towns like Rio Grande City or Roma. Some of the old families still had the property in their family. Anglos, and immigrants such as McAllen, married into Mexican-American families. They were Catholic—or converted—and their mixed-culture children married whomever they liked, and no one thought much about it. They raised cattle, sheep, and horses, as the land between the rivers remained much like it had when the Spanish came in 1749.

Then irrigation came. Then the railroad came. And it all changed in a few short years.

Except for a few settlements with a few dozen families, there were no major towns between Rio Grande City and Brownsville north of the river. Then the Hidalgo Irrigation Company, with its steam-powered engines, found an efficient way to suck the water out of the Rio Grande and spread it over the former ranchlands, which were once considered good for nothing but cattle and sheep.

The St. Louis, Brownsville and Mexico Railway extended its reach into the valley in 1904, creating the whistlestops San Benito and Olmito along the way. A spur made its way west along the river. Outsiders came by train, and land speculators grew rich selling them newly subdivided farmlands.

Half brothers James B. McAllen and John Young Jr., along with some other business partners, formed the McAllen Township Company in 1904 and platted out a town on a portion of the former Santa Anita land grant. They named it after their father, who by then was in semi-retirement living in Brownsville and spending more of his time in his garden. He would pass away at age eighty-seven on February 13, 1913.

As the railroad extension moved west, towns popped up alongside its tracks amongst the scrub brush and cacti: La Feria, Mercedes, Weslaco, Donna, Alamo, San Juan, Pharr, McAllen, Mission, and Mamie, later known as Palmview, all were founded around the same time, about 1907. The ranches were bought up and subdivided into plots. The Rio Grande was sucked dry, and the Mexican government did nothing to stop it. In a subtropical climate ideal for supplying fruits and vegetables to the northern cities, cattle and sheep gave away to onions and citrus. The railroad whisked away the produce to distant markets.

For the most part, the white investors who bought up the land at prices the locals couldn't refuse were Protestant. They saw the local population as cheap labor for the fields and canning factories. They had no intention of marrying into any Mexican-American families or turning Catholic. In fact, within a few years, there arose segregated schools and hospitals, whites-only neighborhoods, city, county and local police dominated by

Highway 83 Through McAllen, 1948. LL Cook Company Collection. Prints and photographs collection. Texas State Library and Archives Commission.

Anglos, and all the trappings of the Jim Crow South. The Tejanos of the valley, whose ancestors had suffered and scratched out a living to settle this inhospitable land, suddenly found themselves second-class citizens.

The Plan de San Diego sought to reverse that through bloodshed. And there was bloodshed.

While the newspapers didn't give Ramos's arrest much ink, word of the plan's content spread throughout the Valley. The Anglos, while now holding all the political power, were still a minority, and were terrified. Even though February 20 came and went without a mass uprising, fear grew. Bandits had launched raids across the border for the better part of a decade, but their incursions were now ascribed to a more organized plot.

The Texas Rangers were called in to help. Governor Jim Ferguson appointed Army veteran and former Houston police chief Henry Ransome as captain of a new ranger company to be based in the Valley. His orders were to eliminate any bandit and revolutionary he could find by any means necessary— carte blanche to perform extrajudicial killings. Ransome hired dozens of new rangers, many of dubious qualifications. Some served as judge, jury, and executioner as they dragged suspected seditionists out of their homes and shot them.

Tom Mayfield was among these new rangers. He was associated with only one notorious event, the discovery of fourteen dead "bandits" in the Alamo city park. Mayfield said he and his fellow rangers found them already killed, then buried them on the spot. He said the rangers had nothing to do with their deaths. The fourteen were added to the list of some 300 Mexicans or Mexican-Americans killed or suspected killed by the rangers.

It wasn't as if there weren't real seditionists and bandits roaming the Valley. James B. McAllen and a housekeeper one day found themselves under siege at the Santa Anita ranch house. The invaders circled his home, shooting through its wood frame, as McAllen returned fire through the windows. He managed to kill two of them before they retreated.

In the town of Olmito, six miles north of Brownsville, Mexican raiders attacked and derailed a southbound train as they shouted Mexican nationalist slogans. They systematically went through each car to rob and kill the passengers. The engineer and two unarmed citizens were shot in cold blood. Ransome and his men galloped after the marauders and searched the brush finding four Mexican men, whom they executed on the spot.

The Olmito raid made national headlines, and while the Anglos of the valley overall seemed to approve of the rangers' shoot-first, never-ask-questions-later tactics, the governor was under increasing pressure to tamp down the brutal practices. Those killed by vigilantes and local law enforcement sent the death toll into the thousands.

President Woodrow Wilson had yet to recognize the Carranza government in Mexico City. Once that happened, and he insisted that the centralists suppress the bandit and seditionist raids originating from Mexico, the violence died down.

The town of McAllen at first was little more than its train station and a few stores and homes. When Wilson called up the National Guard to help quell the border violence, a large camp sprang up overnight. Wherever soldiers went, there were always businesses there to cater to them. While the soldiers did not stay long, the Guard's presence seemed to give the town the kickstart it needed.

James B. McAllen died in 1916 at age fifty-four, only a year after the raid on the ranch house and less than three years after his father. He had never returned there to live, and some claimed the shock of the incident shattered his nerves and led to his rapid decline in health. His widow, Margaret, with four young children to raise, let many of his properties go, although she tenaciously held onto the ranch.

After some eight decades of wars and instability along the Rio Grande, it all came to an end by the close of World War I. State Highway 4, later known as U.S. Route 83, and other federal roads would serve as another conduit for trade between the two nations. Sleepy border crossings from Laredo to Brownsville would thrive as trucks carried goods north and south. That called for modern ports of entry and infrastructure. The political repression and segregationist practices aimed at the Tejano population continued for another sixty years until the first domino fell, up the road in Crystal City.

As for Tom Mayfield, he had arrived by stagecoach as a young man, saw the railroad stretch west along the valley, witnessed the advent of the first state and federal highways, jetliners take off from the local airport and the building of the expressway a few blocks north of the San Juan Hotel. He died on November 24, 1966.

While much that I have uncovered on my trip down Highway 83 in Texas, I owe to chance encounters, that is not the case for the WesMer Drive-In.

Before leaving on the trip, I wanted to know if there were any outdoor movie theaters remaining on Highway 83. I am a big fan of drive-ins. I grew up in the 1960s and '70s, and they were a huge part of my youth. I remember falling asleep in the backseat of my parents' car at the Sky View Theater in Omaha when I was a toddler. I have other fond memories of drive-ins from my teenage years, but those stories are perhaps best left unwritten.

Now that drive-ins are a rarity, I seek them out. My wife and I make an annual pilgrimage to the Hull's Drive-In in Lexington, Virginia, where the community took over the business and turned it into a nonprofit. It's paradise on Earth as far as I'm concerned.

I was delighted to discover that there were two remaining drive-ins along Highway 83 towns—one here and one in Abilene—but the WesMer is the only one that sits right next to the road. It's located between the towns of Mercedes and Weslaco, only a block away from the expressway, making it easy for Valley residents to patronize.

It's an hour till showtime. *Iron Man II* is the feature, followed by *Shrek Forever After*. The ticket booth isn't open yet, so I enter through the exit. I had stopped by earlier in the day and met Josh, the owner's son, who told me his dad would be here about this time. The snack bar is open, and an attendant is getting things ready. The popcorn isn't popping yet, but it soon will be. Josh is there too. He's expecting his dad any minute. He offers me something to drink, and I'm curious about some kind of fruit juice front and center on the counter, Melón Olé. It's a popular drink in Mexico, he tells me, made of cantaloupe. He can't stand it, but they sell a lot of it. I take my first sip. I think it's wonderful.

He has warned me that his father was in a serious car accident and only returned back to work last week.

"I'm just glad you guys are still open," I say. I'm repeating myself. I'm sure I said that four times when we met that afternoon, but it's true.

There were thousands of drive-ins in America in their heyday in the 1950s. In 1933, businessman Richard Hollingshead Jr. opened up the first drive-in near Pennsauken Township, New Jersey. It was said that he was searching for ways to show movies to his overweight mother, who didn't fit comfortably in indoor theater seats. He applied for a patent for the concept and turned it into a business. A year later the idea had spread to Texas, when what some believe to be the third drive-in opened in Galveston. It was a mildly successful venture at first. The early versions relied on speakers placed near the screen for sound, which wasn't ideal. From the get-go, the movie studios didn't do much to encourage the businesses. Since they were selling tickets for only one screening per night, as opposed to four or five per day at the indoor theaters, they offered second-run movies, films that had already been out for several weeks.

After World War II, drive-ins flourished. It was a convergence of technology—namely individual speakers for cars that made hearing easier—with car culture and youth culture. By the 1950s, there were some 4,000 drive-ins, and Texas, with its milder

243

weather, was the king with about 400 screens. The WesMer opened in the 1940s.

And then it all collapsed within a decade. It was always a tough business. The drive-ins in the north had to close all winter. Then VCRs came along, and moviegoers began staying home. Some of the drive-ins tried to survive by showing adult fare and splatter movies. The families stopped coming.

But it was urban sprawl that truly killed off the business. Like endangered animals, drive-ins lost their habitat. American cities expanded into the corn and wheat fields where no one ever imagined they would go. The drive-ins that were once just beyond the city limits had become, by then, the target of land developers. And those folks almost always get their way. The 1980s saw 3,000 of those 4,000 screens close. The WesMer shut down in 1981.

I read the articles back then about the rapid demise of the drive-in movie theater, feeling both denial and grief. But the proof was all around. Omaha's half dozen drive-ins all closed in short order. I grabbed my college roommate and insisted we go to the West-O Drive-In in Lincoln to watch a movie. A year later, a storm blew the screen down, and the owners never bothered to reopen.

But in Texas, those same articles said, drive-ins were still doing well. The warm climate meant they could stay open most of the year. And for the longest time I believed that. Until I did some preliminary research before departing on this trip. Texas is down to sixteen drive-ins, and this is the only one south of San Antonio. Drive-ins were once a fixture in almost every town in the Rio Grande Valley; earlier in the day I passed a sign on Highway 83 without a theater—The Cactus. I looked it up online and found a historic black-and-white picture. It billed itself as one of the most beautiful drive-ins in the world. Indeed, the back of the screen featured a desert scene. To leave the sign out there is cruel, a daily reminder of its loss. The property remains undeveloped. What a waste.

The Cactus Drive-In, 1941 (photographer unknown) and the WesMer Drive-In, 2010

Hector Garza finally arrives.

He's walking with a slight limp and his speech is slurred, for which he apologizes. I insist that there's no need. He tells me about the accident. He was driving in a construction zone on an on-ramp to the 83 Expressway. There was a stop sign there, but he just didn't see it. A truck hauling oranges slammed into the driver's side, T-boning his car. The other driver wasn't hurt, but Hector was close to dead. The emergency room doctor stopped his brain from bleeding and saved his life. But he had a broken pelvis, shoulders, and ribs. He was in a coma for a month. When he woke up he couldn't speak or walk.

"I started physical therapy," Hector tells me. "Once I figured out what to do, I kept going. The doctor said I was a miracle."

He's been in the movie theater business just about his whole life, starting at the age of ten in 1955. His godfather, Lalo Gomez, put him to work on summer weekends doing odd jobs at the Spanish-language Mexico Theater he owned in Raymondville, a town about thirty miles north of here. He swept up, took tickets, and helped at the concession stand. He was paid twenty-five cents an hour. "That first weekend I earned $2.50. Heck, that was a lot of money back then for a kid."

He thought when school started he would have to quit, but Gomez offered him a job sweeping up after classes let out on the condition that he would keep his grades up. "He didn't want my mother getting after him," Hector confesses.

By eighth grade, his boss was handing over many of the everyday tasks to him. He did that through high school until Gomez closed the theater down and took a job in another city. Hector found a job across the street at the Texas Theater, a statewide chain, as assistant manager. At one point, the manager fell ill, and Hector took over his duties. When it was announced that the manager wasn't going to be able to return, they offered him the job.

He was surprised, but he knew he could do it. "Back then, it was very rare for a Latino to be managing an English-language house." He was twenty-one.

Lalo Gomez then reentered the scene when the chain wanted to unload the theater. His godfather bought it, and Hector stayed on as manager. Then he departed again, this time offering the business to Hector for a payment of $200 per month. That began a series of acquisitions. The first was a theater in Mission, where the owner was eager to sell. The asking price was $65,000, but he offered to help him with financing.

"That was when if you knew the banker and he know you, you could get a loan with a handshake," he said. The banker gave him only one condition: he couldn't show X-rated movies. "I said, 'you got it.'"

Hector owned or leased several theaters in the Valley over the next couple decades, including the Buckhorn Drive-In in Mission, which he had for three years.

But the days of independent owners of one-screen theaters was coming to an end. The national corporations and their chains were building multiplexes out by the malls on the expressway. The owner of the Valley Drive-In in McAllen was doing really well, but someone offered him a million dollars for the land.

Eventually, Hector had to let all his theaters go.

He was idle for a couple years until the man who bought and restored the WesMer in 1994 approached Hector about buying it. The drive-in had been closed and overgrown with weeds for a dozen years between 1981 and 1994. The new owner was eager to unload the business and gave him a good deal. By then, the remaining drive-ins were returning to their roots with family-oriented movies or summer blockbusters.

He charges ten dollars per car. If parents want to cram six kids into the minivan, so be it.

The cars are starting to file in. The popcorn is popping, and the smell is intoxicating. Hector offers to refill the drink. He's surprised when I tell him how much I love the Melón Olé. He feels the same way about it as Josh.

The security guard is here. Hector says he's a retired cop. He's not a big fellow, a wiry dark-haired mustachioed man. He doesn't wear a uniform, just plain clothes, along with a perpetual scowl. He looks like he's ready to rip the head off of anyone who gets out of line.

The WesMer seems safe for now. The studios aren't crazy about the ten-dollars-per-car scheme, but there are no other theaters in the vicinity, so they give Hector the first-run movies. He doesn't own the land, but the landlord said he would give him the first option to buy the property if he ever sells. Located between towns, the WesMer doesn't seem to be threatened by development pressure—for now.

I stick around to take pictures, but I don't intend to stay for the whole movie. The sun has just dipped below the horizon and the sunset is coloring the sky with deep blue hues. My wife and I saw *Iron Man II* a week before I left for this trip. She normally doesn't care for superhero movies, unless Robert Downey Jr. is the star—then she's suddenly interested. Besides, watching a drive-in movie by yourself feels odd.

I park the Protegé, tune into the low-wave radio broadcast of the soundtrack, which is barely necessary since all the other cars have it blaring from their stereos. There are no car speakers on poles here. It's a warm night. The majority of the vehicles have their hatchbacks or trunks open, and the patrons are sitting on foldout chairs. Quite a few are sitting in the beds of pickup trucks. The mosquitoes are having a feast. The security guard is making the rounds, letting his presence be known. Good lord, don't anyone light up a joint in this place while he's around, I think.

It has been a long day, and tomorrow will be my last full day of the trip. I feel torn, like I was leaving a baseball game in the seventh inning. So I keep the broadcast on as I drive back to my motel, and listen until the voices of Tony Stark and Pepper Potts fade behind a curtain of crackling static.

It's my last full day on Highway 83. I have done my research, and I have a pretty good idea of how I want to spend it. I want to explore the towns of Harlingen and San Benito, and then see two battlefields, including where the Battle of Palo Alto was fought. That's a lot, because I always seem to come across someone or something unexpected. And that's the case as I'm heading east out of La Feria and spot the 83 Bar and Grill. I'm compelled to stop.

The rudimentary sign has a chef holding out a burger and below it a moveable type sign announces:

$1.00 Daily Specials
Karaoke Wed. 6-9.
New Pool Table
$ Sweepstakes $

It's a long one-story building that looks as if it were hewn from a couple of mobile homes. It sits next to another bar, the much nicer-looking Texas Rose. Signs warn me not to park in one lot if I intend to imbibe in the other. Both lots are empty.

I have seen many businesses along the highway with an 83 in its name, many of them closed. It seems to be a curse. The are only two other restaurants I know of named after the highway, both long gone. The 83 Café, in Coleharbor, North Dakota, had been closed for twenty-five years by the time I came across it. I also found a matchbook cover online for a Bob's 83 Restaurant in Garden City, Kansas. I decide to drive straight to San Benito, where I plan to see its museum, then double back for lunch.

It's time to slip *The Best of Los Texas Tornados* CD in the player.

Flaco Jimenez's accordion kicks things off and the other three members of the band, Freddy Fender, Augie Meyers, and Doug Sahm sing their best-known song, "Who Were You Thinking of (When We Were Making Love Last Night)."

A few miles east I reach the intersection where Business 83 meets Expressway 83. The Longest Main Street in America ends

here. Straight ahead is the town of Harlingen; I bypass it for now
and take the access road to avoid the four-laner.

The CD includes a re-recording of Fender's twice-over hit record "Wasted Days and Wasted Nights," a song he had a minor hit
with in the 1960s, then a monster hit with in the 1970s. Soon
enough the access road takes me past the town's water tower, where
a giant portrait reminds those flying down the expressway that this
is the "Home of Freddy Fender." To celebrate, I change CDs and
insert Eddie Con Los Shades, Fender's alias for a rock-and-roll album he recorded in 1961,
now reissued on Arhoolie Records. I special-ordered this
album before departing on
the trip and have been saving
it for just this occasion. It's
blasting as a I drive down San
Benito's main street searching
for the museum. Fender joins
another Highway 83 Texas
native, Jeannie C. Riley of Anson, with the rare achievement of scoring a number one
hit on both the country and pop charts with the same song, "When
the Next Teardrop Falls" and "Harper Valley P.T.A.," respectively.

The museum, found on a side street, is a three-for-one deal:
it's the San Benito History Museum, the Freddy Fender Museum,
and the Texas Conjunto Music Hall of Fame and Museum. I'm
one of the first in the door and I'm charged three bucks, one
dollar per museum.

Ragtime, jazz, swing, the blues, bluegrass, country, rock
'n' roll, country-western, cajun, and zydeco all emerged in the
United States. The great cultural melting pot and its stew of
various musical styles brought over from Europe and Africa
has created all these unique styles. Almost each has a father
or mother associated with it: Louis Armstrong for jazz, Bill

Monroe for bluegrass, Clifton Chenier for zydeco, W. C. Handy for the blues, and Elvis, the king of rock n' roll. After making my way through the history section of the museum, I enter the Conjunto Music Hall of Fame and find the accordion that once belonged to the late Narciso Martínez. He, and *bajo sexto* player Santiago Almeida, are considered the fathers of conjunto music.

THE HURRICANE OF THE VALLEY

One day in 1928, in a shotgun shack north of Brownsville, a seventeen-year-old Narciso Martínez pulled a dusty accordion out of a closet. It was a relatively simple instrument, he thought. He pulled open the bellows as he had seen other musicians do at wedding dances, and started pressing the keys, listening to the different notes it made. His older brother had purchased the German-made accordion years ago, but didn't have the talent or the determination to master it. Whatever the case, the boy laid claim to it, and was soon practicing on it as often as he could.

The Martínez family were field workers. Narciso was born in 1911 in Reynosa, Mexico, but his parents migrated when he was one year old. He knew little English and had only a few years of schooling, for no one seemed to care if Tejano kids received much of an education.

They picked vegetables on land once owned under a Spanish land grant bestowed to brothers Eugenio and Bartolome Fernandez, two noblemen who had curried favor with the king. After the Mexican-American War, their descendants cut a deal with a retired American Army officer. For the price of half of their land, he would ensure that the families maintained their title to the other half. It was that, or risk losing it all to the corrupt judges in Brownsville.

By the time the Martínez family arrived, the town of San Benito was being built north of them along a dry river bed. The new title-holders of the property, the San Benito Land and Water

Company, saw the arroyo as a means to convey water from the Rio Grande to the parched but nutrient-rich soil. The land was subdivided into smaller parcels, with investors buying up the farms and using cheap labor to do the menial work.

Conjunto emerged from the lowest strata of society in the Valley: the workers who toiled on ranches, farms, and cotton fields. Through the generations, the Tejanos never lost their love of dancing. The wealthy families brought in stringed orchestras, aspiring to mimic the upper crust of the Anglos' society. But on the farms, villages, and ranches, they danced to whatever instruments were handy. Maybe it's called roots music because it came from those who worked in the soil.

The accordions were built in Germany, and could be bought at a reasonable price. Serious musicians called it an instrument for peasants, but its amplified sound and variety of tones made it ideal for celebrations held in makeshift dance halls. Dancing was at first reserved for weddings and other special occasions. The parties could last all night. Then cantinas began using musicians to attract customers.

Martínez had a buddy with the rare skill of being able to memorize and whistle any tune he heard. The pair would play on the house porch for hours as Martínez reproduced on the accordion the melodies his friend had picked up from the radio or other musicians.

Martínez married young, not long after he first picked up the accordion, and he soon had four daughters to support. The family migrated north of the Valley to work in the field near Bishop, Texas, a town settled first by Czechs and Germans. During his three-year stay there, he picked up more tips watching the European-style polka players. He then invested in his own German-made Hohner accordion.

Soon enough, Martínez took the big step of playing in public at a party. He had a lively, bouncy style that made the dancers want to move their feet.

Narcisco Martinez and Santiago Almeida, 1936. Wikimedia
Commons

When Martínez joined up with baja sexto player Santiago
Almeida they helped define conjunto, or "group" music in English. The baja sexto, a twelve-string guitar, gave Martínez's music the exact balance it needed.

A talent scout heard the duo in 1931, and recorded them
for Bluebird Records, a low-budget subsidiary of RCA Victor.
Martínez and Almeida were paid $150 for their first recording
session—a great deal of money in the middle of the Depression—
but they never saw another penny for their work. The record
company received a large return on its investment, distributing

the songs all over the world, even going so far as to repackage them for Polish polka fans as the *Polski Kwartet* and to the cajuns as "Louisiana Pete." In Texas fans knew him by his real name and called him *El Hurucan del Valle*, the Hurricane of the Valley. There was a dance or celebration somewhere every weekend and, later, organized concerts put on by promoters, who would fill the bill with different acts. The duo was were in demand all through the Valley and played as far away as California, but the weekend dances never earned them enough money to quit their jobs working in the fields.

World War II temporarily ended the duo's recording career. Wartime shortages of shellac made producing records prohibitively expensive, and when it was all over in 1945, the major record labels had lost interest in regional music. That didn't mean there wasn't a demand. Two Tejano businessmen, Armondo Marroquin in the town of Alice, some 100 miles north of the Valley, and Paco Betancourt in San Benito, needed music for their jukeboxes. Betancourt was the son of a refugee from the Mexican civil war. His father and uncle were sent by the Diaz administration to be customs agents in Matamoros, but when the dictator lost power, they fled to Brownsville. The family thrived there. Betancourt had many business interests in Brownville and San Benito, including the Rio Grande Music Company, where he sold records and musical instruments and distributed pinball machines and jukeboxes to bars and restaurants. If there were no fresh songs in those jukeboxes— music the people wanted to hear—they wouldn't be dropping in their nickels.

In Alice, Marroquin spent $200 on an acetate recording machine and started playing around with the equipment in his kitchen. How hard could it be? The first recordings he made worthy of distribution were of his wife and her sister singing as Carmen y Laura, and a neighbor accompanying them with his accordion. Soon he was recording Martínez and other acts. Betancourt was responsible for taking the master recordings and having them pressed into records at a plant in California, then reshipped to him for labeling and distribution. The company recorded dozens of musicians in a variety of styles. The Rio Grande Music Company was soon sending boxes full of records all over the Southwest, and the nickels were being pumped into the jukeboxes to play the latest by Narciso Martínez. A rival, Falcon Records, in McAllen, soon emerged. The Tejano music, including conjunto and other styles, was like no other in Latin America. The Mexicans called it *musique del Norte*, music of the North.

Almeida retired in 1950 and moved to the Northwest, but Martinez continued on with other partners. The two businessmen also dissolved their partnership as Marroquin moved on to other endeavors. Betancourt moved the studio and all the master tapes to San Benito, and continued to record and press records. A local teenager fascinated with music, Baldemar Huerta, would come by the studio to do odd jobs and noodle around with the equipment. It turned out he had a great voice, and would later sign with Falcon Records. Betancourt secretly recorded him under an alias, Eddie Medina con Los Shades, a rock-and-roll band that played in their sunglasses. The album spawned hits all over Latin America and Texas. Baldemar would later change his stage name to Freddy Fender.

Betancourt died in 1971. The San Benito building where the studio and master tapes were stored was closed up, and for two decades sat there as an unintended time capsule. That didn't stop Martínez from performing. He could be found in local watering holes on weekend nights pumping the accordion as his sideman strummed along, making the dancers move their feet to the bouncy rhythms. He was still known as the Hurricane of the Valley, although the fame was never enough to allow him to quit work as a field hand.

Almost two decades after Betancourt's death, Chris Strachwicz, a fanatical German-American collector of American roots music and president of Arhoolie Records, found the studio and master tapes untouched. He bought the whole collection and brought it back to his home in El Cerito, California, and began releasing the material on CDs.

The CDs brought Martínez new fans. The National Endowment of the Arts honored his body of work with its National Heritage Award. Arhoolie Records produced two documentaries on the "music of the North" featuring Martínez. The notoriety still wasn't enough to allow him to make music full-time. But he did find a less toiling job feeding animals at the Brownsville Zoo.

Martínez was in more demand than ever as performer when he passed away at age eighty in 1992. Today, San Benito holds the annual Narciso Martínez Conjunto Music Festival in his honor.

I'm back at the 83 Bar and Grill after stopping to explore downtown Harlingen, and now I'm hungry. I've come to the right place.

The proprietor, Marion Schrank—light hair, attractive woman in her fifties, I judge—has sold me on their cheeseburger, and she sits it in front of me with a side of crinkle-cut fries and all the condiments I could ever want.

I've returned at the right time of day, just not the right time of year. It's May, and this bar and the Texas Rose cater to the snowbirds—who have pretty much returned north by now. Relations between the two neighboring watering holes are not good, and Marion made sure I parked in the 83 lot, lest I get towed.

The cheeseburger is everything she said it would be, fat and juicy. ESPN is quietly playing on a TV in the background. The décor is wood paneling and whatever beer posters the distributors have dropped off. The new pool table sits empty. The jukebox is quiet. There is no natural light, which is the way a real dive bar should be, with no reminders of the world outside.

Highway 83 caters to many communities. Custom combine crews like it because it takes them directly from the wheat fields of Perryton to the northern plains. Bikers traveling to the Sturgis Rally in South Dakota love it. Lately, the trucks carrying wind turbine blades use it, as do the drug smugglers and immigrants who cross the border illegally in the Valley. And thousands of snowbirds, retired people from Canada and the north, travel down 83 every fall to escape the onset of winter. Marion and her husband, Garry, were two of those, originally living in Rapid City, South Dakota.

"That road takes us right back home," she says.

Naming the bar after the road that takes them here was a natural choice.

"So many of them come down 83. They live out back. You should see this place in the winter. We have to hire extra help. It's a madhouse."

Marion and Garry normally close in the summer, but this is the first year they are going to try to stay open, she explains. "It's a snowbird bar in the winter and a Texas bar in the summer"— at least that is what she hopes. Everyone disappears around March. I'm one of four customers, but it is the middle of a weekday. An elderly white man comes in to order lunch. He is dressed like a cowboy, but he's an onion farmer, Marion says. And onion prices are currently going through the roof, which I already knew because there was a front-page article about it in the *Monitor* that morning. The spring crop was garnering an all-time high, fetching up to $40 for a bag of yellow onions and $60 for white. Mexican growers were hit with too much rain, and that turned out to be a boon here.

The land from here to the river is sectioned off in squares. Mobile homes where the snowbirds live are near the highway, and fields and orchards go up to the water's edge on the northern bank. Both take advantage of the semitropical climate. The vegetables grow all year around. And the mild winters bring in the winter refugees.

Harlingen, as I found out earlier in the day, didn't start out as one of the train stops on the railroad, but rather as an agricultural paradise. In the 1890s, entrepreneur Lon C. Hill saw the Valley's potential. The early assessment that the land was only suitable for raising livestock was just plain wrong. He witnessed many Tejano families successfully growing their own gardens near the river, where they had access to water. And why couldn't they? The Rio Grande had been carrying nutrients down the river and spreading them over the alluvial plains for millions of years. The problem was bringing the water to where it needed to go. Since the riverbed was actually higher than the land around it, gravity would be the answer.

He went about raising the capital to build the first irrigation channel, which would follow an arroyo north from the river to a spot on the railroad informally named Six-Shooter Junction. The town where the railroad branched west was better known as the living quarters for rangers and Border Patrol agents, a rough-and-tumble

Tourist trailer camp, McAllen, Texas. February 1939. Farm Services Administration and Office of War Information collection (Library of Congress) Taken by Russell Lee.

lot who walked around with their guns strapped on. After forming the Lon C. Hill Improvement Company and raising the capital, he constructed the valley's first irrigation canal in 1903. By 1908, he was running twenty-six miles of canals and irrigating 75,000 acres. Harlingen, named after a Dutch town, was a more appropriate name for attracting families, and the new city was incorporated in 1910. The idea spread west, with one of the towns, Weslaco, actually named after the *W.E. Stewart Land Company.*

As roads improved and Americans began exploring the nation in cars, the Valley turned to tourism with some success. The warm climate and access to Mexico were the big attractions. No one ever built a Disney World or a Six Flags over Texas amusement park here—although Seven Flags over Texas would have been more appropriate. Snowbirds, however, stayed and spent their money for months at a time. Some of the onion fields were converted to mobile home parks.

Finding the Palo Alto Battlefield is no problem at all. Giant brown signs on the expressway point the way to the National Historical Park, which is only about five miles east of the 83-77 Expressway. I spend an hour there studying the movements of the U.S. and Mexican troops and checking out the displays in the interpretive center.

Reproductions of Major Ringgold's flying artillery are placed along the paths, along with signs warning visitors of snakes. It is a truly moving place, as I ponder the misery the U.S. cannons inflicted on Arista's troops.

As night fell after the battle, Taylor's army hunkered down to rest. The next morning they found that the Mexican general had vacated, leaving his wounded troops and dead in place. It turns out his surgeon had deserted him, and his men were not equipped with picks or shovels to bury the fallen. The Americans did what they could for the dying, who begged in Spanish for water. Young Ulysses Grant was among the many who were haunted by their cries for help for years to come.

Arista made a final stand the next day near the river, beside an oxbow lake where the topography would make U.S. artillery ineffective. As a result, the Battle of Resaca de la Palma was mostly hand-to-hand combat. It lasted some two hours before the Mexicans retreated. Those who couldn't swim drowned in the waters of the Rio Grande.

I'm not through with death and war, though. I set out to find the last major historic site on my trip, which is only a few miles away as the crow flies.

All I have to do is cut across the northern part of Brownsville and pick up the last remaining section of Texas Highway 4. After a few minutes, I'm out of the city limits. And there he is! My old friend the turkey buzzard, circling ahead of the car a hundred yards out.

"I missed you, buddy!"

Highway 4 didn't completely disappear when Highway 83 supplanted it. Its last remnant is this twenty-four mile stretch from Brownsville to Boca Chica Beach. I thought it would be a major road leading to the ocean, but there is almost no traffic as I drive between two walls of mesquite and palmito trees, passing a Border Patrol checkpoint on the way.

The battlefield site is easy to spot, with a large interpretive plaque, but this is nothing like the Palo Alto site, which has been cleared by park rangers, with every key maneuver in the battle marked out for all to see. This site isn't developed at all, and there is nothing to see but a wall of vegetation. That is too bad, because it's the location of the last battle of the U.S. Civil War.

PALMITO RANCH

Private John Jefferson Williams of the 34th Indiana Volunteer Infantry spent his days on Brazos Santiago Island doing the same as his fellow Hoosiers—that is, not much at all. They ate. They played cards. Swatted sand flies. Gossiped. Complained. Gazed out at the Gulf of Mexico and watched the tides rise and retreat on this island near the mouth of the Rio Grande. To call it an island was charitable. It was little more than a sand spit with a thin layer of vegetation, no fresh water or shade, and little to keep the mind occupied. On occasion, there was picket duty, or a supply ship to help unload. He was occasionally tasked with gathering driftwood for fires. At least it was something to do.

Williams was a blacksmith by profession, only twenty-one years old, who had volunteered relatively late in the war between the states. The war-weary 34th had seen plenty of action in battles up and down the breadth of the Mississippi, but that was before Williams had joined. Since he'd enlisted and left behind his young wife, the regiment had only carried out garrison duty in the swamps of Louisiana and in New Orleans. Williams had yet to fire his rifle during a battle. It was quite a shock to be pulled away from the excitement of the notorious port city and sent to this miserable speck of sand at the tip of Texas.

The 34th shared the island with the 62nd U.S. Colored Troops, a unit of black soldiers who were mostly freemen or recently freed slaves from Missouri. The colored troops, who were led by white officers, also had never seen battle, having spent most of the war doing menial labor building fortifications in Louisiana. A horrifying number of them had died from tropical diseases rather than wounds.

The Hoosiers were encamped on the northern part of the island, where they monitored a narrow channel between it and South Padre Island. The black troops were camped separately to the south. Aside from the color of their skins, the differences between the two units were remarkable.

The Hoosiers spent their days whiling away the hours, while the 62nd continued to drill and maintain their discipline. For recently freed slaves, the future was uncertain. Here they sat, deep in enemy territory, confined to an island and surrounded by hostile forces. When black soldiers were captured, the

African-American troops dig trenches on Brazos Santiago Island. From Frank Leslie's Illustrated Newspaper, February 13, 1864.

Confederates were known execute them on site. If the 62nd were ever called upon to fight, they were going to be ready.

There was a third force on the island, Tejanos and Texans loyal to the Union. For Texas Confederates, there was no one or nothing lower than their neighbors who had declared their allegiance to the United States. The island hosted some 300 pro-Union civilians, both Anglo and Tejano. From their numbers, the Union officers had recruited enough men to form a cavalry unit, which was cavalry in name only, for there weren't any horses available.

As far as the Mexicans, some of them aligned with Texas in the rebellion, and others took a stand against slavery. Some came from north of the border and others enlisted from the south.

There was, in fact, little slavery along the Lower Rio Grande Valley leading up to the Civil War. Paid Mexican labor was cheap, and the upper-class Tejanos found the practice of slavery abhorrent.

Juan Cortina, whom Rip Ford's rangers had dispatched across the border at Roma in 1859, upon seeing the power vacuum along the border and the ensuing turmoil, returned to wage Cortina's War II. Tejanos who had been mistreated by the gringos were more than willing to join the warlord, although his invasion was crushed easily by an alliance of Texans and loyal Tejanos led by

Colonel Santos Benavides. Later the mayor of Laredo, Benavides was a descendant of the Escandón settlers and had served in the Texas Rangers. He would guard his hometown in the name of the Confederacy for much of the war.

At the war's outset, Colonel Ford was given the task of securing the valley, which was lightly garrisoned with federal troops. With 500 men and the help of Benavides, he took Fort Brown in Brownsville without a shot being fired and negotiated the surrender of eight more outposts all the way north to El Paso.

As the Union formed naval blockades to cut off the South's economic lifeline to Europe, Brownsville, and Matamoros ended up playing a key role during the war. The Mexican town was the only neutral port the Confederacy could ship its cotton through. The Lower Rio Grande Valley was soon called the "back door of the South," and the region saw hundreds of thousands of cotton bales pass through the border towns ever year, providing much-needed cash to buy weapons and materiel for the rebellion. Merchants such as the McAllens grew rich as trade flourished.

The North sought to put a stop to this. The war, which had seemed so far away, came to the Lower Rio Grande Valley in November 1863 as almost 7,000 Union troops landed on Brazos Santiago Island, then began a march up the Valley, setting up posts from there to Laredo. Ford was by then manning a desk in Austin and relegated to pushing paper. The border had few troops, and the state's youth were off fighting in the East.

Colonel Edmund Davis, a West Point educated, pro-Union Texan who had been a political rival of Ford's prior to the war, was instrumental in convincing President Abraham Lincoln to invade the Valley. He organized the 1st Texas Union Cavalry, a force of some 1,500 men mostly made up of Germans and other recent European immigrants from the Hill Country. They promptly took control of Ringgold Barracks. Another 900 Mexican Americans joined the 2nd Texas Union Cavalry. The lightly garrisoned Rio Grande Valley posts were quickly overrun by the force of almost 10,000 men.

Despite their numbers, the Union troops were spread too thin to prevent cotton being smuggled into Mexico. The trade just moved upriver or took place at crossings in the dark of night. Nevertheless, the presence of Yankee soldiers on Texas soil was too much to take for the leaders in Austin. In early 1864, Governor Pendleton Murrah asked Ford to do something about it.

Ford was a fervent Confederate, yet a pragmatist. He had fought Indians and Mexicans all his life but was smart enough to know that there were potential allies among them. He began putting together an army of 1,500 volunteers who were willing to clean the Unionists out of the Valley. They were a ragtag lot, with many men past their prime, or in some cases, barely old enough to shave, but they marched from San Antonio with Old Rip leading the way. By the time the force reached Laredo to join Benavides's men, the Union generals had decided to withdraw most of their forces and send them north to a campaign in East Texas.

The bloodiest battle took place on June 24, 1864, between Davis's 1st Texas Cavalry at a spot twelve miles west of Brownsville. The Battle of Las Rucias Ranch was Texan against Texan, two experienced commanders pitted against each other in a blood feud. It was a rout for Ford and his volunteers, with many of the bluecoats running for their lives into Mexico, and for good reason. They expected no mercy.

Ford prevented his men from hanging forty captured Texans on the spot and insisted that they be treated as prisoners of war and sent to a prison up north. But once out of Ford's control, Davis's men were executed.

Taking Brownsville was considerably harder, but he managed to push the remaining federal troops out of the city, where they retreated to Brazos Santiago. And they remained bottled up on the island for the rest of the war, reinforced by the 64th and the Hoosiers, with the remnants of the 1st and 2nd Texas Cavalry—who no longer had horses—some Confederate deserters, and a few hundred pro-Union civilians taking shelter there. The newspapers, brought there by Union supply ships, came weeks late, but reported mostly good news about the war effort. It was becoming more and more apparent that the South's rebellion was failing.

In March 1865, once bitter foes pitched their tents on the beach at Point Isabel, a neutral spot across the channel from Brazos Santiago. A bone-chilling wind was blowing from the north. Officers representing both armies lit fires and sat down to talk business.

Traveling from the north on a secret mission under the orders of President Lincoln and General Ulysses S. Grant was Union Major General Lew Wallace, commander of the Middle Atlantic Department. He had been in touch with old friends now fighting for the South in Texas, who informed him that there might be an opportunity to make peace in the Lower Rio Grande Valley without any further need for bloodshed. He took this to the president, who had even more serious matters to consider. While the Valley may have been the "back door to the Confederacy," it could soon be the front door to taking on the French Imperial Army. Once America's ally, France was now ruled by Napoleon III, who had dispatched Ferdinand Maximilian to establish a French monarchy in Mexico. The United States supported the elected president Benito Juarez. A day would come when the French problem would have to be addressed.

There on the beach to meet Wallace and his small group of advisors was General James Slaughter, commander of the West Subdistrict of Texas, and his retinue, which included Ford. Slaughter was a Virginian, an outsider, and a rather poor leader in Ford's estimation. The pair butted heads all the time. Despite the old ranger's contributions to the Confederate cause and his intimate knowledge of the Rio Grande Valley, Ford never received an officer's commission. To his loyal troops, he was a general in every sense of the word, but Slaughter remained his superior in rank.

Nevertheless, Ford and Slaughter and the Union leaders found common ground immediately. They agreed that further fighting in the Valley would serve no purpose. The larger war would not be decided in this remote land. As long as the Union forces remained on Brazos Santiago, the Texas troops would leave them be.

Wallace ascertained quickly that while Slaughter was the general, the lower-ranking Ford was the man who knew the lay of the land and had real influence. If he could win over Old Rip, the plan might have a chance.

Over the next two days, huddled in tents and drinking coffee to ward off the cold, they hammered out a peaceful end to the conflict in Texas with a six-point proposal. Moreover, at the war's end, the Unionists and Confederates would join forces and march into Mexico to help Juarez clean out the imperialists.

Both Slaughter and Ford saw this as an honorable way for them to escape the lost Confederate cause. It was by then apparent that the war in the East was coming to an end, and help from Richmond, Virginia, would never come. The Trans-Mississippi area of operations—the lands west of the river—was cut off from the East and the economy was in shambles.

Under the plan, the rebels would not have to lay down their arms, officers and troops would receive amnesty, and most important, the North would not make any claim to Texas's cotton. Ford had been fighting to defend the Mexican border from one threat or another for years. The French would be his next foe. The imperialists were already occupying Matamoros, which didn't sit well with him. He agreed with Wallace that such a campaign would help heal a wounded nation as the public learned that the two forces could work together to defeat a common enemy.

To complicate the matter, it was believed that Confederate commander of the Trans-Mississippi General Kirby Smith was engaged with his own secret negotiations. He wanted to invite the French and Mexicans onto Texas soil as allies to save the South. Ford vowed to Wallace that he would never allow it.

He and his loyal men would turn against Smith and drive the despised Mexicans out.

Ford was entrusted to take the proposal to his superiors, but malaria, which had plagued him his whole life, struck and the courier who took his place never made it past General John G. Walker, district commander of Confederate forces in Texas. The resolute Missouri native ripped up the proposal without forwarding it to General Smith and declared that the South would never surrender.

A few weeks later, on April 9, General Lee signed documents doing just that after General Grant smashed his forces at the Battle of Appomattox Court House in Virginia. It was the decisive, but not the final, battle of the Civil War.

Private Williams stood along with almost 200 of his fellow Hoosiers after a tiring five-mile march along the sandy beach in the darkness down the length of Brazos Santiago. It was May 11, and the heat and humidity made them sweat through their heavy cotton uniforms. About half of those who had been awakened in the middle of the night had spent the previous day trudging through the sand on South Padre Island on an unsuccessful hunt for stray cattle. The others had been tasked with unloading a supply ship. To a man, they were bone tired. And to a man, they despised their commander, Colonel Theodore Barrett. Soon enough, the commanding officer appeared on the beach and began barking orders at them like they were farmyard dogs. The veterans bristled. They had seen a lot more war than Barrett, but they complied with his orders to board some rickety flatboats that would take them to the mainland. Williams had no idea where they were going, or why, but he was surrounded by battle-hardened confident soldiers. He jumped into the boat with his Enfield rifle.

Barrett was a thirty-year-old New Yorker who had advanced in the war through political connections rather than success on the field. Except for some skirmishes with rebellious Lakota Indians in Minnesota, he hadn't led in any battles. He secured the command of the 62nd Colored Troops and joined them in their uneventful occupation duty in Louisiana before they were all sent to Brazos Santiago, yet another dull assignment. When the previous commander was called away, the job leading all the troops on the island fell to him. Shortly thereafter, newspapers arrived announcing Lee's surrender. The news quickly spread through the remote outpost and the rest of the Valley.

Barrett had served for three years and had yet to distinguish himself in battle. He had aspirations to go into politics after the war and needed some kind of claim to fame. And there he sat, bottled up on this sandspit as a big fat prize sat waiting for him and his troops a few miles up the river. Brownsville and its warehouses full of cotton bales were there for the taking. It would be a Sunday stroll. Word had reached him that General Slaughter's troops had been decimated by desertions.

And there was a kernel of truth there. Many, upon hearing of Lee's surrender, simply loaded up their horses and returned to their farms or ranches. Others formally asked for furloughs, which Ford readily granted. Many left without their meager salary. The only way Slaughter could pay them was in Confederate dollars, which no one wanted anymore. There was a truce in place and the war was almost over. Ford had some 300 men under his command remaining in or near Brownsville. Benavides and what remained of his Tejano troops were in far-off Laredo.

Barrett, without seeking permission from any higher-ups, decided to break the Wallace-Slaughter truce and send 250 of the black troops plus fifty men from the recently re-formed, but horseless, 2nd Texas Cavalry on a march of conquest up the river. Soon enough, Barrett guessed, he would be known as the "Liberator of Brownsville."

For the first time, Barrett's black troops had an opportunity to test their mettle in combat. They caught a small contingent of Ford's troops by surprise at an outpost and then took over a ranch between the island and Brownsville. The sixty-five Confederate cavalrymen under the command of Captain William Robinson had to flee, but they didn't go far. The officer sent world to Ford in Brownsville that the Northerners had broken the truce and launched a sneak attack. Old Rip was infuriated. Breaking the truce was an insult of the highest degree to their honor and manhood. He had no choice but to respond. He sent word back to Robinson to hold the Yankee advance at any cost.

After quickly overrunning the outpost and torching the home of a defenseless rancher, Barrett may have believed that the march to Brownsville would be a walk in the park, but Robinson had other plans. The battle-tested Texans mounted on sturdy horses used tactics they had learned from their old foes, the Comanches, to confound the inexperienced troops and their equally green officers. Darting in and out of the brush, they began a series of hit-and-run skirmishes. The Union troops thought there were hundreds of horsemen ahead of them. The Texans fell back for a while, giving the Union troops the impression that they had won, but returned five hours later with an additional 130 horsemen who had left their posts to join the fray.

By the end of the day, Robinson had beaten the foot soldiers back two miles. Barrett was dumbfounded. He couldn't believe that the Confederates weren't falling back to Brownsville in the face of his superior force. In fact, his infantrymen were now deep in enemy territory, led by inexperienced junior officers without the benefit of cavalry or artillery. After coming to the realization that taking Brownsville would be no easy task, Barrett rode back to the island, where he gave the order to call up a battalion of the Indiana regulars.

Back in Brownsville, Ford found General Slaughter eating his dinner and asked him for his orders.

"Retreat," he simply said, while shrugging his shoulders and taking a sip of coffee. He was prepared to abandon the city if necessary. Old Rip couldn't believe what he was hearing. The word "retreat" wasn't in his vocabulary. He had promised to send Robinson reinforcements and he would never leave him high and dry. He railed against his superior officer, forgetting his lower rank, and called him a few choice words. Slaughter was moved enough to allow Ford to do as he wished, although he said he would not be joining him on the battlefield. He and the men under his command would stay behind to guard against Cortina, or the French imperialists, or some such nonsense. The war was over. There was no Confederacy left to defend, according to the latest dispatches. What was the point of shedding more blood? Ford left, his face flushed with anger, but vowing to take matters into his own hands.

After a grueling all-night march, Williams and his fellow Hoosiers arrived to reinforce the Union force at 10 a.m. Barrett had refused to let them take so much as a ten-minute break, and they arrived exhausted. But there was no rest for the weary. He ordered them to load their Enfields and move forward.

Robinson's men had been skirmishing with the Union troops

Private John Jefferson Williams
(Wikimedia Commons)

since dawn, not in an effort to gain any ground, but just to pester them so they couldn't rest before the battle to come. And it was coming.

Barrett continued to drive the line toward Brownsville with a single-minded purpose. Ignoring the weariness of his most experienced troops, he pushed the Hoosiers forward in skirmish lines, while letting his fresher black troops rest.

Williams undoubtedly heard the battalion's junior officers

and veterans carping about Barrett's missteps. They were now twelve miles away from Brazos Santiago, its supplies and reinforcements. Barrett separated the two forces to the point where the Hoosiers didn't know where the 64th and the Texas 2nd were, and they couldn't come to their aid if need be. The wily Confederates seemed to be drawing them farther and farther into a maze of brush, prickly pear, oxbow lakes, and marshes, keeping them at bay just enough to slow them down. And for what? Reinforcements from Brownsville undoubtedly—probably more cavalry and possibly even some artillery. Then what would happen? To top it off, for some inexplicable reason Barrett had ordered Indiana troops the night before to pack only one ration. He had to order the blacks to share theirs just so they could eat.

The Union advance was slow and disjointed. Barrett couldn't coordinate the units into one cohesive line as Robinson's men darted in and out of cover, pulling off shots from horseback, and swiftly disappearing back in the brush.

At one point, a clearly frustrated Barrett rode up on his horse to ask the advice of one of the Indiana junior officers. He was forced to state the obvious.

"Sir, it's pert near impossible for infantry to keep pace with cavalry."

As the day wore on, the overwhelmed Barrett appeared before the troops with a hollow, thousand-yard stare. When asked for orders, he simply said, "advance to Brownsville," and left the details to his junior officers. When one of the experienced Indiana officers took matters into his own hands and tried to instigate a trap, miscommunication sank the plan and it resulted in more confusion.

By that evening the Union forces had retired in defensive positions at Palmito Ranch, after a hard day marching and fighting. They stacked their rifles and began to eat dinner.

Unbeknownst to them, Rip Ford had arrived with another 100 horsemen and an additional fifty artillerymen to man six cannons. While the Indiana troops had been marching the night before, he had gathered every available cavalryman he could find and made a quick trip across the river to parley with his French counterparts. Despite his fervent assertion that he would never allow the imperialists on Texas soil, the French officers agreed to loan him two of their largest cannons, along with a handful of skilled cannoneers. It was the first and final time French troops served in the Civil War. By late afternoon on May 12, Ford and his reinforcements had joined Robinson and his men. Together they had about 250 horsemen, and fifty men to man the artillery. He ordered his troops to advance to Robinson's line in small groups to mask their arrival, and that the cannons be well hidden. Ford, as probably the most experienced scout among them, crept to an ideal spot in the underbrush with his spyglass to survey the Union lines. Like many Texans that day, this was his first glimpse of black troops. Ford used thirty years of experience to note both the weaknesses in the enemy and the terrain to come up with a battle plan. The Union troops had boxed themselves in a bend in the Rio Grande that blocked their way back to Brazos Santiago. He had one-third as many men, but he would counter that with speed and initiative.

Barrett, with his single-minded pursuit of personal glory, and Ford, with his Texas pride and righteous anger, were now locked into a battle that would serve no purpose. To a man, everyone on the battlefield knew that the war was over. The men following Old Rip would have ridden with him to the gates of hell if he had asked, while the Union troops were duty-bound to follow the orders of a man they knew to be vain and incompetent.

Ford put his spyglass down. Apparently the Yankees believed the day was over. It wasn't. The Union force, despite its superior numbers, never really had a chance against Old Rip.

Private Williams stood shoulder to shoulder with his fellow soldiers, who had their bayonets fixed and pointed at the line of charging cavalrymen. None of them were quite sure how it happened, but they were alone, cut off from the main force and now facing certain doom.

After the rebels had launched their surprise attack in the middle of dinner, many of the troops fled to Palmito Hill. It was a good spot to make a stand, with the high ground always being enviable. Barrett ordered two companies from the 34th to form a skirmish line to the west of the hill to serve as a first line of defense.

And then the cannons began blasting. Using some of the flying artillery techniques first employed only a few miles away at the Battle of Palo Alto, Ford's cannons were quickly repositioned to strike. Once the cannon balls began to slam into the side of the hill, Barrett panicked. He ordered a double-time retreat, and the Union force began to evacuate the hill.

Barrett had left the Hoosiers in place to serve as lambs, sacrificed to guard his rear as the main force began its long retreat back to the island. Ford and a company of cavalry came across the troops, alone in the brush, cut off from their main force, and ordered a charge. He watched as his men at full gallop emptied their revolvers then drew their swords. He was amazed to see the Yankees standing tall, with their bayonets defiantly pointed at the chests of the fast horses, not breaking ranks as they faced an overwhelming force. Such valor, he thought, with a tinge of regret for ordering the charge. The cavalrymen soon had them encircled in a cloud of choking dust. They had no choice but to throw down their arms.

When it was over, one man lay in the dirt. Private Williams had been shot through the temple, the most merciful death one could hope for on the battlefield.

The Civil War had taken a terrible toll. Most estimates put the number of soldiers killed in action at more than 620,000. Private John Jefferson Williams would go down in the history books as the last man killed in action in America's bloodiest conflict.

I'm stopped at the Border Patrol checkpoint on my way back, which doesn't bother me at all. They're just doing their job, and it's easy to see how drug or human smugglers could use the thick brush and the road to hide their movements. The only Border Patrol agents I've encountered so far have been locked up in their air-conditioned vehicles, looking fairly bored. And such is the case here. The young Mexican-American agent, probably noticing my camera, road atlas, travel brochures, and other assorted stuff on the passenger seat, takes me at my word that I'm just a history buff. He strikes up a conversation about the battle, and we chat about it for a few minutes, both lamenting the senseless deaths.

The 62nd served with valor as they set up skirmish lines to protect the chaotic retreat, firing volleys to ward off Ford's cavalry, falling back as another set of troops set up another skirmish line, and so on for seven long miles, without losing a man. Barrett at one point sent another group of sacrificial lambs: the Texas 2nd, who were also hung out to dry. Most were captured; others swam the Rio Grande only to be killed by Mexican bandits waiting on the other side to pick clean anyone trying to escape.

Many members of the 34th, footsore, dehydrated, and exhausted after almost twenty hours of nonstop marching and fighting in the soupy humidity, collapsed and could only wait in the dirt to be taken prisoner. The Texans didn't let up their pursuit until it was almost nightfall and their horses were spent. The battered Unionists escaped in their flatboats back to the Brazos Santiago.

After the war, Barrett tried to blame the whole debacle on the Indiana 34th's commander and called him up for a court-martial, but the man was completely exonerated. Barrett retired to live the ordinary life of a civil engineer, and never pursued elected office.

Historian Phillip Thomas Tucker, in his book *The Final Fury: Palmito Ranch, The Last Battle of the Civil War*, notes that one Confederate soldier, Private Ferdinand Gering, a German from Clinton, Texas, was killed in one of the 62nd's final volleys. One of the black soldiers, Private Bill Redmond, died a month after the battle as a result of his wounds. Perhaps they all should be remembered equally along with Private Williams. How many died as a result of this unnecessary battle is still a matter of conjecture. A theory that the Texas Confederates showed no mercy to the largely Tejano and Mexican members of Texas 2nd and that a massacre took place has been lent some credence by the number of human remains found near the battlefield.

In May 1966, a dragline crew excavating fill dirt near Palmito Hill unearthed five skeletons. Finding human bones in the Valley was a common occurrence in the 1960s when the region's exploding population resulted in a construction boom. The bleaching, brittle bones belonged to Native Americans, lone victims of Mexican bandits, those killed by overzealous Texas Rangers, or the honorable dead from the many battles. How many more are out there waiting to be discovered?

Tucker wrote: "Although the opening guns of Fort Sumter have been immortalized, the final fury at Palmito Ranch, which closed the final chapter on the bloodiest war in American history, has been forgotten."

After a long chat with the Border Patrol agent, I'm anxious to go back to town. I could have pressed on east and taken a look at the Gulf of Mexico and the famous beaches, but the sun is sinking and I still haven't explored downtown Brownsville. There are no cars behind us to move me along. But he eventually releases me, and within a few minutes I'm on Business 83-77 making my way to the end of a 1,885-mile trip.

I pass by the old one-story motels that catered to tourists as far back as the 1940s, before the expressway. Some are still open. Others are closed forever. I enter downtown and hit some traffic. Finding a place to park takes a while.

At the beginning of my trip in North Dakota, I drove into Canada and turned around just so I could claim that I have traveled every inch of Highway 83. But I won't be driving the Protegé into Mexico. So If I want to travel every inch of Highway

83, I will have to ignore the warnings of the nice people back in the Panhandle and walk into Mexico.

I entertained the thought of taking the Protegé to a car dealership, selling it for whatever I could get, and then putting the money toward a plane ticket back to Washington, D.C., but I have abandoned that plan. It's not that I'm overly sentimental about the Protegé, it's just that it seems too complicated. It will be easier just to turn around and drive northeast for a few days and hope it has a few more thousand miles left in it.

Downtown Brownsville is bustling. Border crossers stream into the neighborhood to shop in the stores and bring back bags full of goods, clothes, electronics, and shoes. Lots and lots of shoes. Border Patrol agents are ubiquitous in pickups, on bikes, or on foot. But everyone here is crossing legally.

Singer-songwriter and actor Kris Kristofferson was born in Brownsville and lived here through grade school. One of his enduring memories is coming downtown when he was nine years old with his mother for a war bond drive and celebration that featured World War II Medal of Honor recipient Sergeant José Lopez.

Lopez as a boy was orphaned in Mexico and made his way the Valley to seek out his extended family and work in the fields. He had two careers, one in the merchant marine and another as a professional boxer, when he enlisted in the Army at age thirty-one. He earned a Purple Heart and a bronze star on D-Day but became a legend during the Battle of the Bulge. The stocky Lopez on his own initiative saw that his company was about to be outflanked and overrun by German tanks and infantry. He grabbed a Browning machine gun and as much ammo as he could carry and ran to a shallow hole between the retreating U.S. troops and Germans and opened fire. He kept shooting and cutting down enemy troops despite artillery shells landing around him. One blew him over backwards, but he retreated to a dense forest, reset his gun, and kept up the withering fire, running from tree to tree, praying for the Virgin of Guadalupe to spare his life.

He killed an estimated 100 Germans before putting the spent machine gun on his back and returning to his company. The act of gallantry prevented his company from being slaughtered or captured and bought enough time for reinforcements to arrive and for his company to regroup.

Young Kristofferson loved living in this biracial world. He has spent his life speaking up for the downtrodden and he credits that day as a turning point.

"There was a lot of prejudice towards Mexicans then, and at this whole parade we were the only Anglos in the audience," he told an *Esquire* interviewer. "I'll never forget it. That was the kind of things my parents did that gave me a sense of what I should do. That day affected the way I've lived ever since."

After spending an hour walking the streets, checking out the local history museum, and doing a little shopping—namely for clean underwear—I leave my camera, cell phone, and most of my wallet's contents in the car and head for the bridge carrying only a twenty-dollar bill and my passport.

Like most pedestrian border crossings into Mexico that I have experienced, there is no one on the U.S. side to check any documents. I join the stream of folks returning home for the evening, walk through a turnstile, and continue over the bridge. Although I have been hugging it for several days, I am finally crossing the Rio Grande. It's languid here. The channel is full of water, but it barely seems to be moving. There are customs buildings on the other side, but no Mexican authorities.

I arrive in Matamoros, the town I have read so much about. The town attacked by the Republic of Rio Grande forces, federalists, centralists, the merchants' army, and Cortina.

There is little here architecturally that is old. There are more stores—clothing, shoes, and small appliances again. Apparently there are some clothes and TV sets that can't be bought in Mexico, but can be in the United States, and vice versa. The traffic is slightly less organized. Some taxi drivers ask me where I want to go, but I'm really not going anywhere. I am, however,

Gateway International Bridge, postcard undated, and in May 2010.

determined to spend some of my twenty-dollar bill, so I find an outdoor stand, and order a Coke and three beef tacos. The proprietor, a young, mustachioed man, seems nice enough but he doesn't speak any English. I sit at a table with plastic chairs and watch the shoppers go by. It's a soft tortilla and beef that has been in a slow cooker for hours. A fine, simple meal that costs me four bucks. I don't witness any gun battles between Mexican drug gangs, which would have made for a far more exciting ending to my epic journey.

Back at the U.S. side of the border, I hand the Customs and Border Protection agent my passport. He asks what my business was in Mexico.

"Well everyone has been saying don't go into Mexico..."

"... and you just wanted to see for yourself," he says, finishing my sentence, as if he's heard that one several times before. And that's it. He hands me back my passport without another word, and I walk back to Brownsville.

I return to the car, flip open the phone, and call my wife. I had big plans. I was going to check into a hotel, wake up the next morning, see its famous art museum, take pictures of the statue of José Lopez, maybe find a library and do some research. At one point I had aspirations to visit the beach. It's been a long trip and I have a couple days of nonstop driving ahead of me.

My wife answers.

"I think I'm heading back," I tell her.

"When?"

"Like right now," I say, and turn on the ignition.

The street I'm parked on becomes the expressway, and after two weeks of leisurely travel, I'm gunning the Protegé north toward Houston in the twilight. I've got the perfect CD for the occasion: The LeRoi Brothers' *Check This Action*, a raucous rockabilly album that I pop into the player. It only encourages me to go faster. I reckon I have enough money left over from the trip to pay for at least one speeding ticket.

I'm convinced that if I turned around and headed back north on Highway 83 I could write an entirely new book covering what I have left out: the buffalo soldiers' scrapes with the locals at Fort Brown and Fort Ringgold; the plane crashing into the Lady of San Juan del Valle basilica; the World War II internment camp in Crystal City; the famous lawmen of Uvalde, Pat Garrett and the Texas Ranger Joaquin Jackson; and I'd barely touched on the famous Comanche chief Qannah Parker.

But it's time to go home to my wife, where we will begin our lives together without children. After grief comes acceptance. We already spoke about our first trip exploring the world together. We are going to Costa Rica in the fall. And then, who knows? Egypt, Italy, Peru, Santa Fe, New Mexico. We have talked about them all. Maybe I'll even get her to come along on a road trip down a federal highway.

But that freedom we planned to enjoy, that unencumbered life without the burden of little ones—paid for with all that disposable income—will last only fourteen more months, which proves that even the best fertility doctor in town doesn't always know what he's talking about.

UPDATES AND ACKNOWLEDGMENTS

Time may seem to move a little slower in the small towns and back roads of America, and their residents may claim "that nothing ever changes around here," but that's simply not true.

The trip this book recounts occurred in May 2010, and it will be 2017 when it is finally published. I have revisited parts of Highway 83 in Texas since then, but I decided to keep this story confined to my travels during that single month. I have two of the best excuses a writer could have for taking seven years to finish this work. Our daughter, Sophie, was born July 11, 2011. Our boy, Sawyer, arrived March 25, 2013.

Meanwhile, life went on in Texas, and things did change.

For example, the first pages of this book described the beer sellers in the Oklahoma Panhandle catering to "dry" Ochiltree County. The last time I visited, they were boarded up because alcohol sales in Perryton are now legal.

Brent and Brenda Jackson continued to organize and ride the length of Highway 83 in honor of our Vietnam veterans until

2015, when Brent had to stop for health reasons. A small group of about a dozen bikers carried on with an informal ride in the same weekend in March 2016. Brent passed away on New Year's Eve, only a few months before this book's publication. Jim Hudson, *Peryton Herald* publisher, also left us. His belief that "Highway 83 brings people together" has been an inspiration to me.

Not long after I passed through, the town of Menard restored the Presidio San Sabá to what it looked like when the WPA restored it in the 1930s. It looks much nicer now.

It turns out that the man running the antiques store in Ballinger is named Fred Schwake, and he's an inductee in the National Basketball Hall of Fame. I didn't discover this until six years later while doing some fact-checking for the manuscript. I hold myself blameless. I don't think I have ever randomly asked anyone: "Hey, you don't happen to be a member of a major sports halls of fame, by any chance?"

In 2016, the feds swooped in an arrested the mayor and all but one of the city council members of Crystal City, Texas, on corruption charges, an event that made national news.

No area on the highway changed as much as the land south of the Winter Garden area. The southern stretch of the Great Mesquite Forest of Texas had turned into an oil and gas field when I passed through five years later. The once sleepy towns of Asherton and Catarina became boomtowns again as petroleum workers flooded into the region. A pipeline to carry the oil south was being built on the side of the highway. Motels and shiny new gas stations catering to the roughnecks had popped up everywhere, although by the time I passed through the boom was having its inevitable bust. A Chinese family had spent two years renovating the Catarina Hotel, adding updated rooms and a restaurant. When I stopped to visit, it was pretty dead. I wondered if they could hang on long enough for oil prices to go back up.

While that building opened, other businesses closed. Joe LaMaster in Perryton went into semi-retirement and sold his insurance business. Wilson's Ranch Furniture in Anson closed.

Salt Fork of the Red River Bridge: R.I.P.

The 83 Bar and Grill in La Feria is also long gone. But the WesMer Drive-In, Larry's Better Burger, the Hilltop Station, the LoneStar Saloon, and the J. C. Ramirez store in Roma are still open when I last checked. Six years after I first met him, I found Russ Carlson in early December 2015, still selling jerky in the exact same spot near the convergence of Highway 83 and I-35. Attempts to locate Jack Cox Jr. have failed. If anyone knows of his whereabouts, please contact me.

As for Highway 83 itself, the old steel bridge north of Wellington was indeed torn down only months after I passed by. Six years later, I still hear from local residents who haven't forgiven the Texas Department of Transportation.

Improvements were made on that dangerous stretch of road between Laredo and Zapata, and it is hoped that this will save some lives. The 83 Expressway is now known as Interstate 2. U.S. 281 heading north out of Pharr is slowly transforming into a section of Interstate 69, which may end the Valley's isolation if it is ever finished.

This book would not have possible without the continued support of my wife, Nioucha, who allows me to disappear for a couple hours every night to write.

I've made many friends over the years as a result of the Fans of U.S. Route 83 page I administer. Among them, I would like to thank Sharleen Wurm at the Last Indian Raid Museum in Oberlin, Kansas, for sharing the U.S. & Canada Highway 83 Association scrapbook she uncovered in the museum's basement; Russell Stephen Rein for the map of the Great Plains Highway; and MaryLou VandeRiet for the Texas history books.

The Benavides in Roma are wonderful ambassadors for their community, and it was my good fortune to encounter Noel Junior and Noel Senior on the side of the road. I also had the good fortune to be chosen by Jill McCabe Smith at Artsmith and Blasita Lopez of the Laredo Convention and Visitors Bureau to explore the city further in December 2015 during a writer's residency fellowship. The experience greatly improved the book.

I appreciate Midge Coates and Greg Schmidt at Auburn University and Kera Newby at the National Cowboy Museum for helping with the Eddie Rickenbacker and Carl "Big-un" Bradley photos, respectively.

Thank you to my family in Nebraska: my mom, Julie Strnad, and stepdad, Charlie Strnad; my Stapleton cousins; Cindy and Steve Frey; and the Empfields and Karns for their continued support, as well as Monica Harvey and Marcia Hora in Stapleton.

I actually spend a lot more time in small-town libraries doing research than the book indicates. Thank you to the staffs of the Perryton, Abilene, Laredo, Zapata, Rio Grande City and Pharr public libraries for their help.

Barbara Brannon, executive director of the Texas Plains Trail Region, was an enthusiastic early supporter of this book and took on the job to edit it. Thanks to my proofreader, Mary Kalfotovic, and the design advice of coworkers Brian Taylor and Scott Rekdal.

Most of all, I would like to thank the people of Texas for the hospitality and kindness shown to this Cornhusker over the past seven years.

BIBLIOGRAPHY

Ainslie, Ricardo C. *No Dancin' in Anson: An American Story of Race and Social Change.* Jason Aronson Inc., Northvale, New Jersey, 1995.

Alexander, Charles C., *Rogers Hornsby: A Biography.* Holt Paperbacks. New York, 2003.

Allen, Susan C. *They Remember: Recollections of Members of the Carver Community of Abilene.* Hardin-Simmons University, 2000.

Amberson, Mary Margaret McAllen, et al. *I Would Rather Sleep in Texas: A History of the Lower Rio Grande Valley and the People of the Santa Anita Land Grant.* Texas State Historical Association, Denton, 2003.

Ashworth, William. *Ogallala Blue: Water and Life on the High Plains.* The Countryman Press, Woodstock, Vermont, 2006.

Biel, Steven. *Bonnie Parker Writes a Poem: How a Couple of Bungling Sociopaths Became Bonnie and Clyde.* Now & Then Reader, 2012

Bowden, Keith. *The Tecate Journals: Seventy Days on the Rio Grande.* The Mountaineers Books, Seattle, 2007.

Carlson, Paul H. *Dancin' in Anson: A History of the Texas Cowboys' Christmas Ball.* Texas Tech University Press, Lubbock, 2014.

Carlson, Paul H., and Glasrud, Bruce A., eds. *West Texas: A History of the Giant Side of the State.* University of Oklahoma Press, Norman, 2014.

Chartrand, René. *The Spanish Army in North America 1700-1793.* Osprey Publishing, Long Island City, New York, 2011.

Cox, Mike. *The Texas Rangers: Wearing the Cinco Peso, 1821-1900.* Tom Doherty Associates, New York, 2008.

Cox, Mike. *Time of the Rangers: Texas Rangers from 1900 to the Present.* Tom Doherty Associates, New York, 2009.

Cunfer, Geoff. *On the Great Plains: Agriculture and Environment.* Texas A&M University Press, College Station, 2005.

Davies, Pete. *American Road: The Story of an Epic Transcontinental Journey at the Dawn of the Motor Age.* Henry Holt and Company, New York, 2002.

Dawson, Carol, and Polson, Roger Allen. *Miles and Miles of Texas: 100 Years of the Texas Highway Department.* Texas A&M University Press, College Station, 2016.

Dent, Jim. *The Junction Boys: How Ten Days in Hell with Bear Bryant Forged a National Championship Team.* Thomas Dunne Books, New York, 1999.

Douglas, C. L. *Cattle Kings of Texas.* State House Press, Austin, Texas, 1989.

Duff, Katharyn and Seibt, Betty Kay. *Catclaw Country: An Informal History of Abilene in West Texas.* Eakin Press, Burnet, Texas, 1980.

Egan, Timothy. *The Worst Hard Time: The Untold Story of Those Who Survived the Great American Dust Bowl.* Houghton Mifflin, New York, 2006.

Flint, Richard. *No Settlement, No Conquest: A History of the Coronado Entrada.* University of New Mexico Press, Albuquerque, 2008.

Goddard, Stephen B. *Getting There: The Epic Struggle Between Road and Rail in the American Century.* Basic Books, New York, 1994.

Guinn, Jeff. *Go Down Together: The True, Untold Story of Bonnie and Clyde.* Simon and Schuster, New York, 2009.

Gutiérrez, José Angel. *The Making of a Chicano Militant: Lessons from Cristal.* University of Wisconsin Press, Madison, 1998.

Gutiérrez, José Angel. *The Making of a Civil Rights Leader José Angel Gutiérrez.* Arte Publico Press, Houston, Texas, 2005.

Gwynne, S. C. *Empire of the Summer Moon*. Scribner, New York, 2010.

Haley, James L. *The Buffalo War: The History of the Red River War Indian Uprising of 1874*. University of Oklahoma Press, Norman, 1985.

Hämäläinen, Pekka. *The Comanche Empire*. Yale University Press, New Haven, 2008.

Holley, I. B., Jr. *The Highway Revolution, 1895-1925: How the United States Got Out of the Mud*. Carolina Academic Press, Durham, 2008.

Hornaday, William Temple. *The Extermination of the American Bison*. Smithsonian Institution Press; Washington, 1889, 2002.

Hudson, John C. *Plains Country Towns*. University of Minnesota Press, Minneapolis, 1985.

Hutchins, John M. *Coronado's Well-Equipped Army: The Spanish Invasion of the American Southwest*. Westhome Publishing, Yardley, Pennsylvania, 2014.

Hansen, Harry, ed. *Texas: A Guide to the Lone Star State, Revised Edition*. Federal Writers' Project of the Works Progress Administration. Hastings House, New York, 1969.

Higham, Charles. *Brando: The Unauthorized Biography*. New American Library, New York, 1987.

Horgan, Paul. *Great River: The Rio Grande in North American History*. Holt, Rinehart and Winston, New York, 1971.

Hunt, Jeffrey Wm. *The Last Battle of the Civil War: Palmetto Ranch*. University of Texas Press, Austin, 2002.

Isern, Thomas D. *Custom Combining on the Great Plains: A History*. University of Oklahoma Press, Norman, 1981.

Jasinksi, Laurie E., ed. *The Handbook of Texas Music*, 2nd edition, Texas State Historical Association, Denton, Texas, 2012.

Kanfer, Stefan. *Somebody: The Reckless Life and Remarkable Life of Marlon Brando*. Alfred A. Knopf, New York, 2008.

Lewis, W. David. *Eddie Rickenbacker: An American Hero in the Twentieth Century*. Johns Hopkins University Press, 2005.

Lewis, Tom. *Divided Highways: Building the Interstate Highways, Transforming American Life*. Viking Press, New York, 1997.

McConal, Jon. *Jon McConal's Texas*. Republic of Texas Press, Lanham, Maryland, 2002.

McHugh, Tom. *The Time of the Buffalo*. Alfred A. Knopf, New York, 1972.

Meinzer, Wyman, and Chappell, Henry. *6666: Portrait of a Texas Ranch.* Texas Tech University Press, Lubbock, 2004.

Mizruchi, Susan L. *Brando's Smile: His Life, Thought and Work.* W.W. Norton & Co., New York, 2014.

Nathan, Paul D., trans., and Simpson, Lesley Byrd, ed. *The San Sabá Papers: A Documentary Account of the Founding and Destruction of the San Sabá Mission.* Southern Methodist University Press, Dallas, 2000.

Navarro, Armando. *The Cristal Experiment: A Chicano Struggle for Community Control.* University of Wisconsin Press, Madison, 1998.

Nye, Wilber Sturtevant, *Bad Medicine and Good: Tales of the Kiowas,* University of Oklahoma Press, Norman, 1962.

Peña, Manuel. *Música Tejana: The Cultural Economy of Artistic Transformation.* Texas A&M University Press, College Station, 1999.

Punke, Michael. *Last Stand: George Bird Grinnell, The Battle to Save the Buffalo, And the Birth of the New West.* University of Nebraska Press, Lincoln, 2007.

Rathjen, Frederick W. *The Texas Panhandle Frontier,* revised edition. Rept. Texas Tech University Press, Lubbock, 1998.

Riley, Jeannie C., and Buckingham, Jamie. *Jeannie C. Riley: From Harper Valley to the Mountain Top.* Chosen Books, Lincoln, Virginia, 1981.

Robertson, Brian. *Wild Horse Desert: The Heritage of South Texas.* New Santander Press, Edinburg, Texas, 1985.

Robinson, Charles M., III. *Satanta: The Life and Death of a War Chief.* State House Press, Austin, Texas, 1997.

Ross, John F. *Enduring Courage: Ace Pilot Eddie Rickenbacker and the Dawn of the Age of Speed.* St. Martin's Press, New York, 2014.

Roueché, Berton. *Special Places: In Search of Small Town America.* Little Brown, New York, 1982.

San Benito Historical Society. *San Benito.* (Images of America). Arcadia Publishing, Charleston, South Carolina, 2010.

Sanchez, Mario L., ed. *A Shared Experience: The History, Architecture and Historic Designations of the Lower Rio Grande Heritage Corridor.* Los Caminos del Rio Heritage Project / Texas Historical Commission, Austin, 1994.

Sandoz, Mari. *The Buffalo Hunters: The Story of the Hide Men* (1954). Rept. University of Nebraska Press, Lincoln, 1978.

Simpson, Brooks D. *Ulysses S. Grant: Triumph Over Adversity, 1822–1865.* Houghton Mifflin, New York 2000.

Sledge, Robert W. *A People, A Place: The Story of Abilene.* Vol. 1: The Future Great City 1881–1940. State House Press, Buffalo Gap, Texas, 2009.

Stein, Mark. *How the States Got Their Shapes.* Smithsonian Books, Washington, D.C., 2008

Stephens, A. Ray, and Zuber-Mallison, Carol. *Texas: A Historical Atlas.* University of Oklahoma Press, Norman, 2010.

Stevenson, Sue. *Tom Mayfield.* Self-published. 1999

Swift, Earl. *The Big Roads: The Untold Story of the Engineers, Visionaries, and Trailblazers Who Created the American Superhighways.* Houghton Mifflin Harcourt: Boston, 2011.

Thompson, Jerry. *Palo Alto Battlefield National Historic Site.* Southwest Parks and Monuments Association, 2001.

Tucker, Phillip Thomas. *The Final Fury: Palmito Ranch, The Last Battle of the Civil War.* Stackpole Books, Mechanicsburg, Penn., 2001.

Webb, Walter Prescott. *The Texas Rangers: A Century of Frontier Defense,* 2nd edition, University of Texas Press, Austin,1965.

Weber, David J. *The Spanish Frontier in North America.* Yale University Press, New Haven, Conn., 1992.

Weddle, Robert S. *After the Massacre: The Violent Legacy of the San Sabá Mission.* Texas Tech University Press, Lubbock, 2007.

Weddle, Robert S. *The San Sabá Mission: Spanish Pivot in Texas.* Texas A&M University Press, College Station, 1999.

Wheatheart of the Plains: An Early History of Ochiltree County. Ochiltree County Historical Survey Committee, 1969.

Williams, J. W. *Old Texas Trails.* Eakin Press, Burnet, Texas. 1979.

Winship, George Parker. *The Coronado Expedition: 1540–1542.* Rio Grande Press, Chicago, 1964.

Zachary, Juanita Daniel. *The Settling of a Frontier: A History of Rural Taylor County.* Nortex Press, Burnet, Texas, 1980.

A BRIEF NOTE
ABOUT THE SOURCES

My intention is to give credit where credit is due, and to also point readers to some more detailed and excellent books I relied heavily upon. I derived some basic information from various unmentioned sources on the internet, including Wikipedia, which I find has become more reliable through the years. I took great care to verify that what I was reading was accurate.

I referred to The Texas State Historical Society's online resource, "The Handbook of Texas," for about every person, town, and incident of note in the book. Citing every entry I read would be tedious, but rest assured that it was always one of the first sources I checked. My thanks to the society for maintaining this valuable resource.

I stake my reputation on this book being factual. I am not perfect. If a factual error is spotted, please notify me and I will correct it in future editions. stewmag@yahoo.com

For "Conquistador," see Flint, *No Settlement, No Conquest*; Hutchins, *Coronado's Well-Equipped Army*; Williams, *Old Texas*

Trails; and Winship, *The Coronado Expedition*; Weber, *The Spanish Frontier in North America.*

History of Perryton and Ochiltree County and the LaMaster Family: *Wheatheart of the Plains.* For more on the Ogallala Aquifer, see Ashworth, *Ogallala Blue.*

For "Honor and Dishonor," see Haley, *The Buffalo War*; Nye, *Bad Medicine and Good*; and Robinson, *Satanta.* Background on the history of buffalo from: Punke's, Michael. *Last Stand*; Sandoz,' *The Buffalo Hunters*; McHugh, *The Time of the Buffalo.*

Most of the highway history information I interspersed in the book comes from the following sources: Dawson and Polson, *Miles and Miles of Texas*; Goddard, *Getting There*; Holley, *The Highway Revolution, 1895–1925*; Swift, *The Big Roads*; and Lewis, *Divided Highways.* U.S. & Canada Highway 83 Association history is compiled form a cache of documents, correspondence, and newspaper clippings found at the Last Indian Raid Museum in Oberlin, Kansas, by Director Sharleen Wurm.

"The Red River Plunge" is adapted from Guinn, *Go Down Together* and Biel, *Bonnie Parker Writes a Poem.* One of the best sources we have on the Barrow Gang isn't a book, it's a blog: A. Winston Woodward's *Bonnie and Clyde Blog.* "New Info Reveals Wellington As You've Never Known," May 25, 2010, http:// bonnieandclydehistory.blogspot.com/2010/05/wellington-as-youve-never-known.html, retrieved Aug. 29, 2014, provided the best insight into this incident. Also, "Ridin' with Bonnie and Clyde," by W. D. Jones, *Playboy*, Nov. 1968. Information on the bridge is derived from "Historic Truss Bridge: Salt Fork of the Red River—U.S. Highway 83," by Rebecca Snider, *Wellington Leader*, http://texashideout.tripod.com/bridge.html, retrieved Dec. 22, 2009.

About the mesquite tree: "The Ubiquitous Mesquite," *Texas Almanac*, retrieved Nov. 6, 2015, http://texasalmanac.com/ topics/science/ubiquitous-mesquite; "The Maligned Mesquite Gets Some Respect, or the Rodney Dangerfield of Texas Trees"

by Mike Cox, May 8, 2014, retrieved, Nov. 10, 2016, http://www
.texasescapes.com/MikeCoxTexasTales/Maligned-Mesquite-
Gets-Some-Respect.htm

The life of Carl "Big-un" Bradley and the history of the 6666
Ranch from *Texas Monthly*: "The Death of the Marlboro Man,"
Gary Cartwright, Sept. 1973; *Jon McConal's Texas*; Douglas,
Cattle Kings of Texas; Meinzer and Chappell, *6666: Portrait of
a Texas Ranch*; "Marlboro Man at 50 — Icon or Illusion?," Jim
Carrier, *San Francisco Chronicle*, Jan. 7, 2005.

Along with an interview of Pablo Aguillon, he provided a file
entitled, "Vietnam Veterans Memorial Highway: A Chronology of
its Birth," which included correspondence between Aguillon and
lawmakers, State Department of Highways memoranda, American
Legion Post resolutions supporting the effort; Correspondence
between: Aguillon and American Legion Department
Commander Waggoner Carr; State Rep. Ernestine Glossbrenner;
Letter to Aguillon from American Legion Department Adjutant
W. H. McGregor opposing the campaign; Aguillon's response to
McGregor; Aguillon's April 19, 1983 written testimony to state
Transportation Committee; copy of bill HB No. 287 introduced
by Glossbrenner; numerous newspaper clippings. His file was
forwarded to the Texas Historical Commission's Texas Historic
Roads and Highways Program archives.

For "Dancin' in Anson?" see Ainslie, *No Dancin' in Anson* and
Carlson, *Dancin' in Anson*. Also Jeanie C. Riley's autobiography;
Texas Monthly, December, 1986: "No Dancin' in Anson" by Jamie
Aitkin; *Washington Post*, "Footloose or Dancing Free?" May 17,
1987; *Chicago Tribune*, "No Dancin' Has Anson in a Tizzy," April
19, 1987, David Marcus.

Life of Eddie Rickenbacker: Ross, *Enduring Courage*; Lewis,
Eddie Rickenbacker, Sledge, *A People, A Place*.

History of Abilene: Zachary, *The Settling of a Frontier*; Sledge,
A People, A Place; Duff and Seibt, *Catclaw Country*; Allen, *They
Remember: Recollections of Members of the Carver Community of
Abilene*.

For Rogers Hornsby, see Alexander's *Rogers Hornsby: A Biography.*

Bonnie and Clyde in Junction: *Brownsville Herald*, April 29, 1973, "The Day I Met the Real Bonnie and Clyde," by Mrs. J. M. Livingston, Also, Dent, *The Junction Boys.*

For San Saba massacre, see Hämäläinen, *The Comanche Empire*; Weddle's two books, *The San Saba Mission* and *After the Massacre*; Nathan, *The San Saba Papers*; Chartrand, *The Spanish Army in North America*; Gwynne, *Empire of the Summer Moon*; Weber, *The Spanish Frontier in North America.*

For "The Ingrate," see "Twilight of The Texas Rangers," *Texas Monthly.* Feb. 1994; Oral history interview with Joaquin Jackson and José Angel Gutiérrez, 1996, http://library.uta.edu/tejanovoices/xml/ CMAS_012.xml, retrieved May 12, 2016. Gutiérrez, *The Making of a Chicano Militant*; and *The Making of a Civil Rights Leader*; Cox, *Time of the Rangers*; Roueché, *Special Places; New Yorker*, "U.S. Journal: Crystal City, Texas," April 17, 1971, Calvin Trillin.

Catarina: "Texas Tales," Mike Cox, Oct. 6, 2005, retrieved, Dec. 12, 2015. http://www.texasescapes.com/MikeCoxTexasTales/259-Catarina-Texas-Ghost-Town-and-Ghost-Hotel.htm

For Republic of the Rio Grande, see Robertson, *Wild Horse Desert*; Sanchez, *A Shared Experience*; Horgan, *Great River*; Dixon, "The Republic of the Rio Grande: A Story of Its Rise and Fall," from *Romance and Tragedy of Texas History* by Sam Houston Dixon, 1924. http://www.tamu.edu/faculty/ccbn/ dewitt/riogrande.htm, retrieved June 2, 2016.

The Highway 83 tragedy: "Seven Killed in South Texas Crash," *Laredo Morning Times*, Feb. 27, 2005; and "Auto accident deaths shock family, friends," *Laredo Morning Times*, Feb. 28, 2005, Tricia Cortez.

Sources for the history of the Falcon Dam are found within the text. I am grateful for the local historians who compiled all this information and left it for me to find at the Zapata Library.

For Marlon Brando and Anthony Quinn's days in Roma, see Higham's *Brando*; Kanfer, *Somebody*; Mizruchi, *Brando's Smile.*

Roma history: Sanchez, *A Shared Experience*; Ramirez family history, "After 150 years, Roma store still going strong," Travis M. Whitehead, *The Monitor*, undated clipping.

For the Rio Grande Valley and its many conflicts, including Cortina's Wars I & II, The Merchants War, the Mexican Revolution, Plan de San Diego, and Rip Ford, see Robertson, *Wild Horse Desert*; Sanchez, *A Shared Experience*; Horgan, *Great River*; Cox, *The Texas Rangers* and *Time of the Rangers*; Amberson, *I Would Rather Sleep in Texas*; Prescott, *The Texas Rangers*.

Battle of Palo Alto: see Thompson, *Palo Alto Battlefield*; Simpson, *Ulysses S. Grant*.

Life of Tom Mayfield from Stevenson's *Tom Mayfield*.

The life of the McAllen family, from Amberson's *I Would Rather Sleep in Texas*. "Texas Finally Acknowledges Rangers Killed Hundreds of Latinos, Latina, Feb. 2, 2016, http://www.latina.com/lifestyle/our-issues/texas-rangers-kill-latinos, retrieved July 20, 2016.

History of the 83 Expressway: "Snyder Outlines Valley Need For Expressway," *Valley Morning Star*, April 6, 1955; "City Officials Opposing South Expressway Plan," *Valley Morning Star*, Jan. 16, 1957; "Hidalgo Highway Route Approved," *Valley Morning Star*, Feb. 8, 1957; "Expressway Project Ahead of Schedule," *Valley Morning Star*, June 9, 1960; "Dedication Set for Piece of Freeway Scramble," *Valley Morning Star*, May 6, 1971.

Conjunto music: Peña's, *Música Tejana*; Narciso Martinez, http://www.lib.utexas.edu/benson/border/arhoolie2/narciso.html, retrieved, July 25, 2016; Jasinksi, *Handbook of Texas Music*; San Benito history, from *San Benito (Images of America)*.

Battle of Palmito Ranch and the Valley during the Civil War: Hunt, *Last Battle of the Civil War* and Tucker, *The Final Fury*. Also, Amberson, *I Would Rather Sleep in Texas*.

"Skeletons Unearthed at Palmito," *Brownville Herald,* May 31, 1966; "Skeletons Seen Remains of Mexican War Soldiers," *Brownsville Herald*, March, 26, 1967.

For Kris Kristofferson, *Esquire*, "Kris Kristofferson Is Still Living His Epic Life," May 2014, Turk Pipkin.

ABOUT THE AUTHOR

 Omaha native Stew Magnuson is the author of *The Death of Raymond Yellow Thunder: And Other True Stories from the Nebraska-Pine Ridge Border Towns*, 2009 Nebraska nonfiction book of the year. It also was selected as one of Nebraska's 150 most important literary works in celebration of the state's 150th anniversary in 2017. He also penned *Wounded Knee 1973: Still Bleeding*, *The Last American Highway: A Journey Through Time Down U.S. Route 83: The Dakotas*, *The Last American Highway: A Journey Through Time Down U.S. Route 83: Nebraska-Kansas-Oklahoma*, and the novel, *The Song of Sarin*.

He has traveled to 48 countries, all 50 states, and has worked as a foreign correspondent in Cambodia, Thailand, Indonesia and Japan.

He is currently managing editor of *National Defense Magazine* in Arlington, Virginia, where he lives with his wife Nioucha, and children Sophia and Sawyer.

Website: www.stewmagnuson.com

Contact: stewmag@yahoo.com

MORE ABOUT
THE LAST AMERICAN HIGHWAY

For travel tips and trivia about Highway 83, check out The U.S. Route 83 Travel Page at:

www.usroute83.com.

For news, history and updates about the road, read the Highway 83 Chronicles blog at:

www.ushighway83.blogspot.com.

Join the growing legion of members on the Fans of U.S. Route 83 Facebook page for daily postings, photos, events and breaking news.

www.facebook.com/groups/119180393762

Also available from Court Bridge Publishing, *The Last American Highway: A Journey Through Time Down U.S. Route 83: The Dakotas* and *The Last American Highway: A Journey Through Time Down U.S. Route 83: Nebraska-Kansas-Oklahoma*.

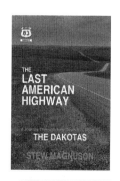

"Stew's book is not exactly a guidebook. It's more of a travel narrative, and like most good travel narratives, it embeds within itself the stories of others." —Tom Isern, Host of North Dakota Public Radio's *Plains Folk* and professor of history, North Dakota State University.

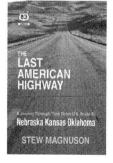

Made in the USA
Columbia, SC
13 August 2017